Coping with Unhappy Children

Edited by
Dr Ved Varma

CASSELL

Cassell
Villiers House   387 Park Avenue South
41/47 Strand   New York
London   NY 10016-8810
WC2N 5JE

First published 1993

British Library Cataloguing-in-Publication Data
A catalogue record for this book is available from the British Library.

Library of Congress Cataloging-in-Publication Data
Coping with unhappy children/edited by Ved Varma.
     p.   cm.
    Includes index.
    ISBN 0-304-32414-0. – ISBN 0-304-32436-1 (pbk)
     1. Depression in children.   2. Handicapped children – Mental
health.   I. Varma, Ved P.
    RJ506.D4C68   1993
    155.45 – dc20   92-38453
                                                   CIP

ISBN 0-304-32414-0 (hardback)
     0-304-32436-1 (paperback)

Typeset by Colset Private Limited, Singapore
Printed and bound in Great Britain by
Redwood Books, Trowbridge, Wiltshire

Contents

List of Contributors

Dr Helen Barrett is a research fellow at the Department of Psychology, Birkbeck College, University of London.

Dr Frank M.C. Besag is medical director of St Piers Lingfield, Surrey.

David Bond is the specialist educational psychologist and audiologist at the Royal School for Deaf Children, Margate, Kent.

Elizabeth K. Chapman is an Honorary Senior Research Fellow at the University of Birmingham.

Dr Fleming Carswell is reader in Child Health at the Royal Hospital for Sick Children at the University of Bristol.

Dr Theo Cox is at the Department of Education, University College, Swansea.

Dr Kedar Nath Dwivedi is a consultant child, adolescent and family psychiatrist in Northampton.

Mrs Deborah Freeman is a writer and a psychiatric social worker in Manchester.

Dr Jeffrey S. Freeman is a consultant paediatrician in Tameside, Greater Manchester.

Dr Conrad Graham was formerly chief educational psychologist at the Child Guidance Service, Brent.

Dr James Gray was at the Department of Educational Studies, University of Oxford.

Dr James Hemming is a consultant educationalist, writer and broadcaster.

Dr David Jones is at the Department of Psychology, Birkbeck College, University of London.

Dr Richard Lansdown is principal clinical psychologist at the Department of Psychological Medicine, Great Ormond Street Hospital for Sick Children, London.

Dr Robert Povey, educational psychologist, was formerly a principal lecturer at Christ Church College, Canterbury, Kent.

Philippa Russell is director of the Council for Disabled Children, London.

Dr Ved Varma has taught at ordinary and special primary and secondary schools in London and Middlesex, and was an educational psychologist at the Tavistock Clinic, London, and in Richmond-upon-Thames and Brent. He is a recognized authority on disturbed children and his publications include sixteeen important books in this area.

Foreword

There is no display of animation more radiant than the fun and excitement that fizzes from a group of happy children. Of course children have their bad times too, when life is darkened by anger, jealousy, hurt and the rest. But, taking the ups and downs together, one can say with conviction that the characteristic mode for children is joy in living, if only because the whole world is laid out before them, fresh and exciting.

The more the pity, then, when children are denied this natural inheritance because some disability or obstructive circumstance clouds their lives. The result may then be children deeply and persistently unhappy because of a situation over which they have no control, and for which they are not responsible. Helplessness and unhappiness are always close partners. Locked into this syndrome is the fact that any disadvantage in the ability to cope with life is liable to generate guilt in the sufferer, and that, too, eats into the capacity for happiness.

Consequently, there are always numbers of unhappy children around. These are a particular challenge to educators today because we now know what are the components of happiness: love, appreciation, encouragement, friendly relationships with others, the actualization of potentialities, achievement, the building of secure self-esteem.

So we find ourselves squarely faced with a central developmental problem: how to help *all* children to attain a happy, purposeful, fulfilled way of life. We know about the psychodynamics of the situation; we still have to struggle to remove the blocks to positive growth. This is a task calling, at the same time, for appropriate knowledge and sympathetic understanding.

It is extremely opportune, therefore, that Dr Varma has assembled a book bringing together a wide range of insights from experts who have dedicated their skills to helping children tackle life-obstructing difficulties, the whole way from learning problems, through functional and physical handicaps, to children beset by dilemmas arising from being exceptionally gifted. Ethnic problems are also sympathetically dealt with.

A fascinating feature of the book is that it brings out, in comment, research and case histories, how approaches generated from a wide range of experiences support one another in identifying the essentials for rescuing children from disabling life situations.

Teachers, parents and other carers will greatly benefit in acumen and reassurance from meeting in varying contexts, and with authoritative backing, the sorts of problems they constantly confront in their lives.

Dr James Hemming, FRSA, FBPsS

Preface

As Sargant (1969) says, in a three-year period in Great Britain, a staggering total of 43 million prescriptions were dispensed for psychotropic drugs to combat states of unhappiness, anxiety and tension in one form or another. Yet this total does not include all the additional tranquillizers, sedatives and anti-depressants used in hundreds of general and mental hospitals in Great Britain, and also in the private practice sector of medicine and psychiatry. And according to Ingleby (1981), doctors in the USA write 200 million prescriptions for psychotropic drugs in the course of a single year.

It is clear, then, that unhappiness is today a matter of great current concern; we are living in an age of unhappiness. But it is not only adults who experience this. Indeed, it can be argued that unhappiness is most evident during periods of rapid change and progress. And since childhood is the period during which we develop most rapidly, then a strong case can be made for unhappiness being especially prevalent in many children. This book deals with unhappiness in children and how we can assist them.

I would like to thank the reader for all her help. As regards my publishing colleague, Naomi Roth, and the contributors to this book, it is impossible to express my deep gratitude in words. It has been a great pleasure to work with them.

Ved P. Varma
London

REFERENCES

Ingleby, D. (ed.) (1981) *Critical Psychiatry*. Harmondsworth. Penguin.
Sargant, W. (1969) Physical treatment of anxiety. In M. H. Lader (ed.), *Studies in Anxiety*. World Psychiatric Association.

Other books edited by Ved P. Varma

Stresses in Children (1973), London: University of London Press.
Advances in Educational Psychology, Vol. 1 (1973) (co-editor Professor W.D. Wall), London: University of London Press.
Psychotherapy Today (1974), London: Constable.
Advances in Educational Psychology, Vol. 2 (1974) (co-editor Mia Kellmer Pringle), London: Hodder and Stoughton.
Piaget, Psychology and Education (1976) (co-editor Professor Phillip Williams), London: Hodder and Stoughton.
Anxiety in Children (1984), London: Croom Helm/Methuen.
Advances in Teacher Education (1989) (co-editor Professor V. Alan McClelland), London: Routledge.
The Management of Children with Emotional and Behavioural Difficulties (1990), London: Routledge.
Special Education: Past, Present and Future (1990) (co-editor Peter Evans), Lewes: Falmer Press.
The Secret Life of Vulnerable Children (1991), London: Routledge.
Truants from Life: Theory and Therapy (1991), London: David Fulton.
Prospects for People with Learning Difficulties (1991) (co-editor Professor Stanley Segal), London: David Fulton.
Resilience and Vulnerability in Human Development (1992) (co-editor Professor Barbara Tizard), London: Jessica Kingsley.
How and Why Children Fail (1993), London: Jessica Kingsley.
How and Why Children Hate (1993), London: Jessica Kingsley.
Management of Behaviour in Schools (1993), Harlow: Longman.

This book is dedicated by the editor, with affection and esteem, to Margaret Procter and Maria and Michael Roe

Margaret Procter, Maria C. Roe and A. Michael Roe: Life and Work with Unhappy Children: An Appreciation

Conrad Graham

To many readers of this book concerning unhappy children the names of Margaret Procter, Dr Maria C. Roe and A. Michael Roe will mean very little. Since all three of them have been known to me professionally and socially for some forty years, Dr Ved Varma, the editor, has asked me to explain to the reader why he has personally dedicated the book to them.

All three were leaders in the field of educational psychology from the 1960s to the 1980s and, along with Jeanne Currie, OBE (former County Educational Psychologist for Durham), Jack Wright, OBE (former County Educational Psychologist for Hampshire), and possibly myself (former Principal Educational Psychologist for the London Borough of Brent), they developed the role of educational psychologists in helping children, many of whom were certainly unhappy.

All of us are now retired and we can look back at thirty years of accomplishment in helping thousands of children. None is medically qualified (Dr here means a PhD in psychology); all are ex-teachers with honours degrees in psychology and postgraduate training in educational psychology; all worked as basic educational psychologists before gaining seniority and taking on more administrative roles.

Margaret Procter retired as Principal Educational Psychologist for the Inner London Education Authority (ILEA) in 1978 after having held that post for 21 years. She had worked as an educational psychologist in London from 1950, and when she retired she was responsible for 55 full-time and 13 part-time educational psychologists. She had established five grades of educational psychologists, with senior specialists in hearing impairment, autism, severe learning difficulty and placement of children with emotional and behaviour difficulty. The twelve inner London boroughs include some of the most deprived areas in the whole country, and the School Psychological Service co-operated fully with Social Service departments.

Margaret trained as a teacher, taught for seven years, and took her psychology degree by evening study at King's College, London University. She then gained a bursary to follow the postgraduate educational psychology training course at the London Child Guidance Training Centre. She worked as an educational psychologist for Wallasey for seven years before returning to London.

In 1965 the Summerfield Committee was established by the Secretary of State for Education to consider the work of educational psychologists employed by local authorities. Professor Arthur Summerfield of the Psychology Department of Birkbeck College, London University, was the chairman and Margaret Procter was a member. She has been an active member of the British Psychological Society, of which she is a Fellow, and has been chairman of the Society's Division of Educational and Child Psychology. Margaret Procter is a quiet and shrewd psychologist who has been highly respected in her long and high-ranking professional life.

Dr Maria Roe retired in 1984 as Senior Staff Inspector of Special Education for ILEA, a post she succeeded to after the retirement of Dr Mary Wilson, OBE, also a trained educational psychologist, who had been Principal Educational Psychologist for Ealing. Maria Roe led a team of six specialist inspectors dealing with hearing impairment, visual impairment, physical disability, mental disability, maladjustment, and child-care staffing for residential establishments. She held this post for ten years and had been an inspector of special education for nine years before this, specializing in physical disability. In 1978 her team was increased to eleven inspectors. In line with the recommendations of the Warnock Report into the education of handicapped children and young people, this team had responsibilities for advice upon and inspection of special educational needs in all phases of education.

Maria Roe was born in Scotland and trained as a teacher of physical education, also qualifying as a physiotherapist. She taught for fourteen years in Manchester and London. In 1956 she took a first-class honours degree in psychology by part-time study at Birkbeck College, London University, and, supported by a university studentship, followed this with a PhD. Her thesis was an investigation into the values and interests of senior grammar school pupils. She undertook her postgraduate training as an educational psychologist at the London Child Guidance Training Centre. From 1959 to 1965 she worked as an educational psychologist for the London County Council. During the period 1961–3 Maria was asked to research into the placement and progress of maladjusted pupils placed in day and boarding schools and tutorial classes. Her report, 'Survey into the progress of maladjusted children', was published in 1965. After this she was the first incumbent of a new educational psychologist post, as liaison officer in placement of maladjusted pupils in boarding schools.

Maria has been heavily involved with the British Psychological Society. She was a member of Council and on the committee of the society's Division of Child and Educational Psychology from 1961 to 1964. She has been a leading light in special education in this country. She was President of the National Association of Special Education in 1972 and was chairman of the International Conference on Special Education held at Canterbury, Kent, in 1975. She has been on countless committees dealing with children with special needs. Maria is a warm-hearted and caring professional who really does take to heart the feelings and views of children, parents and teachers.

After war service, Michael Roe trained as a teacher in London and obtained a first-class general degree in languages. He taught in Middlesex secondary schools for seven years and obtained an honours degree in Psychology by part-time study at Birkbeck College, London University. He too did his postgraduate year's training as an educational psychologist at the London Child Guidance Training Centre, and married Maria in 1956. He worked as an educational psychologist in Kent and became Principal

Educational Psychologist for the London Borough of Bexley in 1965, when the borough was established after London local government reorganization.

Michael has been an active member of the British Psychological Society, of which he is a Fellow. He served for three years as a member of Council and for three years on the Professional Affairs Board. He also served for three years as chairman and three years as secretary of the Society's Division of Child and Educational Psychology. He has been very active in the Association of Educational Psychologists too, where he has been an executive member from the inception of the association in 1961 until he retired from work in 1984. He has also been honorary president twice. Michael is a quiet, retiring professional who, as has been shown, has been most active in the growth of the profession of educational psychology.

All three have brought to the profession good minds, the highest integrity and a total commitment. All have maintained a scientific approach to the diagnosis and provision for children with special needs while showing compassion for the many human tragedies that they have seen. It is in recognition of the doughty spirit exhibited by these three pioneering educational psychologists in fighting for the needs of unhappy children that this book is dedicated to them.

Chapter 1

'Unhappy Children': A Cause for Concern?

Philippa Russell, with a postscript by Richard Lansdown

There is a danger that in looking to the welfare of the children believed to be the victims of abuse, the children themselves may be overlooked. The child is a person and not an object of concern.

Dame Elizabeth Butler-Sloss,
Cleveland Enquiry Report

Childhood is not from birth to a certain age, and at a certain age the child will be grown and put away childish things.
Childhood is the kingdom where nobody dies. Nobody that matters, that is.
Childhood is the kingdom where nobody dies and everybody matters.

Edna St Vincent Millay,
Childhood Is the Kingdom Where Nobody Dies

The Children Act 1989 has introduced a new legislative framework for services for children and their families in England and Wales. For the first time in UK legal history, the concept of the 'paramount welfare' of the child, and the child's right to be heard and taken seriously, dominates family life. In a rapidly changing society, with major social and demographic changes, children, like adults, are frequently victims, sometimes victors. Listening to children can be a painful and cathartic experience. But it is also a challenge to understand better what being a child means in certain families, schools and localities, and to learn rapidly from what we hear about children's lives in a changing society.

Difficult and disruptive behaviour has been preoccupying the minds of the national and professional press in the early 1990s. There appears to be an increasing number of exclusions of 'difficult' children and young people from schools – in part due to the consequences of the 1988 Education Reform Act and local management in schools, but also due to an apparent escalation in the numbers of very disturbed children in local communities. The Staffordshire 'Pindown' Inquiry into residential care similarly identified care staff bewildered and unable to cope with children who seem more unhappy and problematic than any they had to cope with during their training days. But 'difficult' and 'disruptive' behaviour does not occur as an isolated instance in the lives of children.

Martin Herbert (1987) has noted that *parents'* enjoyment of their children diminishes very rapidly and often gives way to anxious concern, and perhaps anger and resentment, when children show signs of abnormal emotions or behaviour. Herbert notes reassuringly that few parents, carers or teachers have *not* observed unhappy children and undesirable forms of behaviour at some time or another. Many emotions (including anger, depression and grief) may be perfectly appropriate in particular situations. The difficulty may be in deciding whether they are definitely abnormal and when to call for further action and support.

SOCIAL CATEGORIZATIONS OF SPECIAL NEEDS: FITTING SERVICES TO CHILDREN, OR CHILDREN TO SERVICES?

Children are frequently regarded as failures or as disruptive when they fail to match up to the standards of achievement or behaviour expected of them. But their 'categorization' may tell us more about the rules and values of the service which rejects them than it does about the children themselves. Very few children's behaviour falls into the convenient categories of 'normal' or 'difficult'. Rather, behaviour (and learning difficulties) tend to occur within a continuum and may be seen as tolerable or impossible according to various criteria, and by different people. Most behaviour is clearly affected by a range of outside factors, including family circumstances, the child's social environment and the school itself. David Galloway (1987), examining the interaction between *schools* and children's behaviour, speculates that:

> The root cause of disruptive behaviour may or may not lie in the structure of society . . . teachers (and parents and other professionals) cannot change the society in which their pupils live (though the children will be changing society for better or worse in twenty to years time). In contrast teachers can change their school and there is ample evidence that schools have a much greater influence in children's lives than was at one time supposed.

Definitions of 'moderate' learning difficulties, or emotional and behavioural difficulties, have always been variable. The Education Act 1944 used the categories of 'maladjustment' to describe children whose behaviour was so problematic that they required special educational provision. But children with the definition of 'educationally subnormal mild' were often interlinked with the current definitions of difficult behaviour, and a number of black educationists in the 1960s (in particular Bernard Coard) cited the growing use of the ESN(M) schools for black children who were theoretically so placed because of learning difficulties but in practice were seen as having difficult behaviour and a range of social problems.

Concern about the misdiagnosis of children with moderate learning difficulties or emtional and behavioural problems has refocused attention on two major studies. The National Children's Bureau's National Child Development Study (Essen and Wedge, 1979) assessed a cohort of children at birth and at 7, 11 and 16 years. The teachers participating in the assessments considered 22 per cent of the children to be 'unsettled' and 14 per cent to show 'irritable behaviour' in the study. A study by Graham *et al.* (1970) found 25 per cent of children in inner urban areas in the Isle of Wight Study to have similar behaviour problems and learning difficulties – both studies in fact endorsed the Warnock view that 20 per cent of children were likely to have some form of learning difficulty during their school life.

Importantly, both the National Child Development and the Isle of Wight studies found a high correlation between difficult behaviour, moderate learning difficulties and wider social circumstances. The Court Committee's Report on Child Health Services (Department of Health, 1976) had already found that 'an adverse family and social environment can retard physical, emotional and intellectual growth . . . and adversely affect educational achievement and personal behaviour'. The National Child Development Study also found that pupils considered to have moderate learning difficulties were ten times more likely to have come from homes regarded as being in social disadvantage. The study described such disadvantage on a scale that included many factors, such as: a child having experienced a period of time in the care of a local authority; large families; poor housing; unemployment; and illness in one or both parents. As there is growing concern about the increased numbers of those living in poverty, the negative impact of social deprivation upon educational attainment seems unlikely to decrease.

However, a social construct of moderate learning difficulties does not in itself clearly indicate how the balance may be changed towards more positive achievements. Martin Herbert (1987), looking at children regarded as 'difficult', has noted that the majority of children who are posing problems and apparently underachieving are not so much difficult as 'unhappy', 'problematic' or 'not fitting in'. Herbert also notes that parents' and teachers' enjoyment and appreciation of a child may rapidly diminish and give rise to anger, resentment or concern when the child shows signs of difficult behaviour or learning difficulties.

Herbert identified three key stages in the identification of real difficulties; that is to say, the point at which 'it is inappropriate to be philosophical about a child's difficulties, when your alarm bells should ring, when you cease to say "Ah well, they'll grow out of it".' He conceptualized three key situations which triggered real anxiety about a child's progress, namely:

- when the child is not *understandable*;
- when behaviour is *unpredictable*;
- when the child is *rebellious* (i.e. when the child is out of control with himself or herself, with peers and with the learning and social environment).

The association between disadvantage/negative life experiences and a learning or emotional difficulty may, however, be difficult to quantify – at least in terms of determining whether it is short-term or longer-term. Kerfoot and Butler (1988) note:

> We know this not only from experience but from major studies of the incidence of such problems in the general population. Social workers for example tend to see such families at their point of maximum stress, when they are striving to cope with an extreme environmental and psychological pressure such as poverty, poor housing, unemployment, illness and death. The children we encounter frequently reflect this adversity. In such circumstances the fact that the child is upset, miserable, cowed or angry is entirely understandable. Indeed in the face of such adversity, a cheerful smiling face might cause us to question the child's perception and assessment of the world about it.

The problems of discontinuity in personal, social and educational experiences are exemplified in the educational experiences of children in care. Sonia Jackson's research (1987) cites a number of groups of young people who have been in the care of the local authority, and describes their real sense of regret at the educational opportunities missed; the negative experiences of family breakdown and the lack of personal esteem which results from such multiple difficulties.

Nationally, there now appears to be a trend towards greater integration of children with a wide range of difficulties and special needs into ordinary services. But moderate learning difficulties associated with emotional and behavioural difficulties can still lead to exclusions – to separate education and the increased use of residential special schools (often in the private sector) as a means of containing a difficult problem. For children with moderate learning difficulties, perhaps the major challenge is in identifying and responding to the specific educational and welfare needs of the *individual* child, while acknowledging that such a child-centred approach may not be effective without attention to the child's actual *environment*. The provisions in the Children Act for 'children in need' may help to resolve the often rigid divide between educational and social care. Unfortunately, at present, as David Galloway (1987) comments:

> There have unfortunately been few serious attempts to integrate sociological and psychological approaches . . . many disruptive or unhappy pupils do have exceptional personal needs which cannot be ignored in any comprehensive treatment plan. Equally important though is the fact that disruptive behaviour is a chronically stressful and time consuming problem in some schools (or other settings) while in others with similar pupils or children this is not the case. Responses to disruptive behaviour – often associated with moderate learning difficulties – must not only recognise the importance of factors in the pupils and their backgrounds but also in the relevance of factors in the institution itself.

Galloway's warning about the importance of acknowledging factors in the supposedly helping services as contributing to disruption and depression is borne out in a number of the contributions to this book. For example, Theo Cox (see Chapter 10) notes the increase over the past decade in the number of children who are experiencing adverse family conditions in line with national changes in the economic conditions, demographic structures and social policies for families in the United Kingdom. Jonathan Bradshaw (1990), in a study for the National Children's Bureau and UNICEF, has shown that the number of children living in poverty has doubled over the past few years. The gap between these poorer families and the rest of the population has also grown wider, which must compound the sense of poor self-esteem and low expectations of what seems increasingly likely to become an 'underclass'. Cox notes that *schools* may have lower expectations of poorer families and their children (perhaps a self-fulfilling prophecy). He also draws attention to the Plowden Report's emphasis upon the importance of providing compensatory environments for deprived pupils in schools, which would include the provision of *extra* resources, such as more experienced and better qualified teachers, teachers' aides, etc., together with a conscious policy of mobilizing *families* to see their children's education as their business. Plowden's forecasts of cumulative adverse effects from neglecting combinations of family poverty, poor education resources and low expectations of children seem sadly relevant. Local management of schools can force hard choices on many schools, and tolerance of 'difficult' or 'disruptive' children diminishes in the light of schools' need to produce credible examination results while working within tight budgets and with less support from the LEA's advisory services.

SOCIAL CATEGORIZATION OF UNHAPPY CHILDREN: SERVICE RESPONSES

James Gray, looking at emotional and disruptive behaviour in the classroom (see Chapter 9), further pursues the theme of positive learning environments in schools by noting that *teachers* themselves can become part of a cycle of disruption and deprivation. Teacher stress is more than an occupational hazard. 'Burn-out' in the health, education and social services professionals is now frequently discussed. And burn-out may in turn diminish the coping capacity and reduce the range of strategies which the services and institutions can apply to making children more successful and better adjusted. Gray notes that while children may become 'disruptive' or 'unhappy' for various reasons, once in the cycle of difficult behaviour it is exceedingly difficult to emerge unscathed. Coping (like avoidance) strategies seem to be minimal, and it is perhaps not surprising that a recent survey for *Young Minds* (March 1992), looking at exclusions from education in a group of children living in residential care, found a very large number of children out of school with no alternative forms of education on offer. Their adverse social circumstances, combined with their perceived threat to the school and low expectations of their capacity or willingness to learn, had been a self-confirming prophecy in terms of their isolation and alienation from the education system. Gray questions the social categorizations made of children by teachers and other professionals:

> If a teacher can be persuaded to translate his or her perception that a pupil is 'lazy' into the recognition that the pupil may feel unable to do the work, it opens up avenues of positive action that the teacher may take. Similarly, if the teacher can translate the perception that a pupil is 'rude' into recognition of the fact that the pupil probably lacks social skills, it becomes possible for the teacher to do something to help the pupil.
>
> (p. 117)

Gray sees such a new conceptual approach as a specific example of 'a move away from categorization of "handicapped" pupils to recognition of their special educational needs as advocated in the Warnock Report'.

EVERYDAY LIVES: FEELING ABOUT DISABILITY, LISTENING TO CHILDREN WITH LEARNING DIFFICULTIES

The past decade has seen a marked swing of the pendulum towards policy-makers and planners seeing *children* as partners in assessment and in planning their own futures. Historically both education and child-care legislation saw children as primarily the responsibility of parents. The Gillick Judgment in 1986, affirming the right of young people of 'sufficient maturity' to seek independent medical advice, was the start of a significant sea-change towards acknowledging the rights of children *and* parents. The Education Act 1981 did not formally acknowledge this new relationship, although Circular 22/89 notes that LEAs will be expected to involve children in decision-making wherever possible. But the Children Act begins with the principle of 'paramount welfare of the child', and envisages a new professional role in working much more closely with children and recognizing that they can make valid choices and that their views must be respected. Attitudes to children with disabilities and special needs, however, have not always been so positive.

Maureen Oswin, writing in 1971 of the lives of children with multiple disabilities, described Jason, aged 5:

Cerebral Palsy had given him permanently writhing limbs and slurred speech. Family rejection had given him a never-eased home sickness. Social provision gave him a hospital to live in. A lively mind gave him an insatiable curiosity about the world.

'Why can't I purr like a kitten?' he asked. This was fairly easy to answer.

'Why did my Mummy eat me?'

'*Eat* you?' This was startling.

'Yes, you told me yesterday I was in her tummy when I was a baby, how did I get there, did she eat me?'

After a while this was sorted out to our mutual satisfaction.

'Where did I keep my tears when . . . I am not using them?' This was a little harder. He may well wonder where they came from, he had known more tears than the rest of us.

'Why do I get sad such a lot of times?' All the past answers from past experience with inquisitive infant children could not rescue me very comfortably from the question.

'Have I got to spend all my life in this hospital?' What answer now?

I thought of all the brave reforms throughout social history, the early crude attempts to help the destitute and improve workhouses, housing, education and factories. There were all the committees, Members of Parliament, journalists, civil servants, the charities, the wealthy and the poor, whose opinions and ideals had shaped English social history over the past 200 years. There were Children's Acts, Housing Acts, Education Acts, Mental Health Acts, the National Health Service and Acts for Divorce, Criminal Justice and Abortion. There were laws to protect women, homosexuals, animals, immigrants, house purchasers, landlords, street vendors and car drivers – the twentieth century, the age of human reasoning and compassion. But where did young Jason and his kind fit into this good age of reform and broad thinking? 'You're not answering me', he said. '*Will* I have to stay all my life in this hospital?'

(pp. 255–6)

Maureen Oswin, like Piaget in the 1920s and Mia Kellmer Pringle in the 1960s, endeavours to reconstruct the world from the point of view of the *child* – and to ask important questions about whether we see children as individuals, or whether we create definitions of children to fit preconceived definitions relating to labels like 'moderate learning difficulties', 'mental handicap' or any other 'category' of special need.

Listening to children like Jason can be a painful experience. Their sharp sense of the realities and limitations of their world profoundly affect their capacity to make educational progress. They also underline the principle of the Children Act – that we should be putting children first and hearing what children say.

David Galloway (1987), cited above with reference to moderate learning difficulties, quotes the case of a 15-year-old boy who had been excluded from his local school:

'My mum said she hated the sight of me – and she said it in Court as well . . . Every time I go to see her, she tells me to piss off home . . . it was always me who got into trouble with the police. Our Dan didn't and our Ben didn't either. If I argue with my mother, our Ben hits me and if I argue with Ben, Dad hits me, so I can't win anyway. I asked to see Miss O again [an educational psychologist] but the deputy head said she was too busy. No-one has time for you.'

But young people can learn to speak more powerfully for themselves. A group of young women with a range of special educational needs participating in a National Children's

Bureau project – *Something to Say* (Bargh and Wertheimer, in press) – wrote their own collective response to their schools, to the other children and to their families, and to themselves, trying to adjust to the loss of esteem and personal identity which they felt their disability had conferred upon them. Their 'imaginary friends', Miss Can and Miss Can't, vividly express their aspirations and their sense of limitation when faced with the gap between what they wanted and what they felt they had achieved. But just as parents can acquire self-awareness and confidence by challenging themselves as well as the system, so the *Something to Say* group found they could help their schools and their parents to help them. Many children with special needs, however, pay a heavy price for striving for conformity in a world where 'norms' are implicitly if not explicitly observed.

The young women in *Something to Say* saw themselves as in many ways more disabled than they were. Their image of Miss Can't presented a young woman who was unattractive, unintelligent and with various physical impediments. None of these categorizations was accurate. Micheline Mason (1981), writing about her realization of the impact of her *physical* disability on her growth and development as a child, says:

> The first time the doubt that I belonged to this particular planet struck me, it was a glorious calm blue-skied day when I was twelve years old. Lying flat on my back in the garden, I was thinking about growing up. Until that moment, I think I had somehow believed that when I grew up, I would become 'normal', i.e. without a disability. 'Normal' then meant to me 'like my big sister', pretty, rebellious, going out with boys, leaving school, getting a job, leaving home, getting married, having children. That momentous day I suddenly realised that my life was not going to be like that at all. I was going to be just the same as I had always been – very small, funny shaped, unable to walk. It seemed that at that moment the sky cracked . . . my girl friend from next door came out and wanted a game as she had done many times before. I remember her look of confusion when I said I didn't want to play any more.

Micheline began the slow process of abandoning her 'handicapped identity':

> Animals have it easy. I mean for example it's very unlikely that a horse wastes much time wondering if she really is a horse, whilst human beings seem disposed to spend vast amounts of time wondering if they really are human beings at all. Well some do.

The growth of the self-advocacy group for people with learning difficulties, People First, has clearly shown that even people with communication problems and severe learning difficulties *do* have clear images of themselves and (although it is often unexpressed) may feel discrimination and isolation as keenly as their peers. Making sense of special educational needs for children with moderate or severe learning difficulties therefore requires communication skills and the time and energy to promote positive self-images and expectations; but above all else to encourage maximum independence and personal autonomy. Such autonomy may be painful for pupils, parents and schools.

David Jones and Helen Barrett, writing about unhappy children with learning difficulties (see Chapter 7), emphasize the importance of acknowledging the special vulnerability of children with special needs, and the possibility that children (like Micheline Mason in the quotation above) may have an incomplete understanding of a complex social world and the behaviours expected in order to survive within it. But they also emphasize the importance of developing coping strategies and acknowledging the possibility of change and development.

Parents have a special role to play in acknowledging their children's special needs and their cognitive capacity, so that they can reduce the causes of frustration and confusion for the children. An extensive literature on the feelings and perceptions of parents of children with special needs has clearly shown both the capacity of parents to encourage positive attitudes in children with special needs, and also the emotional and physical pressures of providing such care. The Office of Population and Census Surveys' reports on the lives of children with disabilities and their families (1989) found that 50 per cent of parents with children who have disabilities or chronic health problems felt that their own health had been adversely affected by the extra burden of care. Similar numbers felt that they could seldom go out and have an ordinary social life; they were financially worse off than their peers without disabled children; and, contrary to beliefs about the universality of the self-help movement, only 38 per cent knew of any local or national voluntary organization which might help them. Helping the children of these families must therefore mean developing positive attitudes to family support, and avoiding simplistic notions of 'integration' or 'normalization' without this support.

COPING STRATEGIES: PEER RELATIONS

David Jones and Helen Barrett (see Chapter 7) underline the importance of peer-group relations, and the difficulties encountered by children who look 'different'. But they also emphasize the importance of looking at coping strategies. Can other children be sources of help and support for unhappy children? Perhaps we underestimate the concept of children as co-workers.

But what do other children think? Ann Lewis (1991) looks at a number of studies of the precise nature of interaction between so-called 'normal' pupils and those with special educational needs. She notes a wide range of shared learning experiences in the best schools, including the use of 'buddies', peer tutoring, co-operative learning and collaborative learning. She finds certain key themes in the studies which are of considerable importance in creating a positive climate of opinion towards integration for children with severe learning difficulties.

1.   When asked to describe their peers with severe learning difficulties, very few of the 'ordinary' children made any reference to their lack of ability. Overwhelmingly the children were described – like other children – in terms of their physical characteristics: 'Some have got brown eyes. Lucy has a red dress.'
2.   The 'ordinary' children generally believed that when their peers with learning difficulties grew up, they too would have ordinary jobs like being teachers, taxi-drivers, etc.
3.   The above belief was, in some ways, often linked to perceptions of the children with learning difficulties as young and therefore as going to 'grow out of it'. Older 'ordinary' children needed some explanation in order to understand continued difficult behaviour or problems with learning. In effect they needed to have some understanding of the internal as well as external features of the other children.
4.   All children are different (with or without formally ascertained special needs). The inclusion of children with severe learning difficulties often contributed to awareness of the 'uniqueness' of individuals and was not a negative experience.

In effect other children are part of the solution to (as well as part of the problem of) unhappiness in the peer group.

CHANGING POLICY AND PRACTICE IN SCHOOLS: WHAT DO THE CHILDREN THINK?

Although there is now a sizeable groundswell of parental aspirations towards integration, the feelings and wishes of the children (particularly those with severe learning difficulties) have been little documented. Popular views assume that children with severe learning difficulties tend to be marginalized and possibly ridiculed, certainly often frightened, in an integrated school environment. But young people with severe learning difficulties are very well aware of being treated differently. The young women who drew 'Miss Can' and 'Miss Can't' so graphically clearly stated their views about 'special' buses and provision, and about being labelled 'stupid' by their neighbours and peers. They also recognized, however, in their book *Bring Back the Thinking Memories* (Bargh and Wertheimer, in press), that the special school head 'always smiled' and that they felt welcome. But is being made to feel welcome enough? Integration is not only about school, it is about what next – and about life in the community.

People First is the first coalition of self-advocacy groups of people with learning difficulties in the United Kingdom. Its members are firmly discounting the belief that people with learning difficulties cannot make their own views known. June Statham (1987) recounts the views of the members of one group. One member, Lorraine, enjoyed her small residential school, saying that 'I wouldn't have liked to go to an ordinary school. I'd be afar behind. I wouldn't be able to keep up.' But her peers took very different views. Eileen, who has Down's syndrome, is graphic in her description of her school days in a special school:

'I went to an ordinary school till I was nine. The headmistress didn't have no time for me. They said I was damaged in my brain and sent me for tests. The tests didn't show anything wrong, but I still got sent to an ESN school. My mother fought it. She went to County Hall, but I still had to go . . . they said it was for a short time but once I got there they didn't bother any more. I couldn't go back. It was horrible. I could have learned a lot but I didn't get any education, nothing at all. I felt I missed out on everything that was going on. They shouldn't have special schools. They shouldn't even have special classes because that's the same really. Like in one school there's a class they called the Lower Class and all the Down's Syndrome children were in that class . . . You're saying "You're Down's Syndrome so you should be shut away".'

Levels of interaction between both groups of children varied in the study. Judy Sebba's research (1983) showed that levels of interaction were lower at the beginning of a school year (when children did not know each other) and at the end of the year, when the 'ordinary children' had moved even further ahead in terms of interests and ability. Sebba suggested that attention should be given to grouping children according to their cognitive or literacy skills rather than on a chronological basis, but noted that this causes social, ethical and educational dilemmas – not least because the majority of children performed at different levels in different activities.

What is clear is that the 'ordinary' group of children produced some interesting 'enablers' who were adept at managing collaborative tasks with their partners with special needs. There was no clear correlation between their skills and having previous experience of disability or of having younger siblings. The 'enablers' came from both sexes and included the less able children. But what they had in common was the ability to sequence and to work effectively on common tasks, drawing on different but complementary skills and avoiding dominance. We need to know more about 'enabling children' – not least because their skills could be utilized with a wider range of children who find life difficult or problematic. They also demonstrate that children with severe learning difficulties, integrated in a mainstream situation, need not be isolated or marginalized if attention is given to nurturing positive peer relationships, if the class has sufficient information to avoid misconceptions or anxiety, and if the abilities of children to act as peer-tutors and co-workers is strengthened and utilized. Integration in terms of peer relationships should be a partnership, without well-meaning but inappropriate 'babying' or dominance, and avoiding neglect. Research suggests that children find living with integration easier than do their parents!

UNHAPPY CHILDREN: THE IMPACT OF LIFE EVENTS

Clinical depression as seen in adults is quite rare in children before adolescence. However, loss, bereavement or other major life experiences can have profound effects on even very young children. Adolescents are particularly prone to periods of misery, disturbed sleep, weight loss, and experiments with diet, drugs or solvent abuse. They may experience considerable anxiety about school bullying, and about school performance. Although the rate of child suicides is low in the United Kingdom as compared to some other countries, such as Japan and the USA, there is a steady annual increase. Many of these young people are regarded by their peers, family or professional carers as having been at some times unhappy, depressed (however defined) or anxious in the periods before their death.

The Isle of Wight Study (Graham *et al.*, 1970) found that as many as one in seven children with a significant health problem or a physical disability had additional behavioural difficulties and emotional problems. There is growing evidence from studies of children in families where there is chronic disability or illness in another family member (for example, Grimshaw's 1991 study of parents with Parkinson's disease) that the role of being a 'young carer', and particularly the gradual erosion of the parents' strength and the increase of their ill-health (which implies a changed identity), may create considerable grief and suppressed anxiety about the future of the family. Donald Winnacott (1962) hypothesized that when a parent had a mental illness, or depression associated with a disability or physical illness, children often developed a 'false self' as a defence against their disturbed environment, and that this 'false self' might have to be broken down before the child could function normally. Child 'carers' who lack good parenting are particularly prone to confused images of reality, and may have low self-esteem and insecurity because of an uncertain future. One child, trying to explain the sometimes bizarre behaviour of his mentally ill mother, described her as 'a parent who is there but isn't there'. Jeremy Seabrook (1983), in a compilation of personal experiences of depression and unhappiness, quotes the story of Paul Collins, the son of a father with muscular dystrophy. Paul says:

> 'My father died of muscular dystrophy when I was 13. The first five years of my life had been wonderful. My father was generous, in love with my mother . . . it was 1946. We had just won the war and he was about to launch himself in a new career. For three months we had the first telephone in the neighbourhood – then we had to have it removed. My mother had been bursting in confidence in her Reg. He was brilliant. But in the end it destroyed both of them. When they had the news that he had dystrophy, it all collapsed. My boyhood from five to twelve was seven years' death.'

Paul goes on to describe his continuing sadness that he could not help his father. Once, feeling better, his father built a metal boat powered by methylated spirits. It was a boat with a real engine. Paul says:

> 'I felt strange recalling a *strong* Daddy in the past, by almost expecting *this* Daddy to sabotage everything. Lo and behold, the boat sailed into the chickweed and some boys on the opposite bank bombarded it with stones. My Dad never really tried to stop them. He could have, I could have, we just stood there. As a child I became passive, shaken, deprived, withdrawn. They had promised me too much and I was selfish to be sad at getting so little. I felt resented, lost, retarded – the house that had seemed a space rocket had a become a haunted tomb.'

Paul felt that no one had the time to see how much he grieved for his 'real father' and how much he hated the actual reality. Bereavement counselling is now frequently offered to adults who have suffered a loss. But it is rarely offered to children – and information on the actual disability and *why* a parent changes is seldom available. Roger Grimshaw (1991), in his study of parents with Parkinson's disease, similarly notes that the children who were not given accurate information and from whom secrets were kept were the most anxious and the most likely to have horrific images of disability and of the consequences for their own lives. Honesty with children may be painful (particularly in a society where open discussion about disease, disability or death is often taboo). But illness in the family is still a common reason for children's admission into the care of the local authority. It can divide and isolate, and the child's perception of events is frequently one, like Paul's, of increasing and overwhelming loss.

But unhappiness and anxiety about illness may not only be due to real difficulties in a family. They may be caused by a situation where a child is propelled into an adult acceptance not only of illness but of prospects of death, and sometimes of a condition which cannot be discussed with friends, school or relatives because of the stigma attached to it. The present author (Russell, 1992), in some case studies of the impact of AIDS/HIV on children and young people, describes two such people:

- *Sadie* is ten years old and has been noted by her class teacher as seeming 'sad, deeply dejected, often tired and sleeping in class'. She has stopped attending the school drama club, which she loves. The school wondered if she was being abused – but preliminary enquiries produced a terse rebuttal and the inadequate information that 'there were problems in the family'. Sadie (not her real name) has a brother with haemophilia. He does not have HIV – but her father and mother do (for reasons quite unrelated to her brother's haemophilia). Her father is well. Her mother is becoming increasingly sick and depressed. Sadie is an intelligent child who watches TV – she knows she and her brother may be orphaned over the next few years. She knows that her grandparents do not (officially) know about AIDS/HIV in the family. She wonders if they will accept her and her brother when the inevitable happens. She would like to talk to her class teacher – but HIV is 'Top Secret' and she knows she must *never* mention it. She takes time increasingly off school to help her mother. She knows she must not ask for help.

- Peter is fourteen. He has a drug-abusing older brother who has frequently been in trouble with the police. Peter has been teased and bullied at school and told he and his brother 'must have AIDS'. The drug connection means that his best friend has been forbidden to play with him. Peter is convinced he *has* AIDS. No one knows where his brother now is – nor do they know if he is HIV-positive. Peter has taken one dose of paracetamol and ended up in casualty. Unlike Sadie, however, his school knew about his brother and the bullying. A whole-school programme on health education and AIDS/HIV, together with the support of a teacher, has encouraged Peter to be more positive. After counselling, he had an AIDS test. It was of course negative. His imagined 'symptoms' disappeared. But without support his unhappiness and real fears that he had a terminal illness could have led to a second and possibly successful suicide attempt.

Sadie and Peter are both facing a 'contemporary' life event – the impact of AIDS/HIV. But a whole range of circumstances may occur to change children's (and families') expectations and to disrupt seriously what might have been thought to be the child (or family's) usual life-style. Kedar Nath Dwivedi (see Chapter 11), writing about the experiences of families from minority ethnic groups, reminds us of the importance of radical changes to family support systems. He describes the experience of dislocation, cultural shock and loss of informal support systems, and the alien, threatening and sometimes hostile culture in which new migrant families arrive. He notes that in Britain '"migrants" are often subjected to a stereotype of themselves and have projected on to them a variety of undesirable characteristics' (p. 136). Children from ethnic minorities may feel hopeless when they experience racial discrimination, bullying, teasing or more overt physical violence, because such discrimination will rarely have been part of the experiences of the ethnic majority.

Similarly David Bond (see Chapter 3), looking at the emotional difficulties experienced by hearing-impaired children, notes the interrelationship of external events which affect the *whole* family in terms of directly impacting on children's behaviour and personal self-esteem. But he also stresses the importance of giving children coping strategies – creating 'opportunities for reciprocal gains for the learner and the adult, e.g. shared pleasure, which makes possible gain in skills and development of positive social relationships' (p. 48). He suggests that children with disabilities or major difficulties need the 'opportunity for improvement of ideas about self' (p. 49), with a recognition of individual skills and interests and the chance to prove independence and responsibility.

In many respects, the challenge of negative life events (particularly if presenting in the context of an already disadvantaged and perhaps emotionally deprived childhood and home environment) is not dissimilar to the challenge of the increasingly acknowledged 'griefwork' which needs to be done when there is serious physical illness or death in a family. Barbara Soricelli and Carolyn Utech (1985), working in the oncology department of the Children's Memorial Hospital in Chicago, have created a framework for coping with grief and loss. The framework follows the well-established 'model' of bereavement or loss, integration (the beginning of coping strategies), renewed bereavement (as the reality and certainty are fully faced and understood), the actual loss (the child or parent dies, a family member is lost through divorce or other reasons), and finally the 'facilitating growth'. The difference between the Soricelli and Utech framework and many others is that it acknowledges that parallel (although not exactly similar) processes of grief and adaptation affect children *and* parents, and that the former, if ignored in terms of coping strategies, may well develop difficult behaviour or – perhaps more sadly – simply never communicate fears and feelings.

The chapters in Soricelli and Utech's book describe a range of children whose 'difficult' or 'unhappy' behaviour occurred in response to a complex world in which they (the children) had been compelled to undertake unacceptably adult roles, and where there had been little appropriate support or even appreciation of the child's real needs. But there are also some positive messages, particularly with reference to children with disabilities, and to the possibility of working with parents as well as children in order to create a community which is more sensitive to individual needs. At a time when child poverty is increasing and when there are radical changes in the organization of health, education and social services, Soricelli and Utech remind us of the importance of listening to and learning from children.

THE KEY TO THE FUTURE?

The Children Act 1989, as noted at the beginning of this chapter, creates a new climate of opinion within which the views and wishes of the child are seen as integral to any decision-making about his or her well-being. In theory, legislation has always listened to children. But in practice their involvement in planning processes, and their wishes and perceptions about their preferred life-styles and futures, have often been paid scant attention. Children may be unhappy for many internal and external reasons. But the key principle within the Children Act – that of partnership with parents *and* children – must be an important step forward in acknowledging that children's feelings about themselves, their lives and their family circumstances will have a direct impact on their future.

In 1971, King, Raynes and Tizard looked at child-care issues in the context of changing patterns of residential care for difficult or disturbed children. Their thoughts are just as relevant to the unhappy or disturbed children of the 1990s, living in residential care or with their own or substitute families:

> Having tried to avoid value judgements . . . we wish to state explicitly our belief that child-orientated practices are 'better' for children and therefore more desirable than institutionally-orientated practices. Kindliness and consideration, an environment in which children are respected as persons, treated as individuals and given varieties of experience seem to us important, in our society and at this time, whether or not they benefit children in measurable terms. And we think that inasmuch as . . . children are treated in a manner which is impersonal and institutional, not only do they suffer but the community also loses something of its human dignity and human happiness. Of course if it could be shown that child-orientated practices had consequences which were actually harmful, one would have to think again. But there is no suggestion that this is a real issue'.

Perhaps, if the overarching belief behind the Children Act – that children's wishes and feelings matter – can be translated into wider professional practice, we shall see fewer disturbed and disturbing children, and we shall overcome some of the obvious tensions of having 'systems' for service provision which are sometimes in conflict with the particular needs of children themselves.

POSTSCRIPT: WHAT MAKES A HAPPY CHILD?

Adults, reflecting on their early experiences, commonly generalize about their childhood: from 'It was idyllic' at one extreme to 'I was miserable for the first seventeen years' at the other. When these experiences are examined it is possible to detect certain threads running through them, threads which transcend divisions of class, culture and the physical or mental characteristics of the people concerned.

First, let us distinguish between an unhappy child and unhappy behaviour. So often, too often, it is assumed that the two are synonymous. There are good reasons for argu-ing that children whose behaviour causes distress to those about them are unhappy in that context, but the converse is not always true: those who conform to the mores of the society in which they live are not always, *ipso facto*, content with their lot. The shy child can easily be passed over in any rating of behaviour disturbance.

For many years there has been an increase in society's sensitivity towards minorities. This sensitivity, although it has culminated in the patronizing absurdity of so-called politically correct language, has justifiable roots: we had to learn to take account not only of the differences between groups but also of the value of alternative ways of life. We have, however, been pushed into seeing these differences as paramount to such an extent that universals of behaviour have been swamped or deliberately ignored as incorrect.

Yet universals there are, in development (all children walk and talk) and in needs. If we can satisfactorily establish the universal needs of children, then we can begin to understand what it is that makes them unhappy. I would like to put forward the view that we can reduce these needs to two constructs, which could be labelled 'love v. cruelty' and 'direction v. letting go'.

The need for love remains throughout life, but the way that the love is shown must change: it is easy for care appropriate for a toddler to become smothering affection when the child reaches puberty. When we look at the direction construct we can see a steady movement from one pole to the other. Neonates are at one end, needing to be directed in most areas of their activity – we would not expect them to decide, for exam-ple, when their nappies are changed. On the other hand, we know that infants can and do influence their care-givers. The sensitive care-giver is the one who responds to the baby's signals, leading to the dance of development in which first the child and then the adult takes a step. Much development can then be subsumed broadly within this con-struct as we observe children moving towards greater autonomy. They move when parents, and later teachers or other significant adults, allow them to and when they have sufficient power within themselves to encourage them to shift – hence the importance of self-esteem. They grow in self-esteem as they widen their horizons and test their limits, a testing that is carried out most successfully against a backdrop of secure paren-tal love and care – hence the continuing importance of the first construct. The active, lively, happy child is one who can constantly experiment in life, knowing that in the end there is someone to fall back on.

We cannot, of course, expect all children to move towards autonomy at the same rate; we cannot expect all to reach the same degree of independence; nor can we anticipate a necessarily smooth transition for everyone.

Can there be such a thing as a test of the above hypothesis? Psychologists make much of tests – is it possible to devise one for happiness? At a basic level we can see whether children are growing, eating and sleeping adequately; three measures which should not be dismissed because of their apparent simplicity. At a more complex level we can ask how many decisions they make, in an appropriate way, about their everyday lives. We can ask about their friendships – a child without friends is an emotional cripple for whom there is no wheelchair.

The Children Act is about looking after children and listening to them. If we do both we have gone a long way towards ensuring, as best we can, their happiness. Unhappiness lies in the mismatch between children's needs at any particular time and the extent to which those needs are met. If we follow the model proposed above, we can see that children whose condition leads to them being teased will be more or less unhappy depending on the extent to which their early and continuing nurturance has built a high level of self-esteem. Children whose physical disabilities, or economic poverty, prevent them from activities that they see their peers enjoying will similarly be unhappy, depending on what else life has given them to offset their regrets. Children who lose their parents, from death or divorce, will be doubly bereft because the remaining parent is also diminished and may then have a distorted view of the child's needs. The parent who neglects or ill-treats a child is a commonplace in the gallery of misery-causing; less obvious is the one whose need to have someone dependent leads to a smothering and a refusal to allow movement from the apron strings, whether the apron belongs to a father or a mother.

Teachers, too, have their role to play in helping children along the journey, of encouraging the individual to flourish while simultaneously providing a bedrock of respected authority. As several studies have shown, schools really can influence the way children behave. Good practice is often seen in primary schools. Sadly, the secondary sector sometimes becomes a battlefield, with baffled, restless teenagers locked in combat, when they are in school, with baffled, cynical teachers.

In the last analysis we talk of a sharing of ideas and ideals. Friends are important because they enable us to share hopes, fears, happiness and sadness. Happy children live in an environment where there is harmony between their expectations, their awareness of what they are capable of and what they need, and the expectations and awareness of those who look after them. This is so for the child who is able-bodied and for the disabled, irrespective of the parental bank balance, and whatever the colour or shade of the child's skin.

REFERENCES

Bargh, J. and Wertheimer, A. (in press) *Something to Say: New Approaches to Working with Young Women with Learning Difficulties*. London: National Children's Bureau.

Bradshaw, J. (1990) *Child Poverty and Deprivation in the UK*. London: National Children's Bureau.

Department of Health (1976) *Fit for the Future. Report of the Committee of Enquiry into Child Health Services* (The Court Report). London: HMSO.

Essen, J. and Wedge, P. (1979) *Born to Fail*. London: National Children's Bureau.

Galloway, D. (1987) *The Education of Disturbing Children*. London: Longman.

Graham, P. *et al*. In M. Rutter, J. Tizard and K. Whitmore (1970) *Education, Health and Behaviour: The Isle of Wight Study*. London: Longman.

Grimshaw, R. (1991) *Parents with Parkinson's Disease: The Impact on Family Life*. Report to the Parkinson's Disease Society of Great Britain. London: National Children's Bureau.

Herbert, M. (1987) *Conduct Disorders of Childhood and Adolescence*. London: John Wiley.

Jackson, S. (1987) *The Education of Children in Care*. Bristol Papers in Applied Social Studies I. Bristol: School of Applied Social Studies, University of Bristol.

Kerfoot, M. and Butler, A. (1988) *Problems of Childhood and Adolescence*. London: Practical Social Work/Macmillan.

King, D., Raynes, N. and Tizard, J. (1971) *Patterns of Residential Care*. London: Routledge and Kegan Paul.

Lewis, A. (1991) Learning together. In B. Carpenter and K. Bouvair (eds), *Children with Severe Learning Difficulties: The Curriculum Challenge*. London: Falmer Press.

Mason, M. (1981) Finding a voice. In J. Campling (ed.), *Images of Ourselves: Women with Disabilities Talking*. London: Routledge and Kegan Paul.

Office of Population and Census Surveys (1989). *Disabled Children: Services, Transport and Education*. London: HMSO.

Oswin, M. (1971) *The Empty Hours*. Harmondsworth: Penguin.

Russell, P. (1992) Affected by HIV and AIDS: cameos of children and young people. In T. Booth, W. Swann, M. Masterson and P. Potts (eds), *Learning for All No. 1: Curricula for Diversity in Education*. Milton Keynes: Open University Press.

Seabrook, J. (1983) *Loneliness*. London: Maurice Temple Smith.

Sebba, J. (1983) Social interactions among preschool handicapped and non-handicapped children. *Journal of Mental Deficiency Research*, **27**.

Statham, J. (1987) Speaking for ourselves: self advocacy for people with learning difficulties. In T. Booth and W. Swann (eds), *Including Pupils with Disabilities: A Curriculum for All*. Milton Keynes: Open University Press.

Soricelli, B. and Utech, C. (1985) Mourning the death of a child – the family and group process. *Social Work*, October/November. Washington, DC: National Association of Social Workers.

Winnacott, D. W. (1962) Treatment for difficult children. In S. Hardenberg (ed.), *The Child and the Family: First Relationships*. London: Tavistock.

Chapter 2

Coping with Unhappy Children Who Are Visually Impaired

Elizabeth Chapman

If you are young, and need to cry,
let nothing stop you;
get it all done early,
don't dam it back or push it down.
For if in middle life the tide still rises,
and the dam bursts,
once begun, you may never be able to stop.
John Stanyon, student, Queen Alexandra
College for the Blind

WHAT'S IN A NAME?

'We're not blind!' declared a group of partially sighted youngsters as they set about making a video on their school activities. Their protestation showed the dislike of being labelled that is predictable, but also a fierce affirmation that they were not in a category which they perceived to be for people more disabled than themselves.

Children, like adults, can mind about being labelled, and also dislike what the label indicates. However, some terminology is necessary in order to provide appropriate educational support services, and to attempt to understand not only individual needs, but those shared by people who have a comparable problem. The term 'visually impaired', rather than the more strictly categorical terms of 'blind', 'low vision' or 'partially sighted', is now generally accepted as referring to people within the visual range from no sight at all to useful but defective vision.

Having established that some reference to visual functioning is necessary if we are to consider issues realistically, can we conclude that unhappiness is an inevitable sequel to defective vision or lack of sight? There are abundant examples of young people in virtually every university in the United Kingdom, and in a wide range of different kinds of employment, whose independent and competent life-styles challenge any assumption that unhappiness and visual disability are by any means inevitably connected. However, the existence of complex additional disabilities as well as sight problems is significant.

Of the Royal National Institute for the Blind's sample of 285 visually impaired children, 56 per cent had additional disabilities (Walker *et al.*, 1992). There can also be a hidden factor likely to affect the success of any training or educational services offered, and that is unhappiness.

Although far from being inevitable, misery does exist among some visually impaired children and young people as a result of their visual disability in terms of the difficulties it can cause them in day-to-day living and learning and, even more significantly, of the way they feel themselves to be perceived by others. Examples of this are poignantly shown in the comments of young people attending Queen Alexandra College for the Blind, Birmingham, during January 1992. Asked about their school experiences these students cited examples of unhappiness arising from bullying and teasing, lack of understanding and homesickness. Of these problems teasing, including name-calling, caused particular unhappiness and threat to self-concept.

An 18-year-old male student suffering from cataracts recalled verbal and physical abuse in both mainstream and special settings, claiming that his psychological bruises were worse than physical ones, but having latterly been helped by counselling. Another 18-year-old with both visual and auditory defects claimed that she suffered severe abuse in her mainstream school, while a 20-year-old also claimed that her mainstream schooling had been made miserable through verbal and physical bullying at both primary and secondary stages, making her at times a school refuser. Both lack of appropriate professional support and teasing were experienced by another visually impaired girl of 17 whose retinal problems made it impossible for her to undertake close visual work without low-vision aids. Some of her classmates responded to her difficulties by taunting her and calling her 'blind'. She found the pace of work in her mainstream school difficult to cope with and feigned illness to avoid going to school. A move to specialist provision had proved to be helpful.

This pattern of avoidance was also evidenced by another female student aged 16. Suffering from bilateral aniridia (see the glossary at the end of this chapter), she was nicknamed 'Blindy', often feigning illness in order to stay at home and feeling above all that she 'wanted to be like everyone else' despite being in a specialist unit of a mainstream comprehensive. A philosophical response to name-calling was shown by a 23-year-old student with retinitis of prematurity and nystagmus. She did not like being called 'specky four-eyes' but realized that other children had derogatory nicknames too. Among those unhappy in mainstream situations because of 'being picked on', a male 18-year-old student with cataracts claimed that his peers poked fun at him and the staff seemed to have little understanding or patience with his difficulties.

Although taunting and verbal bullying seemed more evident in the recollections of students attending mainstream schools, special provision posed some problems too for these young people, principally in the form of homesickness when they first moved away from home. This, however, seemed to be overcome during their first year. In this sample of eighteen students, only two stated that they did not recall unhappiness at school.

Such a small sample of experiences cannot be considered as necessarily reflecting the general views of visually impaired children and young people across the range of educational settings, but it does arouse some cause for disquiet in that so much recollection of unhappiness was evident among such a few young people. On the positive side, the fact that they were prepared to talk so frankly to their tutor and, with her permission, to record their response indicates a developing confidence and trust. When these young people speak for themselves, those providing their education need to listen and to analyse the causes of such unhappiness and help them to seek solutions. In order even to attempt to do so it is crucial to consider the child in the context of the family and to examine the needs of the parents as they themselves express them.

THE TRAUMA OF DISCOVERY

For the parents and family of a child with a severe visual impairment, shock and even disbelief at the time of discovery of the disability is likely to be followed by deep and often enduring unhappiness. The child, an integral part of the family, risks being over-shadowed by this grief, and the extent to which this risk is overcome in some families is remarkable.

The factors which enable the family and child to reach a state of equilibrium and reasonable happiness are complex and difficult to identify, since every family is different in its composition, emotional interaction, economic status and expectations. The single parent and her child are a family, grandparents bringing up bereaved grandchildren are a family, the married couple with several children are a family. The visually impaired child's happiness will be affected by the affection, anxiety or rejection of this family.

There are, however, some well-documented indicators of what kind of aid and support families themselves perceive to be desirable in helping them to cope with their own unhap-piness at the time of discovery of their child's disability and in the early years of child-hood. The way in which information about their child's condition and prognosis is given to parents at this time requires both sensitivity and skill. This need has been explored in terms of disability in general by Lonsdale *et al.* (1979), who stress the difficulty this poses for professionals, emphasizing that the task leaves the teller feeling incompetent and perhaps, even, ignoring the persons most emotionally affected because of embarrass-ment at their grief. The authors cite many instances of parents who recall this time with disappointment or anger at their treatment, and claim that there can be links between their feelings then and their subsequent attitude towards their child's disabilities.

Helping parents

If this is true of disability in general, evidence confirms that it is certainly so when news of severe visual impairment including blindness is broken to parents. The RNIB survey of need (Walker *et al.*, 1992) reports that parents perceived that the presence of a severe visual impairment was the most difficult problem for their child, even when multiple handicap including physical or mental disability was involved. The findings in this survey show that parents still feel undersupported and bewildered at the time of discovery of their child's visual impairment, despite their need for good communication and support at the time. This need has been experienced in practice, documented in research and exposed in literature over a considerable period of time. Langdon (1970) interviewed parents of visually impaired children in the Midlands, and found that feelings of unhappiness at the way in which information about their child's condition had been given to them were widespread, as was their disappointment at the lack of counselling available. The professional implications of these findings are examined by subsequent writers (Chapman, 1978; Chapman and Stone, 1988), but the necessary training and resources to improve the situation still lag behind the demand. Because the provision of counselling by an advocate or adviser is not a statutory requirement, too many parents still feel unsupported at this critical time despite the RNIB survey's claim that 'knowing the causes and nature of impairment can be of great help to the family in accepting and adapting to circumstances' (Walker *et al.*, 1992, p. 2).

Parents may be so shocked and bewildered that they cannot 'take in' the information given to them; additionally, their child may have a complex condition hard to define and describe in terms understandable to the lay person. However, such strongly and continuously voiced experiences of need cry out for attention, through the appropriate training of professionals and a reconsideration of the structure of the multidisciplinary team who support the family. Renewed attention to the 'named person' advocated in the Warnock Report seems timely in the face of the renewed findings of the RNIB survey.

During the first two years of life, the major responsibility for the child's welfare is vested in the health services, after which time the child's needs can be statemented and there is the possibility of visits from a peripatetic teacher or adviser, as nursery attendance may be possible. Since 1972, local education authorities throughout the United Kingdom have increasingly set up teams of peripatetic advisers specializing in visual impairment. These professionals seek not only to support visually impaired pupils in mainstream schools but also to visit pre-school visually impaired children at home, and to arrange and follow up appropriate nursery placements. However, cutbacks in resources reduce or remove the availability of such support, greatly to the detriment of parent and child.

The presence of severe visual handicap has considerable developmental implications, and the value of working with parents from an early stage in the child's life cannot be overstated. Sensible advice and practical help with management can reduce the anxiety resulting from the child's potential or actual difficulties in mobility, communication and self-help skills. It can bring a sense of purpose to parents, which helps to channel their anxiety into activities that reduce passivity or frustration in the young child, especially as the mother of a visually impaired child may experience both physical and emotional strain.

Warren (1984) asserts that the establishment of emotional bonds constitutes one of the most critical processes in the early development of the blind child, forming the basis of the experience of emotional security from which positive concepts and relationships can grow. It has long been well understood that family attitudes can affect the visually impaired child's performance and ability to benefit from early intervention programmes. However, action to help to reduce parental anxiety and to offer positive opportunities for the child to participate in infant programmes is sporadic. In the United Kingdom, for example, there are scattered examples of excellent support for parents and activities for young visually handicapped children, which may have a significant part to play in minimizing their later unhappiness and insecurity.

HAPPINESS IN THE EARLY YEARS

It is worth examining existing examples of pre-school opportunities for visually impaired infants in terms both of the structure of the service they offer, and of the content of programmes. In terms of the happiness of children one has only to visit some of these nurseries to encounter young visually impaired children who arrive with low expectations, possibly with poor mobility and communication skills, and who within months show an improved interaction with other children and an apparent enjoyment of wonderfully noisy and messy activities. Where opportunities exist, they may be set in a special school for visually impaired children, attached to some other voluntary body or academic institution, or be in ordinary nursery provision with or without specialized support.

Specialist provision for young visually impaired children in the United Kingdom, including the RNIB Sunshine House schools, are listed in detail in Travis (1991). The peripatetic advisers for the visually impaired in each local education authority are also listed, and they will be the key source of information on nurseries in their region which will integrate visually impaired children.

There is an increasingly strong policy in some local education authorities to integrate young visually impaired children into ordinary nurseries and play groups. This has the benefit of interaction with neighbourhood children and reduces the impact of the 'handicapped' label. However, it is important for the teachers and carers to have some knowledge of the implications of visual impairment if the child is to flourish happily in such a situation.

In the early years, developmental delay is frequently observed. Reynell (1978) found evidence of social independence normally evident at 3 years of age delayed until 5 years in the case of many children with significant sight problems. This could be the effect not only of the disability itself but of overprotective practice. Fully sighted children learn a great deal incidentally as a result of receiving visual information, and this in the case of visually limited children needs to be replaced by or boosted by direct teaching, including manual demonstration. It is easier to avoid the issue especially when other children are clamouring for attention, but if self-help skills are neglected when the child is ready to learn them, inadequacies can be compounded, with predictable embarrassment and unhappiness in social situations later on.

For most children with visual disabilities, early activities can follow normal developmental play patterns, but more adult intervention will usually be needed as the child progresses from solitary play through parallel play and partner play to group participation. To avoid the unhappiness of being 'left out', activities must be structured so that each child, including the one with sight difficulties, can take part. This may mean ensuring that sound and interesting texture are embodied in toys and materials used, with strongly contrasting colours for those children with residual vision as well as for the fully sighted. Bright visible objects, games that involve movement, singing and percussion music are fun for children who have reduced or absent vision. There is abundant literature giving ideas about activities that can be appropriately used in the mainstream nursery, and young children usually accept each other's differences easily. A generous ratio of child-carers and teachers to children, appropriate activities and awareness of the individual's specific needs can help to avoid the unhappiness and loneliness of being a non-seeing child within a group of the sighted.

Friends and families

The staff at Dorton House, where there is a special nursery, and the nursery attached to the Research Centre for the Education of the Visually Handicapped at Birmingham University have both noted the role of grandparents as well as parents in contributing to the happiness and well-being of young children. A 'grandparents' weekend' at Dorton House in May 1991 offered counselling opportunities, straightforward information on the implications of visual impairments and above all the chance to meet and talk with others in a relaxed atmosphere. It was, not surprisingly, oversubscribed, and revealed many examples of ways in which, within the family network, children with grandparents were helped to cope with unhappiness by people with time and patience to listen and to care. There are of course likely to be inner tensions within a family when there is a child with a disability, and there is a fine line between caring concern from relatives and a perception of interference and taking over, the parents' role. Such issues are well explored in *Facing the Crowd* (Cronin and Fullwood, 1986), an invaluable book for parents in its encouragement of honest feelings and its perception of family grief and possible blame.

SELF-HELP GROUPS AND PRESSURE GROUPS

The parents of visually handicapped children may as individuals or as a group almost unwittingly adopt the role of advisers. Increasingly, as parents are included on the governing bodies of schools and asked to approve statements of educational need, they can perceive the potential power that they have in relation to the educational provision available to their children. Many of the countries in western Europe have influential parent groups, and a National Federation of Families with Visually Impaired Children was formed from regional groups in the United Kingdom in 1991. The Association states that 'visually impaired children and their families have lacked a national voice to express deeply felt concerns for our children's health, welfare and education'. They express unhappiness at the pressure they feel subjected to, claiming that they 'need to be advised, counselled and informed about the various options that are available and what facilities can be provided without constant fear of Local Education Authorities' financial pressure being brought to bear on them, or the professionals assisting in the case' (Catley, 1991, p. 1).

PROFESSIONAL SUPPORT

However, not all visually impaired children are in the situation of a two-parent family. Single parents may suffer considerable stress in the sheer management of the additional time demands involved in bringing up a visually impaired child as well as coping with a job and possibly other dependent family members. There are regrettably a few children in nurseries and schools for the visually impaired whose sight has been damaged as a result of non-accidental injury. There is clearly a vital role here for health visitors and workers in Social Services, whose training should include information on the development of visually impaired children and on sources of more specific advice and help for their parents. The concept of a multidisciplinary team theoretically offers a combination of support and expertise for the visually impaired children and their families. In practice, and especially at a time of scarce resources, this may not be so and the family will be unhappy, feeling underinformed and undersupported, as shown in the evidence previously cited.

UNHAPPINESS AT SCHOOL

Among those who cite the well-established link between parental attitudes and the subsequent adjustment of visually impaired children of school age, Svensson (1990) considers that maladjustment with its associated unhappiness is 'the result of the milieu, in this case, the parents and the way they treat the child' (p. 21). This he claims to be a strong factor in the capacity of the child to adjust to school and to its wider social demands. However, the ethos of the school itself and the nature of its social context may challenge the visually impaired child considerably, and Svensson's own analysis of social interaction exposes some of the problems that children can experience.

Visual disability may not be evident at birth or may develop later in childhood or in adolescence. It can result from accident or illness during the school years, bringing the need for adjustment by both child and family at a later stage and in a different context. The once fully sighted child now has different educational and support needs, and parents at this stage require adequate information if their unhappiness and that of their child is not to be unnecessarily increased by uncertainty and speculation.

In the case of 68 blind pupils in mainstream placements in Sweden, where both specialized support and equipment are of a high level, Svensson assesses the extent to which these pupils were able to relate happily to their classmates. Stressing that his findings reflect evidence comparable to that of other studies on the relation of visually impaired pupils to their peer group in open settings, he shows weak levels of interaction (see Table 2.1). Additionally, among those showing marked mannerisms (stereotype behaviour, rocking, eye-poking) eighteen out of the sample of pupils had very limited peer relations, raising the supposition that those manifesting 'odd' behaviour tended to be frozen out of their peer group.

Table 2.1   *Blind pupils' interactions with classmates in mainstream placements (adapted from Svensson, 1990)*

Type of relation	Number of pupils
Very limited	20
Limited	22
Good	26

Life for children and young people with pronounced visual disabilities can be tough and lonely. Teachers and carers will want to identify the potential causes of these difficulties and to seek ways of helping the visually impaired pupils suffering in these ways to find out and implement their own solutions.

An unusual appearance can be a focus for teasing and name-calling. Unfortunately some visual disabilities do cause disfigurement or uncommon appearance. The flaxen hair of the albino, the keyhole-shaped pupil of the person with coloboma, the never-still eyes of the nystagmus sufferer make them noticeable in a group of children. The use of specialized aids to vision and equipment again makes a child stand out as different from others. For the pupil with no vision or with so little that tactile means of learning must be used there will be specialized braille equipment, tactile diagrams and mobility aids. The pupil will be learning in a different way from sighted children in many of the curriculum areas. Children with low vision may have a particularly difficult role in terms of social integration. They can sometimes have variable sight levels, as in glaucoma, and they give the impression of being fully sighted pupils while having the uncertainties of not being so. They too may be using special methods and equipment that make them evident in a classroom. Low-vision aids can be used in heavy spectacle or telescopic mounts, and magnifiers, task lighting and closed-circuit television may be required for some tasks. The pupils' work needs to be held in a stand to facilitate reading, and the pupil may need to work in an unusual position in order to use any residual vision as effectively as possible.

This situation has been dramatized by Anna Fitch (*Dramarama*, Channel 4, January 1992), herself an albino, who portrays the teasing and abuse she received at the hands of classmates in a comprehensive school because of her unusual appearance and need to use a telescopic visual aid. Pupils may wish to reject the very devices that help them to see more clearly in preference to looking different from their classmates. Such situations call for both knowledge and understanding on the part of their teachers.

Peer-group assistance

Despite the evidence that teasing can occur, peer-group assistance has been encouraged as a normal and natural intervention in many integrated situations (Chapman, 1990). Some children enjoy the responsibility of acting as a sighted guide to a visually impaired pupil, giving a hand in practical situations. A problem here can be over eagerness to help, and a balance needs to be developed between friendship and dependence. It is often in shared interests and enthusiasms that friendships develop, and friendship is a promoter of happiness and a solace in unhappiness. Integrated situations offer opportunities for happiness, but teachers need to be aware that curriculum access is only part of the need for visually impaired children in mainstream situations.

Classroom organization

There is a need to organize the classroom sympathetically as well as efficiently, so that the visually impaired pupil is not cut-off from contact with others by being hemmed in with special equipment. Such a pupil will be helped considerably by receiving clearly prepared material with good contrast between background and print, enlarged if necessary and appropriately lit. Clear instructions as to what is expected in any classroom activity, sufficient time to complete tasks and demonstration of processes as well as verbal explanation will all be helpful for the pupil with defective vision. Detailed information on classroom organization and adaptations and the specific requirements in different curriculum areas is given in Chapman and Stone (1988). An understanding of what is helpful to facilitate learning for a visually impaired pupil can help to reduce unnecessary stress and give the pupil a better opportunity to experience success.

Sharing and encouraging

The minority situation in which severely visually impaired pupils find themselves in a mainstream class can lead to loneliness and a feeling of isolation. Having the chance of meeting others with comparable problems and of sharing experiences and activities with other children and young people can bring an experience of happiness and of being understood. A scheme which was initiated at Refsnaesskolen in Denmark, and which has been adopted successfully in other countries, gives visually impaired pupils in integrated situations the chance of attending a holiday summer school with other visually impaired pupils. The vacation scheme which was started in 1988 in the UK brought 21 visually impaired pupils from different parts of the country together for a week, which proved to be a source of considerable enjoyment and value. Letters from parents commenting on their children's reactions were quoted in Dawkins (1988):

> 'He set out with very mixed feelings but returned a very happy and self-confident young man.'
> 'She made a lot of new friends and would have liked to stay longer.'
> 'He found that he felt happier and more at ease being in the company of people with the same handicap.'
>
> (p. 331)

One parent commented that her son enjoyed the experience of helping others instead of being the only one who needed help.

Integrated placements

Mainstream schooling can offer remarkable benefits for many visually handicapped pupils in terms of proximity to home and the challenge of a wide range of curriculum opportunities, but the happiness of easy social integration does not always occur spontaneously. In order to effect this optimally, teachers and carers need human qualities of sensitivity as well as professional knowledge, together with advice on appropriate adaptations and teaching methods. Verbal encouragement, important to all pupils, is crucial to those who may not see the teacher's face clearly or perhaps at all. Reduced or absent vision reduces or removes the possibility of non-verbal communication through facial expression and body language, and this must be compensated for through increased attention to positive comments and avoiding negative feedback.

Sequels to special-school placements

Homesickness can be a cause of unhappiness in any residential situation, and not surprisingly it is a factor referred to by two of the eighteen visually impaired students at Queen Alexandra College with whom the topic was discussed. Most of the special schools for visually impaired children offer both boarding and daily placements, and the boarding is weekly rather than involving protracted periods away from home. Even so, the residential pupil can have difficulty in initiating and maintaining peer friendships in the home locality when day-to-day activities and their subsequent discussion are not shared. There are likely to be reasons over and above the presence of visual disability

that contribute to the decision to recommend residential special school placement, especially when cost factors are considered. There may be social factors within the family
situation which militate against day-school attendance, or conversely the child may have
determined and articulate parents who are convinced that a particular special school
offers the best education for their child and who press for this, if necessary through
appeals procedure. There can be severely visually impaired pupils for whom advisory
support is too infrequent or who have hearing, physical, learning or behaviour problems
additional to those of sight. The child's happiness within the school placement can be
influenced by the parents' attitude towards it.

Mainstream or special school?

Both mainstream and special-school placements have features which can contribute to
the child's well-being and happiness. Teachers in special schools are usually working
within a smaller community and should be in an excellent situation to encourage individuals and to observe pupil interactions. Their special training, which is mandatory, will
have included considerations of social and personal adjustment in the care of their
pupils as well as the technical support and teaching strategies that they need. The pupils
themselves are in a situation in which the use of specialized equipment is the norm and
in which the need for individual demonstration of processes, unusual work position and
additional time for some tasks is well understood. An individual pupil is unlikely to be
the only albino or the only person with a disfiguring syndrome within the school or even
the class.

The danger here is that the strength and maturity to take on board the challenge of
looking different and working in an unusual way may come slowly and be greatly tried
when an uninformed and unadapted world has to be faced. However, there is evidence
of considerable maturity of outlook among the visually impaired adolescents interviewed by Tobin (1990), all of whom had attended special schools. Of the respondents,
68 per cent had been happy with their placement, instancing smaller classes and more
individual attention from teachers as positive factors. They also claimed that 'people are
used to blindness and partial sight'. Their answer to meeting the challenges of integration was to call for greater public education and awareness, with the inclusion of
evidently blind and poorly sighted persons in public life and media presentations.

Clearly the quality and appropriateness of the school placement is crucial to a child's
happiness, although this may be seen as a sequel to the child's special educational needs
rather than to the actual presence of blindness or partial sight. Both the ethos of the
school itself and the opportunities it gives for enjoyable extra-curricular activities can
be positive factors in increasing potential for happiness. An example is simply described
by a visually impaired youngster who had enjoyed 'lots of trips, we took packed lunches.
We went to museums, the funfair, Chessington Zoo. We went to the circus. I met lots
of friends' (RNIB, 1992, p. 3). Blindness can induce boredom; interesting activities can
need to be structured and promoted more for those with sight problems than for those
with full vision.

The aims of a school for visually impaired pupils will be to encourage independence
and social participation as well as to fulfil the range of curricular areas. Manthorp
(1991) describes RNIB New College, Worcester, as having 'a combination of a family

atmosphere and stress on independence which should, it may be hoped, produce mature, balanced, and if you like, faintly bruised citizens'.

DEVELOPING COPING SKILLS

Coping with unhappiness includes coping with oneself and eschewing the 'learned helplessness' that can be the sequel to an overprotective or overinstitutionalized environment. In referring to the sequels of sight loss in adults, Dodds (1990) observes that in the absence of skill-orientated intervention, such as teaching mobility, with its aim of restoring independence, the client may develop an acquiescent, dependent relationship with sighted others. Even in childhood this can have already developed, but it can be subject to remediation, with resultant improved confidence. Dodds emphasizes that 'individuals who possess a high sense of efficiency will try new things and expect to succeed at them; those with a low sense of self-efficacy will avoid attempting new things because they expect to fail at them' (p. 36).

There are, nevertheless, vulnerable areas in the school situation that can be inimical to happiness, but which if recognized can be addressed. The need for quietness and privacy may be as important to an individual as the need for activity and sharing. Even building design or adaptation can help to make this more or less possible, a factor appreciated by Cave (1989) in designing for people with special needs. The additional demands on time and energy required for the 'hidden curriculum' areas of self-help skills, mobility and orientation need to be monitored if a feeling of exhaustion and overloaded days are to be avoided. The acquisition of such skills will lead to a reduction of stress and the greater chance of easy acceptance in the community in the long term, but there needs to be sensitivity in how and when they are taught and practised. Good verbal communication is essential in teaching and relating to visually impaired pupils. The approving smile and communication through facial expression and body language are reduced or absent. This means that words must be used precisely and positively to encourage and to show approval; for those who see little or nothing, isolation and lack of communication can be experienced all too easily.

Unhappiness can be experienced as a result of feeling a failure in personal terms. The visually impaired pupil will have experienced a considerable amount of assessment, educational, psychological and medical. The implications of this may include anxieties about self-worth and about the future. Will the visual defect be inherited by children? Who will want to marry a blind person? How will I live?

The role of counselling

In helping children and young people to face such inner questionings the place of counselling and of role models is crucial. It is in the pre-adolescent and adolescent years that the availability of counselling is vital, as the young person becomes more self-aware. Inner unhappiness and uncertainty at this time especially can be manifested in unduly passive or aggressive responses to situations. There can be an inability to accept personal responsibility for failure, and to blame either other persons or the presence of visual disability for all failures or lack of acceptance. The experience of success, especially if it is noted, is salutary in such circumstances, and its likelihood is increased by programming work to be just within attainable difficulty. Tasks that are too easy seldom give satisfaction, and the visual demands as well as cognitive ones must be considered. Harrell and Strauss (1988) suggest some perceptive approaches to increasing assertive behaviour in visually impaired people, noting that some may lack effective communication skills although they are academically able, or may have acquired 'learned helplessness' from an early age.

Short courses involving counselling issues around visual disability are offered by the RNIB on an occasional basis and have relevance for children and young people as well as for adults. Family members, teachers and carers can foster helplessness by creating an environment that is not close to reality, so that the response to challenge is helplessness. There is a need to give reasons for failure and success, and to structure situations in which competence and responsibility can be experienced. The difference between assertive and aggressive behaviour needs to be understood, with an appreciation that an ability to identify one's feelings and talk about them to others can be a basis for personal development. This may include finding ways of dealing with the presence of visual disability or the trauma of sight loss.

Expressing feelings

Journal writing, poetry composition, painting and drama are some of the well-tried creative ways of expressing fear, anger or resentment deriving from such experiences. A teenage blind pupil writes:

> My sight was perfect
> My eyes could see everything
> One day
> Total darkness
> Nothing
> I was petrified
> What would I do?
> My mum yelled up the stairs
> I did not answer
> What was the point of answering?
> (DW)

Searching out interests and activities despite sight loss can help to create a situation in which all is not felt to be lost. There may need to be a period of grieving for lost sight, and creative expression of this is manifest in some of the clay models made by blind children, in the paintings of those with some vision, and in the writing of many.

Role playing, too, can give the opportunity for acting out and sharing difficult experiences in a safe situation. It can also be a basis for exchanging both experiences and solutions, centring for example on the dramatization and discussion of feelings experienced when entering an unfamiliar situation such as a room full of strangers.

The influence of role models and potential for social adjustment

Role models can often be encouraging in embodying an achievement or a life-style that demonstrates that visual disability need not be an insuperable obstacle to achievement or to a happy life. There are many examples of visually impaired children and young people who appear to be progressing in a reasonably adjusted way through their childhood and adolescence in both mainstream and special provision. However, evidence of unhappiness does come to light in discussion with some of them, particularly if they have suffered the trauma of sudden sight loss or of deteriorating vision. Crucial too is the way in which they are perceived and treated by others, especially their peer group.

Helping them to come to terms with realistic but difficult facts requires human qualities from teachers and carers. Helping them to develop the confidence to be themselves and to develop their own capacity to find solutions to their own problems can only be effected in a non-discriminating environment which maintains a sensitivity to pupils' interactions and attitudes to each other. It is not enough to give attention only to the curricular adaptations that a child may need because of sight problems; there are social and attitudinal factors which may cause unhappiness if they are not faced.

CONCLUSION

This calls for teachers to be given the opportunity to attend 'awareness' courses, or to have distance-taught or full-time training where appropriate, if they are going to teach or give advice about visually impaired children. Opportunities for parents and teachers to meet and for counselling support to be available also increase the supportive network for an unhappy child. Most solutions have to be individually worked out and there are seldom any short cuts, but the inner resilience of children *can* be strengthened.

NOTE

Thanks are due to K. Hollingsworth, tutor to associate students at Queen Alexandra College for the Blind, for recording the experiences of her students.

GLOSSARY

Albino   person with reduced pigment in eyes, skin and hair
Bilateral aniridia   absence of the iris in both eyes
Cataract   opacity in the lens
Coloboma   unusual-shaped pupil in the eye
Marfan's syndrome   condition in which vision is affected and bones are elongated
Nystagmus   uncontrolled oscillation of the eyes
Retinitis of prematurity   cause of visual disability in premature children

REFERENCES

Catley, P. (1991) Choice is the key. *Look*, **2**, 2.
Cave, A. (1989) Client consultation, the key for designing for people with special needs. *British Journal of Visual Impairment*, **2**, 85–9.
Chapman, E. K. (1978) *Visually Handicapped Children and Young People*. London: Routledge and Kegan Paul.

Chapman, E. K. (1990) Children with physical and sensory impairments. In N. Entwistle (ed.), *Educational Ideas and Practices*, pp. 1070-9. London: Routledge.

Chapman, E. K.and Stone, J. M. (1988) *The Visually Handicapped Child in Your Classroom*. London: Cassell.

Cronin, P. and Fullwood, D. (1986) *Facing the Crowd*. Burwood Educational Series no. 5. Melbourne: Royal Victorian Institute.

Dawkins, J. (1988). Integrated education: progress in partnership. *New Beacon*, **72**, 331.

Department of Education and Science (1978). *Special Educational Needs* (The Warnock Report). London: HMSO.

Dodds, A. (1990) Psychological factors in adjustment to visual handicap. In *Proceedings of ICEVH European Conference 'Europe into the Nineties', Warwick 1990*, pp. 36-43. Warwick: International Council for Education of the Visually Handicapped.

Harrell, R. L. and Strauss, M. A. (1988) Approaches to increasing assertive behaviour in blind and visually-impaired persons. *Journal of Visual Impairment and Blindness*, **21**, 794-8.

Langdon, J. N. (1970) Parents talking. *New Beacon*, **54**, 282-8.

Lonsdale, G., Elfer, P. and Ballard, R. (1979) *Children, Grief and Social Work*. Oxford: Blackwell.

Manthorp, R. B. (1991) RNIB New College, Worcester: what kind of school? *British Journal of Visual Impairment*, **9**, 845-6.

Reynell, J. (1978) Developmental patterns of visually handicapped children. *Child Care, Health and Development*, **14**, 316.

Reynell, J. and Zinkin, P. (1979) New procedures. *Child Care, Health and Development*, **5**, 61-9.

RNIB (1992) *Focus*.

Svensson, H. (1990) Personal adjustment of young people in integrated settings. In *Proceedings of ICEVH European Conference 'Europe into the Nineties'. Warwick 1990*, pp. 21-7. Warwick: International Council for Education of the Visually Handicapped.

Tobin, M. J. (1990) Some aspects of the attitudes of visually handicapped teenagers. In *Proceedings of ICEVH European Conference 'Europe into the Nineties', Warwick 1990*, pp. 28-35. Warwick: International Council for Education of the Visually Handicapped.

Travis, P. (1991) *Directory of Services for the Visually Impaired* (6th edition). Birmingham: University of Birmingham.

Walker, E. C., McKinnell, R. C. and Tobin, M. J. (1992) *RNIB Survey of Needs*, no. 2. London: HMSO.

Warren, D. H. (1984) *Early Childhood Development*. New York: American Foundation for the Blind.

FURTHER READING

Best, A. B. (1992) *Teaching Visually Impaired Children*. Milton Keynes: Open University Press.

Chapter 3

Mental Health in Children Who Are Hearing Impaired

David Bond

INTRODUCTION

Children who are hearing impaired (HI)[1] are reported by many writers to show significantly higher levels of problems of emotional and behavioural adjustment (i.e. 'unhappy' behaviour) than children who have normal hearing. Various writers have described reports in which the behaviour of the hearing impaired was said to be egocentric, possessive, rigid, selfish, lacking in flexibility, superficial, physical, lacking in imagination, regarding issues as being either one or the other with no 'shades of grey', showing an absence of negotiation skills, failing to recognize the rights and needs of others, etc. (see Heider and Heider, 1941; Schlesinger and Meadow, 1972; Levine, 1981; Moores, 1978). Schlesinger and Meadow (1972), reporting on a survey of 516 hearing-impaired students in Los Angeles, indicated that 11.6 per cent of the HI sample and 2.4 per cent of the hearing sample were severely disturbed, and that 19.6 per cent of the HI sample and 7.3 per cent of the hearing sample had had behavioural problems. Vernon (1969), in a study of 413 HI students, found that 22.5 per cent showed severe emotional problems and 5.1 per cent had psychotic behaviours.

Despite the reported high incidence of disturbed and disturbing behaviours in people who are hearing impaired, despite negative social views and 'folk-lore' (e.g. there are those who think the deaf are 'daft'), and despite the pressures on people who are hearing impaired, the majority of hearing-impaired children and adults manage their lives successfully. In Britain, Scandinavia, Australia and North America most hearing-impaired children attend ordinary schools. In Britain, less than 10 per cent of HI children attend schools for the deaf, 15 to 20 per cent attend unit or resource classes attached to ordinary schools, while the remainder are in ordinary classes in ordinary schools (BATOD, 1992). Most hearing-impaired adults function successfully and independently in open society.

Why are some people who are HI successful whilst others are reported to show substantial levels of mental health and behavioural problems? We know that when people who have no significant handicaps are experimentally and temporarily deprived of (or restricted in the use of) their senses, their cognitive and emotional functioning may deteriorate. They may also show diminished ability to solve problems, perceptual responses become less accurate and emotional status may be disturbed (Bexiton *et al.*, 1954). Is it deprivation of sensory input which contributes to higher levels of disturbed and disturbing behaviours among people who are hearing impaired? If we were to accept this thesis, then why do the deaf children of deaf families appear to show a lower incidence of emotional and behavioural disturbance, and tend to achieve at higher academic levels, than the HI children of families who can hear? (See e.g. Vernon, 1969; Moores, 1978.)

To understand some of the factors contributing to the reported higher incidence of mental health problems in people who are hearing impaired, it is necessary to have an understanding of: the causes and effects of hearing impairment; behaviours associated with hearing loss; additional impairments linked with hearing impairment; and the social, cultural and interactional effects of communicational difficulties.

FACTORS ASSOCIATED WITH MENTAL HEALTH PROBLEMS IN PEOPLE WHO ARE HEARING IMPAIRED

Causes and effects of hearing impairment

Severe to profound sensory-neural hearing impairment at birth (congenital) or prelingually (before language develops) occurs at a rate of approximately 1–1.2 per 1000 live births in countries whose medical facilities are well developed. The occurrence of hearing impairment increases with age – older people are more likely to have a hearing loss than younger people.

Hearing impairment occurs in one or both of two forms, sensory-neural-perceptual or conductive. Conductive hearing loss is due to a disorder in conduction of sound from the pinna or ear, through the external auditory meatus or ear canal, to the ear-drum and then via the ossicles – malleus, incus and stapes (hammer, anvil and stirrup) – to the oval window – the entrance to the cochlea. Conductive hearing problems may be caused through abnormalities of the size or shape of the conductive mechanism (e.g. as in Down's syndrome, charge association, etc.), blockages and infections (see, e.g. Tucker and Nolan, 1984). Sensory-neural hearing loss is usually due to damage or lesions in the inner ear, or from the oval window of the cochlea through to the brain. Sensory-neural hearing loss may be caused by a variety of conditions. Prenatal causes may include genetic factors (via syndromes associated with chromosomal disorders (e.g. as in Down's and other syndromes) or associations arising through structural variations in some chromosomes (e.g. partial deletions of the long arm of the thirteenth chromosome), inherited hearing impairment (Waardenburg and other syndromes), viral infections (e.g. maternal rubella, cytomegalovirus, etc.), ototoxic drugs taken during pregnancy, rhesus incompatibility, etc. Perinatal (at birth) factors may include low birth weight, anoxia, etc. Postnatal causes include genetic factors, viruses, conditions such as Refsums disease, infection, ototoxic drugs, tumours, trauma, presbycusis, etc.

The degree of hearing loss is commonly reported in the form of an audiogram in which the vertical axis shows decibels (on a logarithmic scale) and the horizontal axis shows the range of frequencies over which speech normally occurs, i.e. from 0.125 to approximately 8.0 kilohertz (see Tucker and Nolan, 1984). Hearing loss is often

Table 3.1. *Hearing impairment: possible effects on language, behaviour and communication (adapted from Goetzinger, 1972; Bond, 1991)*

		Average hearing loss across the frequencies (0.125, 0.15, 1.0, 2.0 and 4.0 kilohertz)	
Category or degree of hearing loss	Decibels (db HL)	Possible effects on speech and language	Possible effects on adjustment and behaviour
None	0		
Mild	20–40	Slight difficulties.	Confusions. Slight deficit.
Moderate	41–70	Difficulties with normal speech receptively. Some articulation errors. Some functional words.	Some educational difficulties. May show emotional/behavioural difficulties.
Severe	71–95	May show limited understanding of speech. Difficulties in speaking intelligibly. Omissions in spoken language. Limited vocabulary.	Some emotional or social problems. Educational difficulties.
Profound	95 +	May have marked difficulties in understanding speech. Speech may be unintelligible.	Educational attainments may be severely delayed. Behaviour and social skills may be immature.

described in categories which represent the average hearing thresholds of five separate frequencies (see Table 3.1)

For many hearing-impaired children, early identification of hearing loss, early fitting with appropriate hearing aids, effective parent guidance and audiological habilitation, and positive responses to amplification may result in children showing minimal educational, communicational and developmental delays even if their hearing loss is severe. Possibly the most important factor in this process is the effectiveness of the amplification system and the child's improved threshold responsiveness to amplification. Although hearing aids distort 'sound', and listening through a hearing aid may not be a pleasant experience, a child with a 90-db loss whose freefield 'aided' responses (i.e. when wearing appropriate hearing aids) improve to, say, 40 db would appear to have a greater opportunity to develop and understand speech and spoken language than a child whose 90-db loss improves to 80 db. The importance of appropriate hearing aids and management of them, in association with obtaining optimum aided responses to sound, must never be underestimated.

Hearing loss which develops after language has been established (postlingual hearing impairment – the cut-off point is usually accepted as approximately 3 years of age, when the child has a vocabulary of approximately 1000 words) has different consequences from prelingual hearing impairment. Children who have a prelingual hearing loss, particularly those to whom amplification of sound (via hearing aids) gives little benefit, are likely to have significant difficulties in developing speech and verbal language through use of their residual hearing. Their impairment and experience is a sensory deficit which is different from the sensory deprivation of postlingually deafened people. For both groups in comparison with normally hearing people, differences in their sensory reception affect their experiences and view of their world, and their interaction with other people. This difference may lead to differences in perception, behaviour, knowledge, development and understanding.

Behaviours associated with hearing loss

It has been argued that differences in sensory and developmental experience are such that people who are hearing impaired may be 'culturally' different from people who have normal hearing, and that some who are deaf are part of another culture – the 'deaf culture'. To what extent do 'cultural' and experiential differences contribute to perceptions that deaf children's behavioural-emotional adjustment is different from that of hearing children, and is therefore maladaptive or maladjusted in comparison with the behaviour and adjustment of people who are hearing?

Much of the measurement, appraisal, and identification of problems of behaviour and adjustment of people who are hearing impaired has rested on the use of normative measures which were originally designed for use with people with normal hearing. If we can accept that personality develops as a result of social-emotional responses and experiences and cognitive/intellectual functioning, interacting within the cultural environment in which the individual develops, then the use of test data based on tests of personality and criteria derived from, and standardized on, a non-hearing-impaired, non-sensorily deprived, or non-sensorily deficit population would not appear to be a valid way of describing the 'personalities' of people who are hearing impaired.

Hearing impairment may result in differences in communication, speech, and spoken verbal language development. Differences in speech and language are used as indicators for educators to identify children with hearing impairments. Often differences in behaviour will also be used to indicate children who may have hearing impairments. Some possible indicators are as follows:

Speech:

- misses ends of or parts of words, e.g. 's', 'sh', 't', 'ed', 'ing';
- is unable to discriminate (when listening) consonants, particularly those which involve high-frequency energy;
- has poor articulation – slushy speech;
- has difficulty in monitoring/regulating voice, i.e. either too loud or too quiet.

Language:

- has difficulties with reading, spelling, and written language;
- has difficulties with 'phonics';
- has poor vocabulary;
- uses telegraphic sentences – omission of articles, prepositions, etc.;
- has problems with parts of speech, syntax, tense;
- has poor comprehension of spoken instructions/information.

Behaviour:

- is slow to respond to instructions or requests; watches peers and imitates their behaviour after a slight delay;
- may not respond to or answer to his or her name;

- may respond to other stimuli rather than the one intended (e.g. as part of an assess-ment I observed a boy with a severe hearing loss integrated into an ordinary class. A new child had been admitted to the class. His name, which began with 'A', was placed in alphabetical order on the class register. The boy with the severe hearing loss responded when the teachers called out the ninth name – now that of another child. The other children laughed.);
- does not answer, or misinterprets the question;
- often asks for things to be repeated or may ask friends or someone with whom he or she is familiar to repeat the question or statement;
- repeats 'What?', 'Pardon?';
- appears to strain to listen and/or watch; may move/stand up, etc., to watch teacher or fellow pupil;
- cannot locate the source of sound – the speaker – particularly in noisy conditions;
- attention wanders, work habits fluctuate;
- shows poor attention to teacher unless a raised voice is used;
- is more attentive to body language, gesture, mime, etc., than to aural-oral communication;
- appears more able in practical tasks than in academic tasks.

Other writers have developed similar lists, e.g. Webster and Ellwood (1985).

While behavioural differences may be associated with hearing impairment, hearing impairment by itself would not appear to be the cause of the behaviours described at the beginning of this chapter, e.g. egocentric, possessive, rigid, impulsive, etc. These behaviours are not exclusive to people who are hearing impaired: individuals with normal hearing show a variety of levels of the same behaviours, and while these behaviours may occur more frequently or more intensively in some people who are hearing impaired, not all hearing-impaired people show disturbed or disturbing behaviour. There is a wide range of behaviours, needs, abilities and attainments in the population of people who are hearing impaired (see, e.g., Myklebust, 1964; Moores, 1978; Levine, 1981).

Why do people who are hearing impaired show a higher incidence of different and sometimes disturbed and disturbing behaviours? Can contributory factors to these patterns of behaviour be identified? What measures should be taken and what inter-ventions made to prevent or ameliorate behavioural and emotional disturbance in people who are hearing impaired?

Unsuitable measures and means of identifying emotional-behavioural disturbance

Measures which include verbal information, whether it is presented orally or in written questionnaire form, may unfairly assess deaf people. For example, a psychiatrist interviewed a severely deaf man with whom I was working. He asked the man if he 'heard voices'. After some thought, the man replied tentatively, 'Yes, I can hear voices.' He meant that he could hear voices with the use of his hearing aid.

People who are HI may misinterpret or be unable to understand written question-naires, and consequently their responses may be misunderstood. They may also respond from a totally different cultural perspective, which may lead those from a hearing culture to misinterpret the response and incorrectly diagnose or categorize conditions which may not be affecting the person who is HI. These and other problems also apply to the use of projective techniques in assessing people who are HI.

Lack of training and preparation of professionals working with people who are hearing impaired

This may be in respect of diagnosis and assessment of needs, and in intervention and provision to meet needs. Professionals who have inadequate communicational skills may, through their body language, give the wrong messages to the person who is deaf. They may also miss vital information communicated to them by the person who is deaf. If such initiatives are missed, then communication from the person who is deaf will change or cease.

Cultural and experiential differences

These issues are compounded by other factors including the fact that approximately 90 per cent of children who are hearing impaired are born to hearing parents – the estimated frequency of dominant deafness is approximately 6–7.5 per cent (Nance 1976). Vernon (1969) indicates that no more than approximately 10 per cent of the deaf children of deaf parents show emotional behavioural disturbance, in comparison with 18 to 30 per cent of the deaf children of hearing parents. Other factors cited in this chapter may well contribute to this difference.

Communicational/interactional difficulties

Deaf mothers of deaf children are more likely to respond to their children's non-verbal initiatives, and are therefore more likely to establish a responsive learning environment with their child.

Acceptance and understanding of deafness

In general, parents who are hearing impaired are usually more able to accept and understand their child's deafness and needs. Hearing parents of children who are hearing impaired may go through a process of denial, guilt, anger, and rejection before (or if) they come to understand their child's hearing loss and needs. In this process, valuable time may be lost, and the infant's initial communication/interactional endeavours may well be damaged through the inadvertent failure or inability of parents to respond appropriately to the infant's communication initiatives.

Traumatic aetiologies

More hearing-impaired children born to hearing parents have traumatic aetiologies or causes of their hearing loss (e.g. rubella, anoxia, prematurity, low birth weight, mumps, cytomegalovirus, etc.). Most traumatic aetiologies contribute to other handicaps, including brain damage (e.g. Van Dijk, 1982). People who are brain-damaged are significantly more likely to have psychiatric disorders; e.g. Graham and Rutter (1970) reported that 58.3 per cent of children with a brain disorder showed psychiatric disorders. Vernon (1969) reported that 10 per cent of children with a hereditary hearing impairment, 27 per cent of premature and 31 per cent of rubella hearing-impaired children had emotional adjustment and/or behavioural problems. These children may show higher levels of restless, hyperactive, distractable, impulsive, involuntary, and 'irritable' behaviours.

Case study

Margaret (aetiology – rubella), profoundly deaf, severely visually impaired, very severely behaviourally and emotionally disturbed, has mixed learning abilities and difficulties – her functioning in practical perceptual skills is in the average to good average range, and in areas of information processing is in the range of very severe to profound learning difficulties. Margaret showed a range of very severe random unprovoked behavioural outbursts, which were so violent that her family were unable to manage her. Placement was found in a school for the deaf in a department for deaf children with severe additional handicaps. Staff were experienced in working with multisensory deprived children. Communication was through Total Communication – signs supporting English, signing 'over' (i.e. holding the child's hands), etc. Holiday placements were arranged at a psychiatric hospital, where Margaret's behavioural outbursts were so difficult that it was necessary for the hospital staff to sedate her. Hospital staff were not able to communicate with her. The school then spent a period reducing medication after each holiday, since her behaviour was manageable at school. Variations in management and communication techniques added to Margaret's confusion and behavioural disturbance. Self-abusive behaviours increased, and were compounded by her desire to be like her sisters – e.g. to have menstrual periods. She damaged herself in order to bleed like her sisters. When in a temper tantrum she was capable of lifting tables, wardrobes, etc., which would later take two or more men to put back into place. Management and treatment combined the following:

- *Organizational changes*: holiday placements were transferred to a psychiatric unit for deaf people in which Total Communication or British Sign Language was used, and there were improvements in staff–pupil ratio and in staff training.
- *Medical management*: some medication was used to assist in controlling her behaviour. Medication was kept under tight control and regularly monitored and reviewed. Attempts to reduce or remove medication to date have resulted in significantly adverse behavioural responses.
- *Communicational changes*: visual calendars were developed (clear line drawings, good contrast photos and written calendars); Total Communication was improved – e.g. to tell her what is planned in advance, and when and how planned events will happen. The opportunity for Margaret to choose activities was developed, particularly in her free time; and practical and leisure skills were developed to create greater independence.

Now aged 19 years, Margaret is about to move on to another centre which has special provision for multisensory deprived people. It would appear that Margaret is one of the lucky ones who will have the opportunity to continue the substantial progress which she made at her school.

Physical conditions

These may arise through various aetiologies associated with hearing impairment (e.g. Usher syndrome, Refsums disease, Jervel-Lang-Neil syndrome) and those which arise separately from, but may be associated with, hearing impairment (e.g. premenstrual tension, food or other allergies, diabetes, sickle cell anaemia, migraine headaches, etc.).

Case study

Jill, a girl who was profoundly deaf, attended a primary school for deaf children not far from her home. Total Communication (Signed English/signs supporting English) was used at school and home. At secondary-school age she transferred to a residential school. Her behaviour became withdrawn, depressive and non-communicative. Physical functions such as written language deteriorated. It was noted that she showed difficulties with night vision, and in light–dark adaptation – in walking up or down unfamiliar darkened stairways, in the woods, etc. Further investigations revealed a restricted visual field. She was then seen by a consultant eye specialist, who confirmed a diagnosis of Usher syndrome. In this condition there is a progressive deterioration of visual field (the peripheral vision) through retinitis pigmentosa. The pigmentation on the retina may either gradually or fairly rapidly obscure the visual field, causing tunnel vision and possible blindness. Usher syndrome occurs in approximately 4–8 per cent of genetically deaf/hearing-impaired people or in approximately 2–4 per cent of congenitally deaf people (Nance (1976) indicates that approximately 50 per cent of deafness is caused through genetic factors). Jill also showed some symptoms of a motor ataxia and mild difficulties in relating to others prior to the diagnosis of Usher syndrome.

Jill's behaviour became progressively more withdrawn until she would not communicate with anyone via signs, but still wrote. In counselling sessions she eventually wrote that she was going to die in 1988. This idea was repeated frequently in discussion. Finally, in one session she mentioned a friend, a teacher at the previous school, who had died. On further investigating background experience it was found that two other people she had known had died recently. Jill thought her gradually reducing visual field, night vision problems, etc., were symptoms of her dying, as her friends had done. With further counselling and through being taught to use her residual vision effectively, Jill showed a slow improvement in adjustment, which then improved substantially from January 1989. She went through further periods of depression and self-isolation but over the past three years her adjustment improved significantly. Teaching and child-care staff, her family and a specialist nurse for deaf children with emotional-behavioural disorders have all been involved in counselling and guidance. Additional support and advice was provided by staff working with the Usher Syndrome Research Project.

Jill's difficulties were caused by several factors: change in environment, emotional disturbance through the deaths of close friends, confusion created through deteriorating visual field, etc. These difficulties were exacerbated by communicational problems.

The same range of causes which may contribute to emotional or behavioural disturbances in the hearing population

Unfortunately there are still occasions on which professionals fail to investigate fully and treat other potential causes of emotional behavioural disturbance in people who are hearing impaired.

The effects on the family of diagnosis of hearing impairment

These may sometimes include diagnosis of additional difficulties (which occur in approximately 25 to 35 per cent of hearing-impaired students – (e.g. Gentile and McCarthy, 1973). The family's management of their own feelings and emotions may lead to emotional and social restriction of opportunity and independence (Mindel and Vernon, 1976), which may irretrievably harm the hearing-impaired child's development.

'Rejection' and 'failure'

Non-responsive reciprocal interaction – adults failing to recognize and respond to children's initiatives in communication – may start in infancy, causing confusion in the relationship between mother and child. For the child there are no warning or reassuring background sounds, and no information about where he or she is being taken or what people are doing to or with him or her. Adults may respond with controlling responses, commands, and negative responses to attempts to communicate via pushing or pulling. When interaction is pleasurable or rewarding, it increases; when it ceases to be pleasurable, it decreases (Bond, 1981). Wood *et al.* (1986) indicate that a hearing 3-year-old child 'controls' up to 75 per cent of interactions with his or her carer(s). He also demonstrated clearly that when adults 'overcontrol' children's verbal resources through highly 'corrective' teaching, children's responses decrease.

'Rejection' of communication initiatives may occur inadvertently. When parents' attempts at communication are not responded to, their language may become different from that of parents whose children have normal hearing (see e.g. Howarth and Wood, 1977; Gregory and Mogford, 1981).

When the communicative interactive process is inadequate, inappropriate or non-responsive and non-reciprocal, the child would appear to be placed in a situation in which initiatives to communicate are missed or misunderstood, and consequently such attempts are 'rejected'. Behavioural and emotional development is subsequently placed at risk, as is the future success of the child's communication and interaction development. Behaviours involved in an interactive, responsive, communicational context are inextricably linked with behaviours which are crucial in social emotional development and in mental health. Such behaviours may include the following (adapted from Bond, 1991):

Turn-taking:

- awareness of start and finish of others' contributions;
- understanding of others' contributions; awareness of others' body language, language, etc.;
- responsiveness to others' interactions – acknowledging and reinforcing acceptable responses;
- developing and modifying initiatives in response to reactions by others;
- sharing skills, ideas, negotiating, etc.

Learning:

- association of information, generalization, classification, sequencing – organizational skills development;
- recognition, identification and recall of information;
- new rules – linguistic (grammatical construction, syntax, vocabulary, etc.) and social;
- acquiring and using new information.

Establishing roles:

- identifying more or less skilled contributors;
- development of regard/understanding/appreciation of others;
- development of ideas about comparison of self with others, status in social group;
- formation of roles with others, developing relationships;
- modelling, imitating others, customs, fashions;
- developing bonding, trust;
- development of assertive/submissive behaviours, etc.

Rejection of communication initiatives would appear significant in providing the conditions in which alternative means of controlling interactions and of seeking and demanding attention are sought by the child. Consequent reinforcement via adult attention to inappropriate attention-seeking or communication initiatives would then appear to provide a base for these behaviours to evolve into attention-seeking or attention-demanding behaviours in their own right.

Many HI children who show difficult behaviour patterns arising from communicational and interactional rejection and failure also come from homes in which parental relations have broken down. Some of these children have gone into care, sometimes moving from foster home to foster home. Communicational, interactional and behavioural problems have then been exacerbated by changes in environment, changing experiences of communication and, in the child's eyes, further rejection. Many of these children have no faith or trust in relationships with others, are unable to sustain conversations, and may show varying degress of hostile, anxious, depressive and antisocial behaviours.

Case study

George, a 16-year-old who is profoundly deaf, was admitted to a Total Communication school at 8 years, following initial placements in nurseries, a nursery
unit for deaf children, a school for the deaf and a school for children with disorders
of communication. Previous placements had not succeeded for a variety of reasons.
George showed a high level of hyperkinetic behaviours (random involuntary movement such as twitches) and a very high level of activity. He was unable to sit still,
and was restless. He showed attention-seeking and attention-demanding behaviours
and a high level of inconsequential and hostile, physically aggressive behaviours
towards others. His mother had moved frequently, had several changes of partners,
and eventually sought care placement for George. Whenever George saw his
mother, his behaviour deteriorated. Unable to understand or manage this
behaviour, she rejected him by refusing to see him, and for varying periods did not
communicate with him. Foster placements broke down.

As he grew older, George's hyperkinetic behaviours decreased substantially. His
communication skills improved, although difficulties in academic work, which were
affected by significant specific learning difficulties, continued. Behavioural problems decreased through consistent management, structuring his environment to
enable high levels of success, counselling and guidance from various members of
staff, and through brief periods of isolation from other students (with a member
of staff to continue counselling). Repeated rejection (arising through changes of
carers, foster families, etc.) resulted in a mixture of hostile aggressive and depressive
behaviours. While these behaviours were manageable within the school environment, and while George responded to continued guidance and care from the school
staff and his foster family, he remained very vulnerable to emotional disturbance.
Counselling and guidance was based on encouraging self-control and choice,
recognition of his responsibilities towards himself and others, and positive recognition of his own skills and worth.

Inappropriate and inadequate communication

In a study of 250 patients referred to a department for psychiatry for the deaf, John
Denmark (1985) reported that the majority of these patients fell into three categories:

1. those suffering from mental illness;
2. those with problems regarded as directly related to their deafness;
3. those with communication disorders.

In previous papers (1966, 1973) Denmark has linked failure in oral-aural communication educational and communicational approaches for some deaf patients to psychiatric
disorders – e.g. surdo-phrenia, a condition arising from communicational interactional
failure.

On occasions failure and frustration in communication and interaction may be
exacerbated by professional advice to families in which particular systems of communication are advocated as the solution to the child's hearing impairment. Parents
may be told to avoid other systems of communication in case they interfere with or

prevent the development of, for example, speech. If the child is unable to develop the skills required for a particular system, he or she is regarded as a failure, and by implication parents regard themselves as also having failed. It is neither the child nor the parents who fail – it is the system of guidance, assessment and provision, and professional failure to identify needs and abilities objectively and to prepare parents and child through providing 'eclectic' information about provision and intervention to meet the child's needs.

Case study

Ben (not his real name) was almost 8 years old. He was integrated into an ordinary class in the local primary school. Concern was expressed about Ben's failure to learn to communicate in an aural-oral environment and his failure to make progress in language development. The cause of his deafness was unknown. Hearing loss was within the severe to profound range across the speech frequencies. Aided responses to sound (i.e. when wearing hearing aids set at the correct level) were within the severe range, showing a small gain in response to sound, although thresholds across the speech frequencies were in the severe range. Tests of non-verbal ability indicated above average function with no areas of significant difficulty (see e.g. Myklebust, 1964; Bond, 1986). Tests of receptive understanding of spoken language indicated functional understanding at a hearing norm equivalent of 18 to 30 months. When assessed via signs supporting speech, understanding improved substantially.

His parents reported behaviour problems at home (attention-demanding and hostile behaviours), sleeping difficulties, difficulties in communication, moody, restless behaviour, etc. There were differences in wishes between the mother and the father. The mother felt that Ben should transfer to a Total Communication environment in which Signed English (British Deaf Signs simultaneously supporting spoken English acoustically amplified via hearing aids) was used. The father felt that signing would cause the little speech which Ben had to deteriorate. Observed in the classroom in one-to-one, small-group and class lessons, and in the playground, Ben responded to direct instructions from teachers and peers. His peers tended to tell him what to do and how to do it. They occasionally used sign or gesture to support their speech. Interactions tended to be one way – 'controlling' – from peers and teachers. In play and free time, while others engaged in a full range of interactive activity Ben flitted from group to group – always on the fringe, tolerated, occasionally accepted in games where practical or physical skill was required but mostly ignored and rejected.

Recommendations and advice included transfer to an educational environment in which signs were used to support spoken language amplified by appropriate hearing aids. Following a meeting with another professional, Ben's parents transferred him to a school for the deaf in which oral-aural methods of communication were practised.

Two and a half years later, Ben, now almost 11 years, showed a range of attention-demanding, inconsequential attention-seeking and hostile behaviours (Stott, 1974). At this stage, ratings of Ben's behaviour and adjustment indicated severe problems. Parental concerns were great, as was family conflict. Ben was reported to be an 'oral' failure. Professionals and parents agreed that Ben should transfer to a school for the deaf in which Total Communication was used; i.e. Signed English was used for tuition (British Signs simultaneously supporting ordinary speech and amplified by hearing aids) and signs sporting spoken English or British Sign Language were used for communication/interactions.

Ben settled into his new school, showing very rapid and positive learning through Total Communication. As his language expanded, his parents frequently commented to the staff at his new school how his speech had improved. They had been concerned that he would stop talking if he went to a school where signs were used. Ben's articulation had not really improved: he had more to talk about, and was more excited about learning, communicating and interacting with others. Thus talking became a more positive and satisfying activity. At home, a previously silent boy, Ben became more of a chatterbox. Sadly, in the years of inappropriate communication, of failure and rejection of his attempts to control interaction, Ben had developed behaviours which he has difficulty in changing. Attention-seeking, attention-demanding and hostile behaviours have diminished, but Ben has continuing difficulty in sustaining interactive conversation, in asserting himself and in negotiating with others. He is learning techniques of self-control – temper control and techniques of relaxation. Although all members of the school staff, including staff who are profoundly deaf, work to encourage him to take greater responsibility in his life and to manage difficulties positively, what will happen when he leaves the protective and understanding environment of the school?

A sad feature of hearing-impaired patients attending psychiatric facilities for the deaf is that many have had early histories of inappropriate communication, inappropriate provision and consequent failure in communication in the early stages of their education. Despite later placement in facilities where communication is appropriate and where educational programmes, guidance and counselling provide a framework for success, children who are hearing impaired and who have an early history of failure and 'rejection' in interaction and communication would appear to be at risk after they have left educational facilities for hearing-impaired children/students.

In most cases, mental health problems in people who have hearing impairments arise through a combination of several features. To summarize, the major factors which appear to contribute to mental health problems in people who are hearing impaired include:

Physical/psychological factors:

- traumatic aetiologies or causes of deafness;
- additional handicaps;
- allergic conditions which may affect behaviour;
- brain/neurological damage;
- hyperkinesis (e.g. Barkley, 1990);
- deteriorating physical conditions.

Psychological factors:

- psychiatric/emotional conditions arising through the same causes as for other people. These conditions may be exacerbated by hearing loss and any of the other factors outlined in this chapter.

Specific learning difficulties:

- information-processing difficulties, particularly impairments involving short-term memory, sequencing, analogous associative generalization and classificatory reasoning development;
- attention deficits or disorders.

Communication-interaction factors:

- rejection and failure in communication or interaction;
- rejection through inappropriate communication;
- rejection through isolation or non-availability of a peer or social group with which the child can identify;
- cultural and experiential differences, rejection and failure;
- non-availability of peers with whom the child can interact on equal terms;
- significant differences in function, capability and communication between the child and the class or peer group;
- failure in tasks and/or communication – inadequate structuring of communication, the curriculum and the environment to enable success.

Professional issues:

- professional focus on particular issues, rather than on client need;
- inadequate or inappropriately trained and experienced professionals;
- use of inappropriate tools and methods of assessment;
- failure to investigate client needs fully and objectively;
- inappropriate knowledge/awareness about problems and needs linked to hearing impairment;
- inappropriate communication skills/knowledge;
- inappropriate environmental management, placement and support.

Other:

- child abuse (physical, social, emotional, sexual, etc.).

From case histories and professional experience, it would appear that the likelihood of mental health problems increases when any of the factors outlined in the last four groups above occur. The more frequently that any of the above occur in an individual's development, the greater the probability of mental health problems.

ASSESSMENT

As noted earlier in this chapter, patterns of behaviour and adjustment are an area which requires careful and objective investigation in view of the reported high incidence of emotional and behavioural adjustment difficulties in people who are hearing impaired. Investigations of the hearing-impaired client's behaviour or adjustment through projective techniques, written questionnaires and personality tests give dubious results at best, even when the examiner is a fluent user of manual communication. The client may have difficulties in understanding written, oral or signed communication or linguistic structures based on an oral language (Bond, 1986). Norms for the personality structure of hearing people are not necessarily appropriate for the hearing impaired

(Vernon, 1967, 1969). In the case of many people who have prelingual hearing impairment, their world may be perceived as an iconic, ideographic, pictorial, visual-spatial world of movement, into which sound and speech intrude with varying degrees of meaning (Bond, 1986).

To assess the behaviour and adjustment of people who are hearing impaired, observations, both anecdotal and objective, behaviour–analysis, self-reports, and structured and non-structured 'conversations' are useful in identifying areas of difficulty. Where possible, observation of behaviour in a variety of contexts and environments (familiar and unfamiliar) is important. Observations from parents and other professionals also provide invaluable information about the individual and the context or environment in which he or she lives.

A framework similar to the following can be useful in investigating or evaluating need, although the structure and nature of the investigation will vary depending on the problem and the hypothesis established:

Background:

- environment, socio-cultural factors.

Aetiology:

- cause(s) or probable cause(s) of hearing impairment.

Other impairments:

- visual, physical, etc. Careful observation of behaviour, via experience in working with hearing-impaired children, etc., has resulted in diagnosis or identification of previously unrecognized, undiagnosed additional impairments by teachers, psychologists, parents, etc.

Hearing impairment:

- time of onset; nature, degree and extent of hearing loss; aided and unaided responses to sound, speech, etc.

Communication:

- preferred mode – in which contexts or environments?
- optimum mode – in which contexts?
- within school or other environment?
- with peers – in which contexts?
- with family – in which contexts?
- recognition of initiatives in communication versus non-recognition.

Developmental/cognitive/intellectual function:

- non-verbal;
- information processing, e.g. short-term memory: different modes – visual, spatial sequenced, movement, bits of information, pictorial, semantic, etc. – sequencing, analogous-associative reasoning, generalization and classification (all non-verbal). Non-verbal measures should be used. Verbal measures, or tests which have verbal components or which require verbal processing, do not indicate ability – they may indicate the effects of hearing impairment on the individual's test function (see Bond, 1986). It is also essential to recognize that tests are only tools which facilitate

investigation of hypotheses in the process of identifying the clients' needs and abilities. Tests and their results cannot describe the complex myriad of human capabilities, understanding and functions. Test results should be validated against other functional abilities and skills;

- learning;
- attention span (visual, etc.).

Verbal educational development and understanding:

- it is useful to evaluate a hearing-impaired child's level of function in these areas, to compare function with peers (hearing and hearing impaired: see Bond, 1986).

Behavioural and emotional function and development:

- personal-social skills and behaviours (attention control; impulsive behaviour; involuntary-voluntary movement; muscular functioning – gross and fine motor co-ordination, clumsiness; tension; reflexes and reactions; anxiety; honesty; temperament; self-confidence – own views of self, family, peers, etc.; emotional responses; leadership; attitudes and relationships with peers, adults, etc.; attitude to correction and conflict; negotiation/interaction skills);
- work habits and skills (attention to task behaviours; perseverance; motivation; flexibility and adaptability; learning from demonstration or own trial-and-error behaviours; mechanical dexterity and skill; organization, speed and accuracy).

Environmental appraisal:

- staff (attitudes; training and support available; demands on staff; movement in environment (i.e. are there frequent changes of staff, pupils, etc.? are there too many people in the class, etc.?); communication – presentation of information, interaction skills, recognition of child initiatives, etc.; skills in developing the hearing-impaired child's learning, initiative, and independence; structuring and presentation of materials; success levels; methods of behaviour management; expectations – recognition of and provision for needs; use of appropriate aids and equipment; links with family);
- peers (attitudes, understanding – empathy; communication and interaction);
- environment (acoustic conditions; visual conditions; movement; changes in activities, rooms/work places, staff or routines; availability of appropriate aids – support systems to maintain equipment at optimum levels, etc.);
- family (ideas and understanding of child's needs; communication/interactional skills and understanding; attitudes and expectations; support available);
- services (availability – support, etc.).

(adapted from Bond, 1991).

Further investigation may involve more detailed analysis of behaviour, which may include the following:

- detailed behaviour analysis – i.e. how often is the behaviour occurring? When? How long for? Where? With whom? What happened before? What happened after? What happens in different environments? Are there factors in the environment which contribute to the problem (e.g. overcrowding, physical disturbance, poor light, reflective surfaces, cold, heat, etc.)?
- assessment of medical/physical factors;

- assessment of communication and interaction success;
- assessment of rejection, or rejecting features of management, communication or the environment.

Process of investigation

If possible the areas of investigation as outlined above should be explored or investigated with the client in order to obtain his or her views. It may be necessary to use the services of an interpreter, particularly if the client uses sign and the psychologist is unable to sign or unable to understand fine nuances of sign. Other sources of information should include family, teachers and educational assistants. Explorations of client needs with deaf professionals can also be particularly useful. There are occasions when behaviour and adjustment vary significantly from environment to environment and from person to person. This raises other questions.

Questions which should be asked in all aspects of an assessment or investigation with people who are deaf include:

What sources of information do I need to explore in order to carry out an unbiased objective and valid assessment so as to fully identify the client's needs?

Have I the skills to carry out this assessment in view of this person's communication needs? Is my communication at an acceptable level?

Is the interpreter and the interpretation accurate, reliable, valid, objective, unbiased and non-political?

How reliable are the views of observers and the client? Are they objective, accurate, valid, unbiased and non-political?

What are the reasons for differences in observations or perceptions?

Have there been any changes or shifts in outlook, behaviour or adjustment? Are changes and differences related to anything in particular?

The following case illustrates the importance of careful analysis of behaviour and case history.

Case study

An adolescent with a very severe to profound familial genetic hearing loss displayed excessive uncontrolled behavioural outbursts, mood changes, and aggressive and hostile behaviours which included physical attacks on authority figures and damage to property. She spent time in psychiatric prisons, psychiatric hospitals, ordinary prisons, etc. One professional who had charge of the case ascribed the behaviour to her deafness.

When she was referred (after some three to four years of very severe behavioural problems), I collected all records and reports about behaviour (from previous schools, the family, the client, social workers, courts and the police). It was possible to show that the major behavioural difficulties occurred at approximately monthly intervals. After a considerable and unfortunate delay, further medical investigations revealed a hormonal imbalance, and premenstrual tension was diagnosed. The client was subsequently offered a simple, effective medical treatment (Bond, 1986). The early years of inappropriate treatment, interaction/communication and management have left lasting scars on the personality and adjustment of this young woman, although the treatment effectively controls her condition.

INTERVENTION

Elimination or amelioration of conditions identified in assessment may contribute to a reduction in mental health or behavioural problems. For example, a small group of children who had severe hearing losses and additional handicaps (aetiologies involving rubella, cytomegalovirus, low birth weight, prematurity and meningitis) showed high levels of involuntary impulsive behaviours, poor on-task behaviours, poor sleep, skin conditions and upper respiratory tract infections. Treatment through removal of, for example, cow's milk, white sugar, additives and preservatives from their diets was arranged, and target behaviours were monitored. Decreases in impulsive behaviours, temper tantrums, and destructive behaviour were shown, as were improvements in sleeping, attention span and other behaviours in approximately 30 per cent of the cases. The same cases showed reversals back to the original pattern of behaviour when returned to an ordinary diet (Bond, 1985, 1986).

As many of the problems faced by children who are hearing impaired arise through inappropriate management (communication/interaction, learning environments, and professional assessment and advice), intervention should target general principles which should assist identification and development of effective treatment programmes. The general principles outlined below were developed from the work of Wood *et al.* (1986) and Glynn (1987). As already noted, disturbance of the interactive process through deprivation or abnormality of input is likely to lead to disruption of communication and a distortion of personal development, which may then result in disturbed or disturbing behaviour (Bond, 1991).

Critical interactional features in intervention include the following:

- Control over initiating, continuing, sustaining, changing or ending communicative interactions should be shared between the adult and the child.
- The task or focus of interaction should be shared between the child and adult, i.e. activity has to mean something if learning is to occur.
- There should be opportunities for reciprocal gains for the learner and the adult, e.g. shared pleasure, which makes possible gain in skills and development of positive social relationships, which in turn enable the less skilled contributor to learn from the skilled or experienced participant(s).
- Learning requires a responsive context in which both parties recognize each other's initiatives and contributions.
- Feedback should assist learning by containing content information rather than corrective information. When the response to initiatives is corrective the less skilled contributor reduces his or her contribution, whereas reinforcement of appropriate contributions and behaviours by partial inclusion/repetition and approval encourages learning and responsiveness.
- The more experienced contributor in interaction must encourage development of independent skills in the less experienced participant.
- Time is needed to process information, to self-correct and to review contributions.
- Compatible communication systems and environments in which the learner is and can be a successful communicator and participant in interaction is essential.

- Learners must have peers with whom they can identify, communicate and interact on equal terms.
- More skilled participants should have expectations and the capability of structuring interactions and demands to enable the learner's needs and abilities to be appropriately met, and their skills extended through progressive opportunity for success.

(adapted from Bond, 1991, pp. 39–41)

In addition to restructuring or changing the environment to ensure opportunity for communicative and interactive success, it may be necessary to employ techniques which are utilized in the case of sad or disturbed and disturbing children who are not hearing impaired (see, e.g. Hoghughi *et al.*, 1988). Techniques used successfully with children who are hearing impaired may include the following:

- improvement of communication systems – e.g. use of pictures and photographs to enable planning ahead, so that children know what is happening and have additional opportunity for choice;
- ensuring of ample opportunity for constructive, rewarding occupation of leisure time;
- monitoring of TV/video watching to avoid films which include violence. Children who are hearing impaired appear to be more readily desensitized to violence via TV or video, particularly following periods of watching TV/video without discussion; e.g. in observations of hearing and hearing-impaired children following physical violence on a TV film, the hearing-impaired children showed a significantly higher level of physical activity ('kung-fu kicks') in the playground than their hearing peers did. They also had greater difficulty in appreciating that their actions were dangerous and could hurt others;
- opportunity for improvement of ideas about self – recognition of individual skills/interests; photographic books about self; opportunity for independence and responsibility;
- positive management programmes;
- group guidance – utilization of peers in social skills training, e.g. increasing awareness of others' feelings, concerns, skills and abilities; increasing awareness of consequences of their own behaviours; encouraging responsibility for their own behaviour management; effective communication training; developing and managing feelings; relationship and health/sex education; developing positive constructive assertiveness skills;
- use of puppets, role play and drama training in social skill training;
- use of peer courts/counselling;
- information feedback about behaviour via photos, video, mirroring, discussion;
- relaxation training (e.g. breathing, massage, aromatherapy);
- self-management of aggression, tension or anxiety via self-isolation/relaxation, self-monitoring or self-appraisal of behaviour.

CONCLUSION

Effective implementation of the above and other techniques to assist sad, disturbed and disturbing deaf children to develop more successful strategies (not just cope) in self-management of their behaviour is dependent on positive and successful interactional skills and strategies. Early identification, appropriate assessment and intervention, and staff and family training support and awareness would appear to be key factors in the development of enabling interactive environments. When we provide positive, enabling, responsive learning and interactive contexts and environments for children who are hearing impaired, then we may see a reduction in unhappy, disturbed and disturbing behaviours.

Our greatest concern and effort should be directed towards the preventable contributions to mental health problems in the HI. Placement in environments in which the HI child is not enabled to compete, interact and communicate on equal terms with peers who have similar needs is a major and preventable factor. Professionals and managers need to be more aware of the damage which may result from inappropriate assessment, intervention and provision.

NOTES

Thanks are due to the many hearing-impaired children, teachers, families, care staff and other professionals who have contributed to the writer's understanding, learning experience and hopefully continuing development, in appreciating the needs of children who are hearing impaired.
1. The terms hearing impaired and hearing impairment are used throughout this chapter to encompass and describe the whole range of hearing loss and deafness. This includes hearing losses which are mild through to total deafness. Some people who have severe to profound hearing losses may prefer to be called 'deaf' rather than 'hearing impaired'.

REFERENCES

Barkley, R. A. (1990) *Attention-deficit Hyperactivity Disorder: A Handbook for Diagnosis and Treatment*. New York: Guilford Press.

BATOD (1992) Surveys on staffing, salaries, etc. *Mag. British Association of Teachers of the Deaf*.

Bexiton, W. H., Heron, W. and Scott, T. H. (1954) In D. O. Hebb (1958), *A Textbook of Psychology*. Philadelphia: W. B. Saunders.

Bond, D. E. (1981) Hearing loss, language cognition, personality and social development. In A. Jackson (ed.), *Ways and Means III. Hearing Impairment*. Globe Educational for Somerset LEA.

Bond, D. E. (1985) Managing behaviour: an alternative diet. Paper presented to International Conference for Educators of the Deaf, Manchester, 1985.

Bond, D. E. (1986) Psychological assessment of the hearing impaired, additionally impaired and multi-handicapped deaf. In D. Ellis (ed.), *Sensory Impairments in Mentally Handicapped People*. Beckenham: Croom Helm.

Bond, D. E. (1989) Communication and interaction with multi-handicapped hearing impaired children. Paper presented to a course at the Newcomen Centre, Guy's Hospital, London, May 1985.

Bond, D. E. (1991) The hearing impaired child with additional handicaps. Unit 17: Distance Learning Course for Teachers of Hearing Impaired Children. Birmingham: School of Education, University of Birmingham.

Denmark, J. C. (1966) Mental illness and early profound deafness. *British Journal of Medical Psychology*, **39**, 117–24.

Denmark, J. C. (1973) The education of deaf children. *Hearing*.

Denmark, J.C. (1985) A study of 250 patients referred to a department of psychiatry for the deaf. *British Journal of Psychiatry,* **146**, 282-6.

Gentile, A. and McCarthy, B. (1973) *Additional Handicapping Condition among Hearing Impaired Students, United States 1971-72.* Washington, DC: Office of Demographic Studies, Gallaudet College.

Glynn, T. (1987) Contexts for independent learning for children with special needs. *Journal of the Association for Behavioural Approaches with Children,* **11**, 5-16.

Goetzinger, C.P. (1972) The psychology of hearing impairment. In J. Katz, *Handbook of Clinical Audiology.* Baltimore: Williams and Wilkins.

Graham, P. and Rutter, M. (1970) In M. Rutter, J. Tizard and K. Whitmore, *Education, Health and Behaviour: The Isle of Wight Study,* London: Longman.

Gregory, S. and Mogford, K. (1981) Early language development in deaf children. In B. Woll, J. Kyle and M. Deuchar (eds), *Perspectives on British Sign Language.* London: Croom Helm.

Heider and Heider (1941) Observation of children's play. *Psychological Monographs,* Vol. 53 No. 5.

Hoghughi, M., Lyons, J., Muckely, A. and Swainston, M. (1988) *Treating Problem Children – Issues, Methods and Practice.* London: Sage Publications.

Howarth, C.I. and Wood, D. (1977) A research programme into the intellectual abilities of deaf children. *Journal of the British Association of Teachers of the Deaf,* **1**, 5.2.

Levine, E.S. (1976) Psychological contribution. In R. Frisina (ed.), *A Bicentennial Monograph on Hearing Impairment: Trends in the USA. Volta Review,* **78**.

Levine, E.S. (1981) *The Ecology of Early Deafness.* New York: Columbia University Press.

Mindel, E.D. and Vernon, M. (1976) *They Grow in Silence: The Deaf Child and His Family.* Md: National Association for the Deaf.

Moores, D. (1978) *Educating the Deaf. Psychology Principles and Practices.* Boston: Houghton Mifflin.

Myklebust, H.R. (1964) *The Psychology of Deafness. Sensory Deprivation, Learning and Adjustment.* New York: Grune and Stratton.

Nance, W. (1976) Studies of hereditary deafness: present, past and future. In R. Frisina (ed.), *A Bicentennial Monograph on Hearing Impairment: Trends in the USA. Volta Review,* **78**.

Schlesinger, H. and Meadow, K.P. (1972) *Sound and Sign: Childhood Deafness and Mental Health.* Berkeley, CA: University of California Press.

Stott, D.H. (1974) *Bristol Social Adjustment Guides.* London: Hodder and Stoughton.

Tucker, I.G. and Nolan, M. (1984) *Educational Audiology.* London: Croom Helm.

Van Dijk, J. (1982) *Rubella Handicapped Children: The Effects of Bilateral Cataract and/or Hearing Impairment on Behaviour and Learning.*

Vernon, McK. (1967) A guide for the psychological evaluation of deaf and severely hard of hearing adults. *The Deaf American,* **19(a)**.

Vernon, McK. (1969) *Multiply Handicapped Deaf Children: Medical, Educational and Psychological Considerations.* Washington Research Monograph for Council for Exceptional Children.

Webster, A. and Ellwood, J. (1985) *The Hearing Impaired Child in the Ordinary School.* Beckenham: Croom Helm.

Wood, D., Wood, H., Griffiths, A. and Howarth, I. (1986) *Teaching and Talking with Deaf Children.* Chichester: Wiley.

Chapter 4

Coping with Unhappy Children Who Have Asthma

Fleming Carswell

Asthma can produce considerable disability, both physical and psychological, in children. Nevertheless, with modern, appropriate treatment designed for the individual child, the great majority should be able to lead a full, normal life. Asthma can either be the cause of a child's unhappiness or can affect an unhappy child to make him or her even less happy. Emotional distress is only rarely the direct cause of an asthma attack and there is no evidence that unhappiness can start the child being asthmatic.

WHAT IS ASTHMA?

Children with asthma have attacks of wheeze, cough and breathlessness episodically. These can occur rarely or can inhibit their activities, especially exercise, in a major way. Asthma causes more than 10 per cent of the school population to seek clinical help each year.

The disease usually starts before the child goes to school, and the more severe sufferers tend to have begun having features of it before their first birthday. In children, asthma is twice as common in boys as in girls, but the sex ratio (male/female) becomes 1 in middle age. We do not know the fundamental cause of the asthmatic state but it is certainly more likely to occur if there is a strong family history of asthma. In other words, if both parents have asthma, there is a six-fold greater chance that their child will develop asthma than that the child of two parents who do not have asthma will develop it.

Many children adapt psychologically to its continuing presence and assume it is normal not to be able to run or play games involving running, or that other children are similar and have regular need for chest medicine. Those who so adapt are better able to carry out and to enjoy the activities available to them, but undoubtedly they miss out. Sadly, this disability is largely unnecessary, as asthma is eminently treatable and almost always compatible with a full, normal life. I have severe patients on major treatment who have completed Outward Bound courses, one competing at international level in triathlons, and one who is a regional sprint champion.

The knowledge that this unmerited disability is inhibiting one's life can of course lead to unhappiness, though most people adapt. Teenagers, particularly, seem to feel aggrieved by having the disease and commonly seek to deny it. This can lead to stopping the treatment that is reducing their physical disability because taking medicine negatively affects their body image.

The disease is defined as episodic reversible obstruction of the inner chest air-tubes or airways. As there is no single test that defines the presence of asthma, one has to diagnose it by its manifestations, of which the wheeze is the most characteristic. This is the wheezy or musical noise commonly heard throughout the chest in attacks. The wheezing and other respiratory effects may appear abruptly and disappear in minutes or days, either spontaneously or as a result of specific asthma treatment. No other common childhood disease presents with these features. Present research leads to the suspicion that there is not only a genetic predisposition to develop asthma, but that the things the foetus and more especially the child of less than 1 year of age is exposed to may set up the asthmatic state. Evidence for this includes the finding that asthma tends to be more common in children who are born in or just before the grass-pollen season or who are exposed to other allergens such as house-dust mite or birch pollen, or to general lung irritants such as tobacco smoke or gas fumes. This is a controversial subject; although some researchers have observed these associations, workers elsewhere have failed to confirm their existence. Nevertheless, as only one in five identical twin pairs develops asthma, despite having identical genetic constitutions, one must assume that the environment to which the child is exposed has some part in the causation of the disease.

HOW ASTHMA IS MANIFESTED

The classical features of asthma are wheeze, breathlessness, cough and occasionally spit production. Various combinations of these features occur. The features of asthma are usually clear, because the asthmatic child would have had previous episodes and an attack is likely to respond to anti-asthma medicine quite rapidly (10 minutes is usually sufficient for inhaled medicines such as bronchodilators to produce a response).

- Asthma can occur without observed wheeze, and it is clearly important in the group of patients for whom this is so that tests are carried out and asthma treatment tried, as it can be of great physical and psychological benefit.
- Breathlessness occurs in asthma probably because the airways are partially blocked and much more effort is needed to pull and push the air in and out of the lungs. The breathlessness becomes particularly dangerous when it is so severe that the child cannot say a single word or the lungs' ability to exchange the blood gases is so reduced that blood in the warm places, such as the lips, is blue (cyanosis) because of the lack of oxygen. In approximately 1 in 20,000 asthmatic children a year, this can lead to death in an attack (Carswell, 1985).
- The asthmatic cough is usually an irritating, spasmodic, dry, repeated cough which is not usually associated with spit production. A modest proportion of asthmatic children do, in fact, bring up spit particularly at the end of attacks.

This description of the disability produced by asthma is important, as an essential part of coping with asthma is assessing its severity and therefore the likely difficulties and danger. Parents and children need to be able to assess this and to have appropriate coping strategies. One can judge to a considerable extent how bad individual attacks are by comparing them with such descriptions. Another significant measurement is whether the child's heart rate is much more rapid than usual. This reflects under-oxygenation of the blood and is an important warning sign, produced by difficulty in obtaining sufficient gas exchange in the lungs. Severe indrawing of the lower chest, tummy or neck, indicating that large pressures are being used to drive the gases in and out of the chest, are other useful indicators. Nowadays, however, one must say that the best indicator of the severity of an attack that is readily available is the peak flow rate. Peak flow meters that measure this can be purchased for £10 from the National Asthma Campaign (Providence House, Providence Place, London N1 0NT) and doctors can supply them on prescription. If a child can blow reproducibly into such a meter, the maximum flow rate recorded gives a very useful measurement of how open the chest air-tubes (bronchi) are. In normal children, the peak expiratory flow rate (PEF) rate is related to height; any reduction from the predicted rate in asthmatic children indicates the current severity of the disease. Thus, in a very bad attack, a 14-year-old child who could normally blow at a rate of 380 litres/minute might only be able to blow at less than 30 litres/minute.

An index of how often the asthma had interfered with the child's life over the last year would be the reduction in activity produced. Thus chronic inability to play games, absence from school or playgroup, the need for extra medicine, including cortico steroids, and any hospital admissions all give an indication of the disease's severity. This assessment of the severity of both the acute attack and of the chronic state is very relevant because, as there is no cure for asthma, specific treatment has to be adjusted to the particular child's problem. Each child should have its treatment specifically tailored to its needs. There are, nevertheless, general as well as individual guidelines for treatment.

GENERAL GUIDELINES FOR TREATMENT

The principle that cannot be stated too often is that asthma treatment will only be effective for asthma. Therefore, one must have assessed the asthma before and after treatment to know the effect of that treatment on that patient. Asthma medicine will not remove unhappiness that is *not* produced by asthma. It is best to reassess a new treatment, taken daily, after at least a month of major usage rather than earlier, and to start with this after a base-line assessment of one month without regular treatment. The child and family then commonly feel more convinced that the treatment is needed and will continue it when not obviously unwell. Many parents find an asthma diary invaluable: for five minutes a day a record can be kept that is useful both to the parents and to the doctor. This allows easy comparison of the different months of treatment. The assessment of complaints is commonly linked to the regular measure-ment of the peak expiratory flow rate, which provides a complementary and objective record of asthma severity. The effective working of the peak flow meter needs to be checked, both as regards its mechanical function and to ensure the child is using it correctly. A particular problem encountered at doctors' clinics is that sometimes, to please their physician, some children write up their diary card in the waiting area. This creates considerable difficulties in the management by the doctor, and I suspect a similar situation not uncommonly occurs in the house when the parent is supervising the child. Explanation of the need for the medicines and reassurance on their correctness (such as pointing out that famous athletes take them) are gentle, positive support and reminders that help to ensure that medicine is taken effectively and regularly, if required.

The major present treatment of asthma involves the administration of substances which suppress the manifestations rather than cure the disease, so asthmatic children have to keep taking the medicines. There is a bewildering array of these and many different techniques are often available to administer a particular drug. Literature such as that produced by the National Asthma Campaign should be obtained and read by children and parents.

GENERAL PRINCIPLES OF DRUG ADMINISTRATION

Modern therapy commonly uses the principle that delivering the drug through the air-routes into the lungs achieves maximum concentration there and reduces the likelihood that unwanted effects will be produced elsewhere, because lesser concentrations reach the other areas of the body than if the drug was given by mouth or injection. This may be achieved by inhaling the medicine as dry powder. Such a system requires a loading device and that the child can be taught to suck the powder down into the lungs by a major inhalation. Although occasionally children less than 2 years can be taught this technique, it is usually not practical unless they are at least 3 years old.

An alternative delivery system is though pressurized inhalers, which have the active substance and an inert gas as a propellant. The child holds the canister to the mouth and presses to release the given dose of the drug just after starting a large slow breath. Unfortunately, this demands that the child can co-ordinate pressing the inhaler and taking the breath in at the same time. Also, for greatest delivery of medicine to the lungs, it is desirable that the child inhales from the canister at a steady rate rather than as quickly and as hard as possible (as is required with the dry powder technique). To alleviate these difficulties, a variety of spacer devices has been developed. These essentially involve a chamber which is designed to match the nature of the propellant in the canister. The active substance is held in suspension in the chamber air on activation of the canister. When the child takes a big breath in, the active medicine empties into the lungs. There is commonly a valve at the entrance of the spacer which prevents the child blowing into the chamber and removing the active contents. Spacers come in a variety of different forms which are rapidly changing but, as with all these mechanical aids, the basic technique is to check the instruction leaflet provided with each of them and directly observe whether the individual child is using the device effectively. Direct demonstration by the parents on themselves of the technique and the acceptability of the medicine helps.

When these devices are used to deliver a drug that relieves attacks rapidly, it is easy to observe their effectiveness; when they are used to deliver drugs to prevent attacks, it is more difficult, as one can only observe whether they achieve their therapeutic objective over a month or so. Failure to inhale effectively is a common reason for the apparent failure of a drug. Another potential cause of failure is change in the quantity of the drug given. Many inhaler medicines come in different doses, which means that the child could be taking less than the correct amount if a lower dose than was previously used has been accidentally prescribed. It is well worth while knowing and ensuring the actual quantity (weight) of drug/dose the child is taking, in order to avoid this.

Hopefully, all children will have the proposed technique for their device demonstrated to them at a clinic and will be subsequently shown how to use it effectively. However, some children cannot perform any of these manoeuvres. For these children, an alternative way of giving treatment is to drive a gas, commonly air from a compressor or oxygen from a cylinder, through a device (a nebulizer) which contains the medicine in liquid form. This produces small, moist particles of drug solution (aerosol) in the stream of air/oxygen. This mist can be delivered to the lungs via a tube in the child's mouth or by face mask, so that the child's breathing co-operation is not required. It is important to emphasize that such a compressor/nebulizer system is only a method to deliver the drug to the lungs. Other systems, as described above, will produce the same effect, if given in equivalent dose. Unfortunately, the nebulizer/compressor demands moderately expensive apparatus (costing about £100), not routinely available on the National Health Service. Using it may make the family anxious and over-protective, as they may feel that only such complicated medical therapy will control the child's symptoms.

The clinic should have the aim of liberating the child from the disease and teaching parents and children how they can manage their own asthma and enjoy a full and normal life. This is entirely possible with the great majority of asthmatic children. What every child requires is careful assessment, adjustment of treatment and reassessment *until that aim is achieved*.

TECHNIQUES FOR THE MANAGEMENT OF ASTHMA WHICH DO NOT INVOLVE MEDICINE

Techniques such as hypnotherapy and relaxation exercises have a place in the management of childhood asthma. Homeopathy may also have a place, but doctors like myself are anxious that such a treatment does not involve the stopping of effective conventional treatment.

I have in the past found that breathing classes, where physiotherapists teach the full, controlled utilization of breathing muscles, have been of considerable value, particularly for children identified by their parents as nervous or in some way unwilling to use physical drug-inhalation techniques. It can provide major reassurance and reinforcement of their using the treatment to see their peers or older children willingly taking it effectively and without embarrassment in a group. The physical maneouvres taught may also increase comfort in attacks.

Apart from these psychological techniques, there are others which do not involve the giving of medicine. Asthma attacks may be provoked by particular chemicals known as allergens. If one can avoid contact with these allergens, it may be possible to avoid an attack. The trouble is that many asthmatic children are in fact allergic to a range of substances and may not react immediately on contact. The child and its family may not be aware of which substances provoke attacks. Some useful information on allergens can be produced if the doctor carries out skin-prick tests. If there is a large skin reaction, it is expected that the lungs will react similarly. This may be particularly helpful if there is a suggestion that a pet is involved, as a large reaction to that species makes it more likely that this is, in fact, the case. Of course, there are often particular social and family reasons why a pet cannot be removed and clearly, if the object of the exercise is to make the child happier rather than more unhappy, the family may decide that a balanced position of reduced exposure to the pet – for instance, by excluding it from the child's bedroom or washing it weekly – would be sufficient in the domestic situation. Alternative solutions to problems caused by pets may appear if the family assesses the situation as truly causing the attacks. Thus, I find suggesting two weeks' boarding of the pet away from the family home, while they extensively vacuum and clean, may provide necessary evidence of the pet's effect. It is especially useful in that situation to have a diary record of peak expiratory flow rates and symptoms before, during and after the temporary removal. With allergic children, it is undesirable to introduce furry pets into the household, as they will commonly become allergic to them. I have a limited success in suggesting fish as alternatives!

Skin-prick testing may reveal sensitivity to moulds, including those present widely in the atmosphere and in the house. This is only rarely a problem for the asthmatic child, and of course is best treated by removal of the moulds. A much more common problem, which is more difficult to remove, is the house-dust mite. This ubiquitous pest apparently can sensitize and provoke asthmatic children to such an extent that it is the commonest cause of positive prick reactions. It is very difficult to remove it effectively but its presence can be reduced in the child's bedroom by removing carpets and replacing them with washable coverings, avoiding furry toys and washing soft toys regularly. Washing should be carried out at high temperatures on machines. If a new mattress is being bought, it is worth covering it completely with an airtight plastic covering, which can be dusted weekly. A variety of chemicals are becoming available which are said to kill house-dust mites. They often do this in the test tube and sometimes in houses in experimental situations, but they have not yet been convincingly shown to be of value in routine treatment – and there is a small risk that the children will become sensitive to them. Similarly, especially powerful or modified vacuum cleaners have been advocated, but these are less likely to reduce the house-dust mite population enough for an observable effect on an asthmatic child. Air-filtration systems have also been advocated and may produce an effect, but they are expensive, inconvenient and occasionally actually spread the allergen.

The direct and sensible advice is to ensure the child is not in the room when vacuuming and bedmaking are done, as these are the two major causes of mite particles being released into the air. Again, as the object of the exercise is to increase the happiness of the family, they should be encouraged to reach their personal solution, after careful presentation of the facts. It is necessary in this context to remember that the convenient treatment which suppresses symptoms is practically always effective when carefully adjusted, and its side effects are minimal even if the drugs are continued for years.

Other factors are commonly implicated in attacks, such as emotion, expecially excitement before an event such as a birthday or tiredness at the end of a busy or emotionally demanding day. Exercise commonly promotes attacks, particularly out of doors in cold weather, and it may be useful for the child to take a bronchodilator regularly before exercise known to provoke an attack commonly. Usually, such bronchodilators can be taken in addition to other preventive medicines, and it is probably preferable for a child to take them in order to reduce the social disruption produced by the illness. Such a balance must be decided by the child and family after they have been informed of the potential benefits and risks. An asthmatic child, like any other child, is commonly happier when carrying out many activities with peers. Asthma need not inhibit this.

WORRIES ABOUT ASTHMA

Worries about death are more commonly present in the parents than in the child because most children are egocentric and probably do not appreciate that death could occur to them, at least before the age of 10. As a worried parent can lead to an unhappy child, it is clearly important to deal with the parents' concern about death in an attack. This occurs, as stated earlier, in approximately 1 in 20,000 asthmatic patients a year, and in fact that figure is likely to be a considerable overestimate of the true likelihood, as it is derived from the last 20 years' experience – often before the widespread use of modern, effective therapy. All the studies have implied that those children that die have chronic asthma, which has usually been untreated or inadequately treated. Failure to deliver effective treatment, or even to seek it, was present in the majority of deaths; so people's fear of a sudden, overwhelming attack in a previously well-controlled child is unrealistic. In nearly all the children who died, there was time to seek additional help – perhaps the major positive message from such studies is to remember that each treatment has limitations but there is always a more powerful alternative available – so seek help if the usual remedy is not working.

Parents also worry about their child taking regular medicines, as they fear he or she will grow into a drug addict. There is no evidence that severe addiction to the present effective remedies occurs. Children do not become truly addicted to their inhalers, though they can become dependent on them, particularly if they do not have adequate attack-free time because the basal medicine is not sufficient to allow them daily freedom from the emergency medicine. The remedy then is to increase the basal medicine and to increase the child's security, rather than attempt to get them to tolerate a much severer degree of physical disability because of the asthma. Sometimes, children have quite severe attacks which are not recognized by their parents or medical practitioners. For example, one child was referred back to my clinic for possible reduction in treatment. Before doing this, I asked the mother about the particular attacks the child had had, after she reassured me that the child had had perfect school attendance throughout the year. At this point, the mother very proudly said she always went to school though, admittedly, she had had to give her the kiss of life on two different occasions when she fell to the floor because of breathlessness – but she was fit enough to go to school half an hour later! It turned out the mother was grossly underemphasizing the severity of the attacks and that these were potentially fatal episodes, which were abolished when we increased rather than decreased the medicine. A further worry is whether the effectiveness of the medicines will wear off over time because of regular use. The answer is usually not to any important degree.

A reason for failure to obtain adequate control for a lot of asthmatic sufferers is failure to persuade the child to take the medicine. This is particularly the case in adolescence, when the adolescent commonly feels that taking the medicine sets him or her apart. Adolescents may have the idea also that if they can deny their illness by not taking the medicine, the illness will not truly exist. This is dangerous and it is important that one tries to teach them the opposite version – that, because they have the disadvantage of the disease, they are entitled to the appropriate medicine. It should be emphasized that very famous and effective people, including Olympic athletes, have had asthma and successfully achieved world records while necessarily taking their medicine. The Amateur Athletic Association recognizes the specific disability of asthma and people who have this disease can take drugs, such as bronchodilators, for the particular alleviation or prevention of their attacks, even in record-breaking attempts.

Another reason advanced for not taking medicine is the idea that children will grow out of their asthma and therefore it is not worth treating it, or that treating it will delay the growing out of it. The latter is not true. While many boys do tend to have a reduction in the severity of their asthma in adolescence, only about half actually stop having attacks, and this can be after 15 years of troublesome asthma. It is important that proper treatment is delivered as soon as asthma is identified in the child.

The question of whether separation from the parents is good or bad for asthma depends on the family. Though it has reasonably convincingly been shown that sometimes this can be of benefit, more often it is an advantage to increase the child's asthma medicine, counsel the family and help them to reach a more satisfactory, working, interpersonal relationship. Much of the foregoing relates to the fact that sufferers do not always take their medicine, even though the need may have been eloquently and persuasively argued by the doctor. This can happen because the explanation was misunderstood or was not appropriate for the parent's perception or wishes for the child's life-style. Such non-compliance of course is an indication of the need for discussion and investigation of its reasons, and for additional attempts to ensure that the proposed solution is satisfactory to the child and parents. It is very important that non-compliance is admitted to in consultation, as otherwise there is no chance of realistic instructions from your adviser. If you cannot speak to your adviser, change to another one and save both your time!

SUMMARY

Coping with unhappy children with asthma requires detailed assessment, therapeutic trial and reassessment, and detailed counselling of the child and its supporters within rational practical management.

REFERENCE

Carswell, F. (1985) Thirty deaths from asthma. *Archives of Disease in Childhood*, **60**(1), 25–8.

Chapter 5

Coping with Unhappy Children Who Have Diabetes

Jeffrey and Deborah Freeman

Diabetes alone seldom causes permanent unhappiness in a child, or the child's family, although it is always an unwelcome presence in the home. However, when there are pre-existing emotional or social difficulties in a family, we believe diabetes may exacerbate them. These difficulties may also have a profound effect on the clinical course of the condition.

Several surveys have pointed out that insufficient information on diabetes is available to people in the field of education. Our aim in this chapter is to provide basic information about diabetes in both the medical and emotional context. We believe that coping with unhappy children with diabetes means first and foremost understanding diabetes itself.

Over several years we have learned a great deal about diabetes and the way it affects children and their families. One of us is a consultant paediatrician in a district general hospital and has for ten years run a diabetic clinic, catering for children up to age 16. The other is a psychiatric social worker and a writer. Between us, we have brought up three sons, one of whom became diabetic at the age of 7.

WHAT IS DIABETES?

Before the introduction of insulin into clinical use in the 1920s, juvenile diabetes was a fatal disease, life expectancy being measured in weeks. Insulin transformed this scenario. Diabetes is now a chronic condition which is compatible with a normal life-span. In order to achieve this, however, the diabetic patient must adhere to a regime of insulin injections, regular urine or blood tests, and dietary control. With all that, the life expectancy of the average diabetic can still be reduced by the long-term complications of the disease; and the quality of life, short-term and long-term, can often be impaired. Yet most diabetic children appear healthy in all respects and live normal lives. It is against this somewhat paradoxical background that behavioural issues in diabetic children need to be seen.

When dietary carbohydrate is absorbed into the bloodstream of a non-diabetic, specific cells in his or her pancreas (called the beta cells of the Islets of Langerhans) automatically produce the hormone insulin. This ensures that blood-sugar levels remain within the 'normal' range (normal blood sugar = 3.3–8.5 mmol/litre). Insulin enables sugar in the blood to enter the cells of the body and to be used by the body as an essential energy source. A diabetic is a person whose pancreas has ceased to produce insulin in sufficient quantities.

The basic problem for the diabetic patient is that the ability to control the level of sugar in the blood has been lost. Absence of insulin causes blood-sugar levels to rise, and when the levels pass a certain threshold the sugar spills over into the urine. This causes weight loss (due to loss of calories from the body) and, most importantly, the loss of large quantities of fluid. The untreated diabetic child will pass large volumes of urine, then feel thirsty, and drink to excess.

There are two main types of diabetes. In Type I (or insulin-dependent diabetes), the insulin-producing cells are destroyed. This affects children and young people, and virtually all sufferers need insulin injections on a daily basis. Type II, or non-insulin dependent diabetes (though insulin may be required in severe cases), affects older people, and is caused by the wearing-out of the insulin-producing cells. It can often be controlled by diet or tablets. Type I diabetes is not treatable by tablets.

Diabetes is becoming commoner. Current data suggest 1 in 500 children under the age of 16 is affected. Siblings of diabetic children stand a greater chance of developing the disease than other children, and so do their offspring.

Causes of diabetes

The causes are not known with certainty, although there is some evidence of a genetic predisposition in some families. Most newly diagnosed children, however, have no other affected family member. Another factor may be the occurrence of a viral infection in the weeks before diagnosis. The fact that most children are diagnosed in the autumn and winter months supports the theory that viruses are implicated. There may be other as yet undiscovered environmental factors.

Signs and symptoms of diabetes

Weight loss, thirst and the passage of large quantities of urine (and bed-wetting in a child who has previously been dry) are the early symptoms of uncontrolled diabetes. There may also be loss of appetite, lethargy, moodiness, irritability and pallor. These symptoms are eliminated when the insulin deficiency is corrected, but may return if the control of the diabetes deteriorates.

Left untreated, the child will become very seriously ill with diabetic keto-acidosis, which can itself be fatal. (See the diabetic emergencies section below.)

Management and control of diabetes

The object of diabetic control is to maintain blood-sugar levels as close to the normal range as possible for as much of the time as possible. This is a difficult task. It is like maintaining the central heating in a house at a constant temperature when the thermostat is broken. The tools available are: injected insulin, a regulated diet, and exercise.

Injected insulin

The mainstay of treatment is the insulin injection. Each patient will have an injection regime worked out by his or her diabetic clinic. The precise insulin dose is not rigidly fixed, but will be changed from time to time by the doctor, patient or patient's parent.

Once injected, insulin works to lower the blood sugar, irrespective of the level of the blood sugar at that time. If the blood sugar is high, insulin will bring it down; if it is already normal or low, insulin will operate regardless and still bring it down. Injections are usually given by a plastic syringe with a very fine needle, but in recent years many patients have started to use specially designed pen-injectors. The insulin is injected under the skin. Favoured sites for injection are the upper arm, thigh, lower abdomen or buttocks. Babies (in whom diabetes is rare but not unknown) and small children will need to have the injections given by their parents or carers, but older children (from age 6–7) can learn to inject themselves. Injection problems are one obvious cause of 'unhappiness' in diabetic children.

Different types of insulin, pork or beef-based, have been used over the years. Nowadays most patients use synthetically manufactured human insulin. There are different types of insulin:

- Short-acting insulins, which are transparent in the phial, start acting within half an hour, reach peak activity at 2 hours, and start to lose effect at about 4 hours.
- Medium-acting insulins, of cloudy appearance, start acting 2 hours after injection, peak at 4 hours and act for 10 to 12 hours.
- Long-acting insulins, also of cloudy appearance, start acting 4 to 6 hours after injection, and have maximum effect at 8 to 24 hours.

Patients are controlled on various combinations of these insulins given in one to four injections a day. Some patients are controlled on pre-prepared mixtures of insulins.

A regulated diet

In the past it was recommended that diabetics should have a low-carbohydrate diet, as they were unable to handle carbohydrates. Improved understanding of the metabolic consequences of different types of diet has led to a revision in this recommendation. Experts now suggest a low-fat, high-carbohydrate diet, the carbohydrate being derived from slowly absorbed, high-fibre sources. Rapidly absorbed, highly refined sugars should be avoided. The diet should contain enough protein and calories to ensure adequate nutrition and growth. The carbohydrate content is spread throughout the day, the exact quantities being calculated according to the child's age and weight. Some children are taught to measure their carbohydrate in terms of 10-gram portions, or 'exchanges', of which they are allowed a certain number per meal.

So lots of roughage, plenty of good-quality protein and a modest amount of fried and fatty foods is the ideal diabetic diet. This diet can be quite expensive, although pulses, excellent foods for diabetics, are cheap. (The problem with pulses or beans is getting the children to eat them!)

One crucial postscript to the subject of diet: whenever the blood-sugar level falls, has fallen or is falling rapidly, the diabetic must eat something – immediately, if possible. (See the information about hypoglycaemia in the 'diabetic emergencies' section below.)

Exercise

Exercise has the effect of lowering the blood sugar. The ideal way for a diabetic to take exercise is as regular, controlled exercise throughout the day. The way most children exercise is sporadic, erratic and vigorous. This of course will complicate the task of controlling the blood sugar.

For games and PE lessons in school there should always be supplies of rapidly absorbed carbohydrate available – a tube of glucose tablets or a bottle of sweet drink, preferably a glucose drink. This is important not only for prolonged, sustained exercise such as cross-country running, but also for brief but intense exercise such as squash or swimming.

Other factors which influence blood-sugar levels are:

- The weather. Blood-sugar levels tend to run at a slightly lower level in warm weather, perhaps because of more rapid absorption of insulin from under the skin, perhaps because children take more exercise.
- Illness. Most day-to-day, minor illnesses such as colds and flu, diarrhoea, etc., will affect diabetic control to some degree, making blood-sugar levels higher than normal. Insulin doses may need adjustment.
- Mood. Emotional tension or upset can sometimes have an adverse effect on blood-sugar levels.
- Menstruation. In some girls, diabetic control becomes erratic around the time of menstruation.

Monitoring of diabetic control

Diabetic patients need to monitor the level of sugar in the blood by one of two methods:

1. The direct method: the child takes a drop of blood from a fingerprick. Specially made strips allow him or her to estimate the blood sugar through changes in colour. These same strips can be used in portable electronic meters.
2. The indirect method: the child measures the amount of sugar in his or her urine with special chemical strips.

Most of this testing will be done at home, and little at school except perhaps in the case of emergencies. Further tests are done at the diabetic clinic. The aim of monitoring is to inform the child, the parents and the diabetic clinic about the level of diabetic control. The attitude of children towards the daily routine of monitoring varies (usually from unenthusiastic to very unenthusiastic). The younger the child the more the parents will be responsible for monitoring.

Diabetic emergencies

There are two types of diabetic emergency, those due to low blood-sugar level and those due to high blood-sugar level.

Low blood-sugar level emergencies – hypoglycaemia or 'hypos'

When the child has had insulin but not enough carbohydrate, has had exercise and not enough extra carbohydrate, or has had to wait for a meal or snack which may be late, he or she will (in diabetic jargon) 'feel hypo', 'go hypo', 'be hypo', or 'have a hypo'. The initial symptoms of hypoglycaemia may include *all* or *some* of the following: loss of concentration, vagueness, uncharacteristic mood change (silliness, anger, extreme irritability), lethargy, sweatiness, pallor and shakiness. The child may or may not be conscious of these changes. If the child or supervisor notices the hypoglycaemia, it should be dealt with. The child should have something sweet – liquid, if possible, or glucose tablets. The onset of these symptoms may be very rapid even though the symptoms themselves may be vague. The time-scale is unpredictable – anything from two minutes to an hour, depending on how fast the blood-sugar level is falling.

Further symptoms of untreated hypoglycaemia may include *all* or *some* of the following: intensification of the initial symptoms, which may progress to inco-ordination, loss of consciousness and convulsions. At this stage do not attempt to give the child anything by mouth. Call an ambulance quickly.

It is far better to prevent hypos by making sure the child always has food to hand, particularly during sports lessons. Even if the child comes to you during a tables test asking for a sweet, please give him or her the benefit of the doubt. Schools educate children not to eat during lessons; but the needs of the diabetic must make him or her an exception to this rule.

High blood-sugar emergencies – hyperglycaemia and diabetic keto-acidosis

Blood-sugar levels in diabetic children fluctuate, often being highest around breakfast time. The odd high blood sugar is to be expected; but when sugar levels remain high for days, or 'very, very high' for a day or two, the original symptoms of diabetes return. If this process continues unchecked (by insulin, diet or exercise), the body cells, unable to utilize sugar, will start to burn fat as an energy source. This process releases ketones and acids into the bloodstream, causing abdominal pain, vomiting, rapid breathing, drowsiness and a smell of acetone on the breath. This condition, left untreated, will lead to diabetic coma and death. The condition can occur as a result of acute infections, missing insulin injections, severe emotional upsets, and very occasionally at the time of menstruation. It is more likely to occur where the basic level of control is poor.

Vomiting in a diabetic child should *always* be taken seriously. *Never* attribute it to a stomach upset; seek medical advice. An unwell diabetic child who does not feel hungry should *not* be encouraged to miss an insulin injection.

Long-term complications

Long-term complications very rarely affect children; but the billboards of our streets display posters from the British Diabetic Association, which mention them unequivocally. Parents of diabetic children, and older children themselves, will be aware of the issue.

The main complications are kidney disease, circulatory problems, heart problems, eye problems including blindness, and neurological problems. Good control lessens the chance of complications; and some of the complications, particularly eye problems, are amenable to treatment if detected early. The issue of such complications, however, may weigh heavily on the diabetic and his or her family. For children it is not the complications but the fear of them which is the problem. This fear can be a potent cause of unhappiness in diabetic children. It can induce depression, anger, apathy, despair, and a fatalistic approach to diabetic control, especially where teenagers are concerned. The real pain around this issue needs to be acknowledged and handled sensitively. There is no need to be afraid to recommend specialist counselling.

Bear in mind that diabetes, like life itself, is full of paradoxes. Unfortunately plenty of non-diabetics die young. Lots of diabetics live full and healthy lives. But ignoring the fact that a worry about complications may be there in the background is, in our view, no help to anybody.

THE SOCIAL/EMOTIONAL FACTS ABOUT DIABETES

The best-laid plans of the diabetic clinic can be and often are confounded by the realities of what it is like to have diabetes and to live with it. In the rest of this chapter we highlight the social and emotional context of diabetes, and suggest guidelines for coping with unhappy children where diabetes may be implicated in the unhappiness (though, as we stressed at the start of the chapter, it need not always be so).

Diabetes is not a condition which can best be dealt with by stoicism, a stiff upper lip, or doing your best to forget it. Whatever the rights and wrongs of it, you cannot allow yourself to ignore diabetes – somebody must be mindful of it, on an almost hourly basis. The diabetic or the parent (and it is usually the mother) has to be aware of what has been eaten, when, and what food is available for the next snack-meal. The diabetic and his or her family cannot go out for the day without making sure that insulin, snacks and blood-sugar measuring equipment are all available. Maintaining normality in the life-style of the child takes a huge amount of work behind the scenes. However significant the role of the diabetic clinic, no doctor or nurse stays by the diabetic child from morning till night to check all is well. Perhaps more than in other illnesses, clinical responsibility has to be shouldered by the child and the family.

COPING WITH UNHAPPY CHILDREN WHO HAVE JUST BEEN DIAGNOSED AS DIABETIC

When diabetes is diagnosed, the impact on the child and the family is profound. This impact will vary according to the age of the child and the structure and type of family, with particular reference to the family's economic, social, cultural and educational background. It will also vary according to the severity of the child's condition at diagnosis. Here is an extract from a piece written by a 15-year-old, remembering diagnosis at the age of 7:

> In the very early stages of my diabetic life, I had no idea of the full implications. I didn't think I was going to be ill for long. I thought that I would spend seven days in hospital and then come out fighting fit. I did . . . but I wasn't cured. I had a condition that would stay with me for life. This fact still hadn't hit me . . .
>
> I was started on a regime of one injection a day. The moment when I had my first insulin injection sticks in my mind so vividly that whenever I think of it goose-pimples prick up on my back . . .
>
> I was sitting on my bed when the Sister came over to me. She was carrying a small silver tray on which was a syringe containing twelve units of fast-acting insulin. She picked up the syringe, looked me in the eye, and spoke to me in an ice-cold voice, telling me I had a condition which would stay with me for life. She told me I had to have the injection or else I would get very ill. I remember not really believing her. But when she picked up the syringe and moved towards me, I was horrified at the thought of her sticking that needle in my thigh. I grabbed her hand, and tried to push it away, but her stronger arm moved the needle closer and closer to my leg. In about two minutes, she had the needle on the surface of my skin. She pushed it forward and into my leg. I was surprised at how little it hurt, but my mind was conjuring up pictures of pain, so I continued to scream and bawl until the needle was taken out. My mother and father were there watching the whole thing. I could not understand why they were allowing Sister to be so mean to me.

The initial parental reaction is usually one of shock at the discovery that the child has a life-long illness for which there is no cure – combined often with relief that the child who has been getting paler, thinner and less energetic by the day is not dying of cancer after all. Any previous experience with diabetes, perhaps through a relative or friend, will colour this. A grief reaction may occur, especially in parents and in older children. The child has lost many normal expectations, and can only continue to live a normal life by following the complex routines and procedures described above.

For children of all ages, the social and emotional level of functioning of the family will profoundly affect how the child adjusts to the diagnosis. Families with poor communication skills will be especially disadvantaged. There is so much to learn, and to understand, and so much that needs talking through.

THE DIABETIC CHILD IN SCHOOL

The overriding task for a teacher has to be to understand the language and concepts of diabetes, so that when a child of any age communicates with you regarding blood sugars, hypos or exchanges, you know what he or she is talking about.

For the pre-school child, the main issues are likely to be:

- problems with injections and blood-tests, and the fear that they engender;
- problems about eating. Food is one of the most powerful weapons a toddler possesses, in that battle of wills otherwise known as 'early childhood'. But the stakes in food-refusal are much higher if the child has already had insulin.

The dramas around these issues will be mainly enacted at home, but a small child recently diagnosed as diabetic may show signs of emotional distress in the nursery. On the other hand, the child may well blossom initially because of the extra attention, while his or her siblings may be noticing the lack of it. You can offer help when a toddler has been diagnosed as diabetic by offering a listening ear to the mother, as well as to the child, and believing what they tell you. Keep a sweet drink or a packet of glucose tablets always to hand in the nursery for emergencies. Try not to give the rest of the class sweets as rewards for games – they are bad for their teeth anyway.

Primary school

Children of primary-school age are developing an understanding about death and danger, though they may not be able to articulate this. They may have dreams which relate to the diabetes; their art-work may show symbolic representations of syringes, blood, etc. They are becoming increasingly socialized, and the attitude of their class-mates to the diabetes will be significant. You can help by, for example, inviting the child to bring diabetic equipment into school, and maybe give a short talk to the class. It is a mistake to keep the diabetes a secret. On the other hand, it is also a mistake to turn it into the class talking-point for the year. Other than where specific diabetic needs are concerned, the child should be treated like other members of the class. One of the worst things about having diabetes in childhood is being 'different'. The child should be allowed to eat snacks in class without this becoming an issue, but should be discouraged from turning the eating into an attention-seeking device.

In the nursery or primary school the situation ought to be manageable. There is likely to be a small number of teachers, all of whom know the child. School dinners are closely supervised, and there should be communication between teachers and parents. School trips may be a problem area, but are not prohibited, provided a responsible and knowledgeable adult is prepared to supervise. The teacher will need to be responsible for the child's equipment, and an adequate supply of food will have to be available at all times.

Secondary school

Children who are diagnosed in adolescence may be beginning to question authority, rulings handed down for seemingly no reason, life-styles and family structure. The self-image of the adolescent will be undermined both bodily and emotionally by the diabetes. Adolescence is a time when peer-group identity is all-important. The diagnosis will threaten this. Anger, depression, self-doubt and even despair are common reactions in the newly diagnosed adolescent – though of course there will be those youngsters who are perfectly resilient, and quite able to get on with their lives.

Many studies of the psychiatric status of diabetic youth show that there may often be raised levels of anxiety as a result of the diabetes. But it is not always the case that an enhanced level of anxiety indicates poor diabetic control. On the contrary, it could indicate super-awareness of the need for good control. We cite some research papers at the end of this chapter, which seem to endorse our view that diabetes is a very difficult condition – to live with, to assess and to research. This is because diabetes is intrinsically bound up with all the processes of childhood – eating, self-awareness, growth towards physical and emotional autonomy, and awareness of mortality.

Tips for secondary-school teachers include the following:

- *General*   The diabetic pupil may have to eat in class, as well as in exams, even though snacks are officially scheduled for break-times. Uncharacteristically poor concentration in class may be a sign that the pupil is suffering from hypoglycaemia (low blood sugar).
- *Discipline*   The diabetic pupil should not be immune from discipline because of the diabetes, but you should never give a detention to a diabetic pupil without advance warning. The pupil must know in advance in order to have an extra snack to hand. The parents should not be put through the anxiety of the late arrival home of their teenager – they will be visualizing their child unconscious and hypoglycaemic by the roadside.
- *Exercise*   Diabetes is no reason for missing PE and games – diabetics benefit from exercise. But exercise means the diabetic must have the opportunity to keep his or her blood-sugar levels up by consuming carbohydrate before, during or after the exertion. This is particularly crucial in sustained exertion, such as cross-country running. It is not a sign of vigour, strength and health for the pupil to 'manage without' his or her glucose during sporting activities (though we once met a PE teacher who thought it was).
- *School trips*   These should not be a problem for a secondary-school diabetic, although at this stage they may involve overnight coach-journeys, ferry sailings, etc. The child may wish to be left to his or her own devices by this stage, but it remains crucial that people with the child, and the families/hostels he or she stays with or at, should be aware of his or her condition.
- *Teenagers*   Should you be called upon to offer help to an unhappy teenager with diabetes, do not expect too much of yourself. The twin tasks required of the diabetic teenager are firstly to accept the reality of diabetes, and secondly to learn to control the condition as autonomously as he or she can. Smoking is even more harmful to diabetics than to the general population and should be discouraged. Many older teenagers will consume alcohol despite the fact that it is illegal for them to buy it. One or two units of alcohol should not do any more harm to the diabetic than to the non-diabetic, but getting drunk is *dangerous* – alcohol induces hypoglycaemia. Growth and puberty proceed normally in the well-controlled diabetic but may be delayed where there is poor control. This will do nothing to enhance the teenager's already threatened self-image.
- *Career prospects*   There are only a few careers that are closed to youngsters with diabetes, such as active military service, driving public service vehicles, being steeple-jacks and flying civil aircraft. Career counselling should provide the necessary information.
- *Driving*   A person with diabetes may hold a driving licence but this needs to be renewed every three years following a medical examination.

SOURCES OF INFORMATION AND HELP

These include the following:

- the diabetic clinic at the hospital.
- the general practitioner. The medical care of the diabetic child is likely to be

hospital based. General practitioners with a special interest, however, are playing an increasing role.

- The British Diabetic Association (BDA), 10 Queen Anne Street, London WlM 0BD (tel. 071-323-1531). There is a youth section, and the BDA produces a wealth of literature on diabetes, as well as a bi-monthly journal, aptly named *Balance*. It also runs workshops for diabetic children and their families, and summer camps for children.
- The local BDA support group.

When the problems of the diabetic seem unsurmountable, it may be necessary to enlist the support of the child and family psychiatry service, the clinical psychology services, or the social services department – depending on local availability. There are a few residential schools for emotionally disturbed children with various medical conditions.

THE PRINCIPLES IN PRACTICE

In the above we have given you the principles, as we understand them, of coping with unhappy children with diabetes. With the following extract from Simon's story we illustrate how they work out (or fail to work out) in practice. Simon, aged 9¼, has been a diabetic since age 5.

Day 1

7.00 a.m.   Simon wakes up with a very low blood-sugar level, because the previous night he played football out in the street, and only ate one digestive biscuit before going to bed.

8.00 a.m.   Simon's mother is late for work, but has ensured Simon has his normal insulin before breakfast. Simon eats a regular breakfast – which is a mistake. He should have had two extra slices of toast.

9.00 a.m.   Simon reaches school, and luckily realizes he is quite hypo, not a usual state for this early in the day. He takes two biscuits from his snack-bag. His friend Colin remarks enviously, 'Lucky Simon, eating all the time.' This remark hurts Simon.

9.45 a.m.   Simon has a tables test. He finds, to his puzzlement, that whichever way he does it, $8 \times 8 = 2$. Luckily for all, he has the presence of mind to realize that the two biscuits were not sufficient extra carbohydrate. This time he approaches the teacher for a glucose tablet. The teacher hesitates, but eventually fishes a glucose sweet out of her drawer and hands it to Simon, saying rather scathingly: 'I hope you really need this.' Simon then eats one of his spare apples. The crunching sound echoes round the classroom. The class and teacher choose to ignore it.

12.15 p.m.   School dinner: it is ham salad and mashed potatoes, and the dinner-lady makes sure Simon gets three spoonfuls of mashed potato. Simon now has only just enough snack-food left in his bag to last him until 3.15, and hopes to play football again during the lunch-hour. He eats two dollops of mashed potato. By the time he gets to the third, it is cold. Simon hates mashed potato – impasse. If he takes the last snack from his bag, he will be left with no reserves. What is he to do? He forces himself to eat the cold potato, but with tears of self-pity in his eyes.

3.15 p.m.   Simon's mother fetches Simon and his younger sister Dawn from school. Dawn has been dreaming for weeks that a day will come when Mummy says 'How are you, Dawn?' before she says anxiously, 'How are *you*, Simon?' Today is not the day. Simon has the presence of mind to mention to his mother that he almost ran out of food, and that he was almost hypo in school. Dawn hits Simon surreptitiously in the back of the car. As a result, Simon's mother, who has had a bad day at work, finds it hard to concentrate on driving.

6.30 p.m.   Simon's mother realizes the implication of the day's events. She is a perfectly normal mother, who happens to be in the middle of an argument with her husband. Dawn has brought a letter home saying she must have more reading practice out of school. Simon's mother rushes out to the late-opening grocers to buy apples for Simon to take to school in the morning.

9.30 p.m.   Simon's mother resolves once and for all that if Simon's blood-sugar is low at night, he must have a proper snack. If he is getting hypo in school, they must reduce his insulin. She helps Simon measure his blood-sugar level. To everyone's surprise the level is quite high. Why? Who knows? Possibly he overdid the extra snacks during the day; or maybe, unlike yesterday evening, he spent this evening lying on the floor watching television.

Day 2
9.45 a.m.   Reluctant now to change the insulin dose without consulting the clinic, and not even sure that the dose needs changing, Simon's mother lets him go to school the next day with his dose unchanged. She feels anxious and confused during the day. She is torn between wanting to protect Simon from low blood sugars and hypos now, and high blood sugars with complications when he is grown up. She phones the doctor from work. The doctor hears the anxiety in her voice, asks what the erratic blood sugars were, but suggests leaving the insulin as it is for the time being. The doctor suggests that there is no need to be quite so anxious about minor fluctuations in blood sugars. Simon's mother tries to control her anxieties and get on with her life.

Simon has a particularly fun day at school, and has fish-fingers and chips for lunch, which he loves. He does not give diabetes a thought all day – until he sees his mother again at 3.30.

In the evening he plays football out in the street, and scores four goals. That night his blood sugar measures . . .

CONCLUSIONS

Diabetes permeates the social fabric of life, and is a constant and unwelcome presence. We have offered information about it in both its medical and social context. An educationalist responsible for a diabetic child will be better placed to offer effective help in direct proportion to his or her awareness of the intricacies and complexities of the condition.

REFERENCES

Bradbury, A. J. and Smith, C. S. (1983) An assessment of the diabetic knowledge of school-teachers. *Archives of Disease in Childhood*, **58**, 692-6.

Court, S., Sein, E., McCowen, C., Hackett, A. F. and Parkin, J. M. (1988) Children with diabetes mellitus: perception of their behavioural problems by parents and teachers. *Early Human Development*, **16**, 245-52.

Fonagy, P., Moran, G. S., Lindsay, M. K. M., Kurtz, A. B. and Brown, R. (1987) Psychological adjustment and diabetic control. *Archives of Disease in Childhood*, **62**, 1009-13.

Halford, W. K., Cuddihy, S. and Mortimer, R. H. (1990) Psychological stress and blood glucose regulation in Type 1 diabetic patients. *Health Psychology*, **9**, 516-28.

Menon, R. K. and Sperling, M. A. (1986) Childhood diabetes. *Medical Clinics of North America*, **72**, 1565-76.

Tattersall, R. B. and Lowe, J. (1981) Diabetes in adolescence. *Diabetologia*, **20**, 517-23.

Warne, J. (1988) Diabetes in school: a study of teachers' knowledge and information sources. *Practical Diabetes*, **5**, 210-15.

Wrigley, M. and Mayou, R. (1991) Psychosocial factors and admission for poor glycaemic control: a study of psychological and social factors in poorly controlled insulin dependent diabetic patients. *Journal of Psychosomatic Research*, **35**, 335–43.

FURTHER READING

Baum, J.D. and Kinmonth, A.L. (eds) (1986) *Care of the Child with Diabetes*. Edinburgh: Churchill Livingstone.

Craig, O. (1981) *Childhood Diabetes and Its Management*, 2nd edn. London: Butterworths.

Elliot, J. (1989) *If Your Child Is Diabetic: An Answer Book for Parents*. London: Sheldon Press.

Farquhar, J.W. (1981) *The Diabetic Child*, 3rd edn. Edinburgh: Churchill Livingstone.

Sonksen, P., Fox, C. and Judd, S. (1991) *Diabetes at Your Fingertips*. London: Class Publishing.

Chapter 6

Coping with Unhappy Children Who Have Epilepsy

Frank Besag

What singles the child with epilepsy out from others who have chronic or recurring conditions? There are many similarities but also some notable differences. Epilepsy is a particularly 'hidden' condition. Although children with asthma and diabetes may also be said to have 'hidden' conditions, there are factors which frequently bring them to the attention of others; for example, the dietary restrictions and importance of regular meals in the case of diabetes or the use of prophylactic inhalers together with the occasional audible wheeze which may occur in asthma. The greater public awareness and peer acceptance of these conditions also makes it somewhat easier for the child and the family to acknowledge that 'He has diabetes' or 'He has asthma.' The statement: 'He has epilepsy' is likely to bring a very different reaction. Why? It is not just the sudden, paroxysmal, unexpected nature of epilepsy. The condition of epilepsy engenders many irrational fears: death, brain damage, serious injury, 'swallowing the tongue', not coming out of the seizure. Many people would not have the slightest idea of how to manage a seizure. Furthermore, those who consider that they do know what is required may do more harm than good. If people do not know how to cope with a seizure they may ignore it or act in an aggressively defensive way. They will certainly fear the seizure. This makes it particularly difficult for the child with epilepsy to cope and can lead to great unhappiness. Ignorance about epilepsy and how to manage the child who has this condition can result in major consequences for the child, including unnecessary and excessive restrictions.

UNHAPPINESS IN THE CHILD WITH EPILEPSY

Self-esteem may be damaged by overprotection, rejection and guilt. Parents and other authority figures may respond to the situation by overreacting to the possibility of harm befalling the child. Overprotection devalues the child by emphasizing what he or she must not do and, by implication, what he or she cannot do. The paradox which then arises is that by trying to protect the child the parent is making him or her even more isolated; the attempt to help makes matters much worse. The child then has to cope not only with the sadness of not being able to take part in pleasurable, adventurous activities but also with the feelings of isolation. This is a double punishment.

Overprotection and rejection are often considered to be opposite extremes of the way in which parents might react, but they have much in common; they can both result in feelings of isolation and despair. Because it is the parent, who is usually the child's source of love and support, who is causing the feelings of rejection and isolation, the main source of help and comfort is cut off, increasing the feelings of isolation even more.

A less common situation arises when the parent feels unable to cope at all with the epilepsy and openly rejects the child. This can be very damaging. The mother of a child known to me would implore, 'Don't say that word', referring to the term 'epilepsy'. She eventually decided to have no contact with the child because she could not cope. The parent who cannot cope cannot help the child to cope.

It is not only the parents who may overprotect or reject the child. Restriction from taking part in school subjects and activities such as home economics, climbing, gymnastics, swimming and other sports can be very damaging to self-esteem. If the epilepsy itself has already made the child feel different, the restrictions are likely to make matters far worse.

Peer-group relationships are important for a child of any age but they are particularly important for the teenager. Anything which singles the teenager out as being different from the group is likely to be a source of acute embarrassment. If the child is openly teased, this can be particularly damaging to self-esteem. Counselling the individual child or the family may be of significant value in this situation. Offering the child specific strategies to cope with the teasing can be a great help.

Guilt

The 'hidden within' element of epilepsy and the fact that it begins in the brain, which is considered culturally to be the source of the will or the self, are factors which contribute to the idea that epilepsy is somehow the fault of the person who has the condition. Because young children feel 'omnipotent', tending to think that they have magically caused anything that happens, they are especially likely to feel responsible for and guilty about their epilepsy: 'It must be my fault', or 'No one has done it to me, so I must have done it to myself.'

Many of the phenomena of epilepsy are closely related to disturbances of the conscious mind. This seems to emphasize the possibility that it may be the child's fault. Since the disturbances of perception in partial seizures occur in consciousness, the child is all the more likely to blame himself or herself.

Our culture and language are very negative in relation to seizures. The common expression 'I almost had a fit' implies that this is a way in which an individual may react to or cope with a difficult situation. It suggests that the cause or the focus of the epilepsy lies in the individual as part of his or her personality, and that its expression is one way of dealing with the world. It also easily translates to a common form of teasing used when children with epilepsy are the target. If the group wants to reject the child with epilepsy, this is easily achieved through the jibe, 'Oh go away and have a fit.' Again, the implication is that the epilepsy is within the control of the individual and is consequently his or her fault. It is something about which the child should feel guilty.

The situation is further confounded by the phenomenon of non-epileptic seizures. This is now the preferred term for what were previously called 'pseudoseizures'. The reason for the change in terminology is highly relevant to the subject under discussion. 'Pseudo', again, has very derogatory connotations. The implication is that a person who is described as 'pseudo' is one who is wilfully trying to appear to be something he or she is not, for his or her own self-gain. Such a person would deserve no respect. Because of these connotations, the term 'pseudoseizures' may lead to rejection, not only by the family, friends and teachers of the child but also by medical staff: 'Don't waste my valuable time', or 'Tell the child to pull herself together'. The truth of the matter is that the person with non-epileptic seizures has a problem. Doctors and other professionals have the role of trying to help people with problems, using their skills to do so. Rejecting them is unlikely to help. Discussing the cause of the problem and managing it sensitively is the appropriate professional response.

It is important, at this point, to distinguish between psychogenic seizures and non-epileptic seizures (pseudoseizures). There is much confusion in the literature over the terminology. Fenwick (1991) has suggested that the term 'psychogenic seizures' be used for genuine epileptic seizures which are brought on either intentionally or unintentionally by psychological factors. He has distinguished two categories of psychogenic seizures: primary psychogenic seizures are those which the person attempts to precipitate by will, whereas secondary psychogenic seizures are brought on unintentionally by thinking or mental activity. Subjects with primary psychogenic seizures have learned to go through some mental process which they know will precipitate a seizure. A study by the Maudsley group (Fenwick, 1991) indicated that a surprisingly large proportion of the patients attending their clinic could precipitate or stop seizures by an act of will. These were genuine seizures brought on by 'psychological' activity. They were true psychogenic seizures of the primary type.

An example of unintentionally precipitated (secondary) psychogenic seizures brought on by mathematical calculations is quoted by Fenwick from the work of Wilkins *et al.* (1981). This is an example of a psychogenic form of reflex or evoked seizures. Another example of a psychogenic seizure in a child, drawn from my clinical practice, was a lad who only had seizures when he was excited or upset. He became very excited on the day the Princess of Wales was due to visit his school and he had a seizure just before he was due to meet her. Fortunately he recovered in time to see her. It was clearly not in his interest to have a seizure at that time and he did not wish to have it. This was an example of a genuine psychogenic seizure.

In contrast, some people may simulate seizures. According to Fenwick's classification, such episodes are not psychogenic seizures but non-epileptic seizures (pseudoseizures). These subjects almost always have some experience of epilepsy: they may have epilepsy themselves or they may have witnessed seizures in others. Those who have epilepsy themselves simulate seizures in addition to having, or in the past having had, genuine seizures. The group which does not have epilepsy, but which has experience of the condition, enabling them to simulate seizures, includes members of the nursing profession and, relevant to the present discussion, children who have witnessed seizures at school or elsewhere. This situation illustrates another paradox. Epilepsy may make children unhappy and unable to cope. However, the seizures themselves may become a mechanism for coping. They are a way of escaping from difficulties which arise in the child's life. Both the genuine, intentionally precipitated seizure and the simulated seizure may be used in this way.

There is a further situation in which simulated seizures may be used as a coping mechanism. The idea is not new, although the terminology and heightened awareness of the possibility are relatively new. The concept of using someone else to have a simulated 'attack' or 'funny turn' is part of our literature and culture. In the Kingsley Amis novel *Lucky Jim*, the university lecturer arranges that, if the lecture is going badly, a colleague will swoon to draw attention away. A recent British Telecom television advertisement uses a similar idea – 'He's had one of his turns' to enable those concerned (not just the subject himself) to escape from an embarrassing predicament. Most paediatricians will now be very familiar with the concept of 'Munchausen syndrome by proxy', described by Meadow (1982). The parent presents with a history of some disorder in the child. This is commonly an epileptic seizure, but another example is haematuria. In the latter case diagnosis may be easy when analysis reveals that it is the mother's blood in the child's urine, intentionally placed there to simulate medical illness. The parent has used the simulated illness in the child to escape from or cope with a difficult situation. Not uncommonly, the parent will present repeatedly to the casualty department giving the history that the child has had a seizure. Although there is no definitive test, as there is for maternal blood in the child's urine, close examination of the case may leave little doubt about the fact that the seizure was fabricated by the mother and not real. Such seizures are, of course, never witnessed by a reliable informant or during hospital admissions. Gentle confrontation may be necessary at some stage. Very careful and sensitive use of a provocative sentence may be of diagnostic and therapeutic value here. When rapport appears to be well established and the time seems right, I have frequently used the sentence, 'You must have felt like throwing him out of the window when he's like that.' Contrary to what might be expected, this sentence, sensitively used, has never generated apparent outrage or offence in a parent. The response is often just the opposite. A look of enormous relief comes over the parent's face: 'He understands!' The door is opened to honest dialogue, correct diagnosis and the possibility of helping the unhappy family to find a more acceptable way of coping, by acknowledging the problems facing them.

Non-epileptic seizures, whether simulated by the child or fabricated by the parent, are an unsatisfactory way of coping. The role of the professional is to assist the family to cope in more acceptable ways.

The predicament of the child with epilepsy

Taylor (1979) has distinguished very clearly between disease, illness and predicament. It is possible for a child to have a disease – for example, an early cancer – without being ill. It is also possible to be ill without any discernible disease process, a situation which the lay person would describe as 'psychosomatic illness'. The predicament of the child, however, does not depend simply on the disease or illness; the whole situation may very much determine how the child responds, copes and feels. For example, the reactions of the family, to which reference is made in the next section, can affect the predicament to a major degree. Predicaments may be altered by understanding the child and by offering support to the family. The professionals involved can play a very important role in this regard.

The effects of epilepsy on the family

The effects of epilepsy on the family have been discussed in detail in the symposium *Epilepsy and the Family* edited by Hoare (1988). There, I consider the reactions of the parents and the relationships of the child with siblings, parents and others (Besag, 1988). It is now accepted that the management of the child with a chronic or recurring condition involves the management of the family as a whole. Parental attitudes have already been mentioned. The response of the siblings may be a very strong one. A type of bereavement reaction in the family has been described. This may lead to disbelief, panic, anger and sadness. Managed appropriately, the parents and siblings will be encouraged to work through these feelings to achieve acceptance of the condition and, more important, reacceptance of the child. The family will then be better able to support the child emotionally. However, other reactions may occur. The siblings may have fears, either real or imaginary, of developing the condition themselves. In a few families there is a strong history of epilepsy and this fear may be a very real one. Generally, however, the incidence among siblings is not sufficiently high to cause real concern.

Siblings of the child with epilepsy sometimes react in a very negative way, becoming jealous of the attention being given to the child who is perceived as needing it. This may lead to attention-seeking behaviour in the siblings with consequent unhappiness in the family and additional difficulties with which the child who has epilepsy must cope.

Am I going mad, doctor?

The phenomena of partial seizures can be bizarre. Most complex partial seizures probably arise in the temporal lobe, although they can arise elsewhere, notably in the frontal lobe. The temporal lobe has a major role in integrating perceptions and feelings. If this function is impaired by an epileptic discharge, perceptions or emotions may be altered in a disturbing way. The strange feeling in the epigastrium (upper middle part of the abdomen) is a common aura (simple partial seizure). Other auras include odd smells or tastes, flashing lights, feelings of *déjà vu* or *jamais vu* and the unpleasant dysphoric aura (a feeling of being ill at ease). It is very important to ask the child about such phenomena. The initial questions should be relatively unstructured and non-specific; for example, 'Do you ever know when a seizure is coming?' 'Do you have any warning?' These questions may, if necessary, be followed by more direct enquiry, asking about funny feelings in the tummy, head or elsewhere. It is best to put such questions in a way that gives the child a choice of many possibilities. This style of history-taking involves less leading questions and the information is consequently much more reliable. More dramatic ictal (during the seizure) phenomena may include hallucinations, delusions, depersonalization, derealization, disordered perception and disordered thought processes. O'Donohoe (1985) has provided a good summary of such states. If any of these odd phenomena are experienced, the child may feel that he or she is going mad. Some children cautiously seek reassurance from their peers or parents, in the hope that they will be told that all children experience these phenomena. More often they keep their experiences to themselves because they realise that reassurance is unlikely to be forthcoming, either from their peers or from their parents. The child should be told that these phenomena are quite normal in the form of epilepsy he or she has and that 100,000 children in the UK have epilepsy. This simple intervention may be of enormous value in reassuring the child that he or she is not going mad and is not alone: many other children with epilepsy experience these things. Much unhappiness in the child may be lifted or prevented by providing this type of information.

The child may also think he or she is going mad because of behaviour exhibited which is abnormal or out of control. The child may not be aware of having exhibited this behaviour until he or she hears others describing it. The interaction between epilepsy and behaviour is discussed in detail elsewhere (Corbett and Besag, 1988; Besag *et al.*, 1989). In brief, behavioural disturbance may result from the epilepsy itself, from treatment of the epilepsy or from reactions to the epilepsy. Some people with epilepsy experience a prodrome, lasting typically between and hour or two and a day or two, which is characterized by non-specific symptoms such as irritability. These symptoms resolve when the seizure occurs. Repeated auras or other forms of simple partial seizures, because they occur in consciousness, may be much more disturbing than full-blown tonic-clonic seizures, of which the child will have no recollection. Post-ictal changes, occurring immediately or soon after the seizure, can take a variety of forms, from tiredness and irritability to depression or, rarely, short-lived psychosis. These changes usually resolve quite quickly and are best managed by supportive measures, but occasionally medical treatment is necessary. Some anti-epileptic drugs can cause gross behavioural disturbance. In children, phenobarbitone and clonazepam are especially notorious in this regard. Anti-epileptic drugs can also, rarely, cause distressing abnormal mental phenomena such as delusions or hallucinations. The relatively new anti-epileptic drug, vigabatrin, causes transient acute psychosis in 1–5 per cent of those treated. It is my impression that the incidence is somewhat higher in subjects with learning disability. Lethargy and other signs associated with depression may be the direct effect of anti-epileptic medication in some people; for example, ethosuximide can cause lethargy and weight loss. Psychological management of these drug effects would be inappropriate when what is needed is a review of the medication.

It is not surprising that some people with epilepsy become depressed. This subject has been reviewed by Robertson (1988) and Betts (1982). A careful evaluation of the cause of the depression allows rational treatment to be given.

A few people with epilepsy develop a schizophreniform psychosis requiring specialist psychiatric treatment, but these cases are almost invariably in adults who have had epilepsy for many years.

Although absence seizures are not very likely to make the child think that he or she is going mad, they can certainly cause considerable inconvenience. These seizures result in brief interruptions of consciousness and may go unnoticed by the casual observer. The teacher may think that the child is inattentive or daydreaming and may remonstrate with him or her because of this. Other children may also be critical. One boy under my care recounted that the other boys shouted at him for allowing the ball to go into the goal when he was playing football. He was unable to stop it because he was having an absence seizure at the time and was briefly unaware. This boy's mother thought that he might be having as many as 20 absence seizures daily: specialized monitoring showed that he was having over 200 absence seizures per day. Data recently collected on young people have shown that some can have thousands of absence seizures in a single day (Besag, 1992) . It is not surprising that such children may appear quiet and withdrawn, and that they may have some difficulty coping with life.

All of these phenomena, together with reactions to the epilepsy, including over-protection, rejection, teasing and guilt, can cause great unhappiness and difficulties in coping. If the doctor takes a careful history, identifying the key factors considered in the foregoing discussion, he or she will be well placed to educate, counsel and support the child and family. These interventions can do much to alleviate and prevent distress by helping the child to cope.

PROBLEMS CAUSED THROUGH MISDIAGNOSIS OR DELAYS IN DIAGNOSIS

Episodes which are not epilepsy may be misdiagnosed as epilepsy, and epilepsy may be misdiagnosed as not being epilepsy. Examples of episodes which may be misdiagnosed as epilepsy but which are not include simple faints, night terrors, breath-holding attacks, benign paroxysmal vertigo and temper tantrums. Complex partial seizures and absence seizures are examples of epileptic seizures which may be misdiagnosed as something else or may not be diagnosed at all. The failure to make the correct diagnosis within a reasonable period of time may lead to much unhappiness and despair in both the parent and the child. The child may think that he or she is being blamed or is being accused of 'putting it on': 'The doctor has found nothing wrong with you, so there is nothing wrong with you.' In my experience, this situation may prove to be very difficult indeed for the child and the family. The best way of coming to the correct diagnosis is by taking a careful history from the child, the parent and any other witnesses of the episodes. Education and counselling of the child and family can, as already indicated, be invaluable.

CONCLUSIONS

Epilepsy can cause much unhappiness in children and their families, who may find coping with the condition very difficult for a number of reasons including fear, ignorance, diagnostic incompetence and inadequate management. There are certain key factors in preventing this distress and in assisting families to cope. Correct diagnosis depends on taking a good history from an informant who has witnessed the attacks and from the child. Correct management depends on correct diagnosis. The importance of listening to what the child has to say and reassuring him or her that the strange phenomena he or she describes are normal for his or her form of epilepsy, if that is the case, cannot be overemphasized. Education, counselling and support of the child and the family are invaluable elements of the management.

A careful, sensitive and perceptive assessment of the child with epilepsy is the first step to rational management which can, in turn, do much to assist the family to cope with the condition in a capable way, avoiding the preventable unhappiness and distress which otherwise so often occur.

REFERENCES

Besag, F. M. C. (1988) Epilepsy, the family and the residential school: a time of transition for the family. In P. Hoare (ed.), *Epilepsy and the Family: A Medical Symposium on New Approaches to Family Care*, pp. 77–83. Manchester: Sanofi UK Ltd.

Besag, F. M. C. (1992) Lamotrigine: paediatric experience. In A. Richens (ed.), *Lamotrigine Treatment in Uncontrolled Epilepsy: A Clinical Update*. International clinical practice series, pp. 53–60. Tunbridge Wells: Wells Medical.

Besag, F. M. C., Loney G., Waudby, E., Fowler, M. and Brooks, N. (1989) A multidisciplinary approach to epilepsy, learning difficulties and behavioural problems. In F. M. C. Besag (ed.), 'Epilepsy, learning and behaviour.' *Educational and Child Psychology*, 6, 18–24.

Betts, T. (1982) Psychiatry and epilepsy. In J. Laidlaw and A. Richens (eds), *A Textbook of Epilepsy*, pp. 227–70. London: Churchill Livingstone.

Corbett, J. A. and Besag, F. M. C. (1988) Epilepsy and its treatment in children. In B. B. Lahey and A. E. Kazdin (eds), *Advances in Clinical Child Psychology*, 11, 369–94.

Fenwick, P. (1981) Precipitation and inhibition of seizures. In E. H. Reynolds and M. R. Trimble (eds), *Epilepsy and Psychiatry*, pp. 306–21. London: Churchill Livingstone.

Fenwick, P. (1991) Evocation and inhibition of seizures. In D. B. Smith, D. M. Treiman and M. R. Trimble (eds), 'Neurobehavioural problems in epilepsy,' *Advances in Neurology*, 55, 163–83.

Hoare, P. (ed.) (1988) *Epilepsy and the Family: A Medical Symposium on New Approaches to Family Care*. Manchester: Sanofi UK Ltd.

Meadow, R. (1982) Munchausen syndrome by proxy. *Archives of Disease in Childhood*, 57, 92–8.

O'Donohoe, N. V. (1985) *Epilepsies of Childhood*. London: Butterworths.

Robertson, M. M. (1988) Epilepsy and mood. In M. R. Trimble and E. H. Reynolds (eds), *Epilepsy, Behaviour and Cognitive Function*, pp. 145–57. Chichester: John Wiley.

Taylor, D. C. (1979) The components of sickness: diseases, illnesses and predicaments. *Lancet*, 2, 1008–10.

Wilkins, A. J., Zifkin, B., Anderman, F. and McGovern, E. (1981) Seizures induced by thinking. *Annals of Neurology*, 11, 608–12.

Chapter 7

Coping with Unhappy Children Who Have Learning Difficulties

David Jones and Helen Barrett

It would be much too simplistic to suggest that learning difficulties are causally related to unhappiness in children. Certainly a child's learning difficulties may be a cause for concern and a source of stress for the parents and for other carers. It follows that these stresses may well have indirect effects on the child's emotions. There is also good evidence that, for many children, self-esteem is influenced by perception of apparent differences between self and others (for example, Ruble, 1983). For children with learning difficulties the very acts of living and attending schools bring frequent, daily examples of failure relative to others. Whether or not these experiences provoke unhappiness will depend on many factors including the nature and pattern of the difficulties, the child's security of attachment to his or her family and peer group, and a whole range of influences in the school environment and in the wider community in which the child and family live. A brief review of some of the ways our society has struggled with finding satisfactory ways to label and educate children with learning difficulties may facilitate an awareness of some of the contextual factors which pose a threat to the development of self-esteem and individual dignity.

STIGMA AND SEGREGATION

As long ago as the reign of King Edward I a distinction was made between the 'born fool' and the 'lunatic'. By the sixteenth century we find that 'idiocy' was being used as a generic term to describe a broad group of individuals considered to be without understanding, ignorant or lacking in education. Early definitions tended to focus on concepts such as arrested or incomplete development of mind and usually included some reference to social incompetence, or even degeneracy, as illustrated by the following much-quoted passage: 'Feebleminded women are almost invariably immoral and if at large usually become carriers of venereal disease or give birth to children who are as defective as themselves' (W. E. Fernald, 1912, quoted by Sarason and Doris, 1969). Classification imposed by legislation gave a measure of protection to individuals with disabilities, but it also allowed for compulsory segregation and institutionalization as a means for preserving and protecting the wider society and its moral values. Despite a concern to guard them from dangers, the happiness of individuals did not figure highly in early care programmes.

The Mental Deficiency Act of 1913, as well as formalizing previous thinking and practices on care and education, provided a classificatory system which identified three levels of severity of mental deficiency, namely, idiots, imbeciles and feebleminded. At the highest level of severity, idiots were described as 'persons so deeply defective in mind from birth or from an early age as to be unable to guard themselves against common physical dangers'. Sadly, the Act retained the long-held view that such individuals were unlikely to benefit from education or training. At the next level, imbeciles were distinguished from idiots by their ability to attain some benefit from training and to develop basic communication abilities, although they too were thought to be in need of protection. At the lowest level of severity, the feebleminded (or 'morons' in US terminology) represented the highest grade of mental deficiency and were considered capable of benefiting from training and, possibly, of being able to achieve some degree of independence in adult life. One has only to reflect on the way in which all of these labels have become incorporated into everyday language as terms of derision or abuse to become aware of the stigma attached to both the labelled individuals and their families.

Changes in educational practices followed the Education Act 1944 which defined as 'educationally subnormal' (ESN) children who were educationally retarded by more than 20 per cent for their age. Within this group, children with more severe disabilities were deemed 'severely subnormal' (SSN) and ineducable. Their care and training was made the responsibility of health, not education, authorities, a situation which was not altered until the passing of the Education Act 1970 (Handicapped Children).

A more detailed system of classification, suggested by the World Health Organization in 1968, placed greater emphasis on the measured intelligence quotient (IQ) to identify categories in terms of level of functioning. Individuals with an IQ below 20 were referred to as having 'profound' mental retardation, a category roughly equivalent to the older term 'idiot'. IQs in the range of 20–30 and 30–50 were designated, respectively, 'severe' and 'moderate', while mental retardation in the IQ range of 50–75 was labelled 'mild'. That problems can arise from over-reliance upon a single criterion such as intelligence for a classification system is amply discussed elsewhere (for example, Berger and Yule, 1985; Richardson, 1991), and many authorities (such as Grossman, 1983) have preferred to place greater weight on measures of social functioning, particularly in the case of older children.

In 1971, a step was taken towards integrating children with more severe learning difficulties into the national education curriculum when, following the Education Act 1970, responsibility for the education of all children was devolved upon local education authorities. Children with IQ levels below about 50 were now referred to as 'severely educationally subnormal' and were placed in ESN(S) special schools. Those in the IQ range 50–70 were regarded as 'moderately educationally subnormal' and were usually placed in ESN(M) schools. Despite these considerable advances, this pattern of special education provision still involved the labelling and segregation of children deemed educationally subnormal. Further, the tendency to push into the ESN(M) category children who were underachieving and out of control in mainstream schools gave rise to additional problems, since the emotional and educational needs of these children were often quite distinct from and incompatible with the needs of other children in ESN(M) schools.

After the lengthy discussions which led up to and followed the publication of the Warnock Report (DES, 1978), the term 'learning difficulties' came into widespread use. Here, there was an intention to minimize the stigma attached to low educational achievement both by altering the way that children needing special education were described and by extending, as far as possible, the principle of choice of school for parents of children with learning difficulties. Under the Education Act 1981 which followed these discussions, the option was made possible, at least in theory, for special needs to be provided for within mainstream schools. The Act defined a child as having 'special educational needs' if 'he has a learning difficulty which calls for special educational provision to be made for him'. It further defined the child as having a learning difficulty if '(*a*) he has a significantly greater difficulty in learning than the majority of children of his age; or (*b*) he has a disability which either prevents or hinders him from making use of educational facilities of a kind generally provided in schools, within the area of the local authority concerned, for children of his age' (DES, 1981, p. 1).

In these terms, 'learning difficulties' were identified as being associated with a wide range of behaviour patterns, in many of which below-average intellectual functioning was not implicated (for example, physical disability or emotionally disturbed behaviour). A category label as broad as 'learning difficulties' allows for considerable discretion in interpretation and there has been some resistance to its use, since it blurs provision requirements. Further, to ensure that local education authorities provided for children with learning difficulties, the 1981 Act required that statements were prepared for all children considered to have special educational needs. This system of statementing, despite its intention to keep parents informed, can still be felt by both parents and children to involve a formidably formal procedure in which they have little power to influence the professionals who are seen as passing judgement.

It seems fair to say that, for children with learning difficulties, the National Curriculum (DES, 1987) may not represent any serious departure from the aims of the Education Act 1981 in that there remains, in theory, the intention to minimize the pejorative effects of categorization and to maximize parental choice of schooling. It would seem precipitate at this stage to comment on the possible effects of changes introduced for children with learning difficulties, though it seems reasonable to suggest that rapid and radical restructuring in a climate of economic recession inevitably places stress on all participants, and those by definition less well equipped to cope with change may well experience greater distress. In addition, the attempt to integrate children with special educational needs into mainstream schools, despite the good intentions of the Education Act 1981, has in many cases been highly problematic, in part because of resource limitations. This situation must, in some instances, have created extra pressure for children with special needs (Montgomery, 1990).

IN WHAT WAYS ARE CHILDREN WITH LEARNING DIFFICULTIES DIFFERENT?

As the previous section has indicated, conceptualizations of the group of people with learning differences have undergone major changes throughout history. At the present time, it seems as relevant to ask how children with learning difficulties are like other children as to ask how they are different. Being such a very heterogeneous group, differences within the group of children with learning difficulties are probably at least as numerous as differences between them and other children. Clarke and Clarke (1985) have pointed out that, over the latter half of the present century, several factors have contributed to encourage a less punitive or 'normalising' (Craft, 1987) approach towards individuals with learning difficulties. These include increased knowledge about genetics, nutritional and social factors, as well as optimism about the efficacy of some remedial programmes. A decrease in fears of national degeneracy and 'a more humane and tolerant attitude towards at least mild forms of social deviation' is now thought to prevail (Clarke and Clarke, 1985, p. 31).

The definition of mental retardation proposed by the American Association on Mental Deficiency (AAMD) was as follows: 'subaverage general intellectual functioning which originates during the developmental period and is associated with impairment in one or more of the following: (1) maturation, (2) learning, and (3) social adjustment' (Heber, 1959, p. 3). This definition needs quite a lot of unpacking, but effectively draws attention to the different sorts of evaluation of children which need to be made at different ages.

Early recognition of causes of learning difficulties, particularly in cases such as hearing loss where remedial action can be taken, has obvious importance in terms of children's happiness and well-being. Delays in the maturation of such skills as sitting, walking and talking will be particularly important in the evaluation of development during infancy and the pre-school years. During the school-age years, learning defined as the ability to acquire academic skills provides a measure of adaptive behaviour. Social adjustment assumes greater importance as the child gets older and faces increased expectations that he or she will function independently in the community.

When preparing a statement of special educational needs, professionals in the UK will use a wide range of scales to provide an estimate of social, intellectual and cognitive abilities. Examples might include the Wechsler Intelligence Scale for Children – Revised (WISC-R; Wechsler, 1974), the Stanford-Binet (Terman and Merrill, 1973), the McCarthy Scales of Children's Abilities (McCarthy, 1972) and the British Abilities Scales (Elliott *et al.*, 1983), though many other methods of testing are available (Wodrich and Kush, 1990). However, there has been a move away from absolute reliance upon performance in standardized tests which can be strongly affected by motivation, self-confidence, mood, etc., and which often constitute a highly stressful experience for children. Other sources of information used in assessments might include school records, classroom observations and a wide range of social contextual factors (Quicke, 1984). Nevertheless, it can be seen that low IQ is often a feature of learning difficulties, and the use of IQ measurements may be the most convenient and easily available as well as, in some people's view (for example, Clarke and Clarke, 1985), the best estimate of developmental delay.

Both the AAMD definition and the British Education Act 1981 focus on the current needs of the child rather than the cause of conditions. At great risk of oversimplifying causal factors, it is possible to differentiate between a smaller group of children with learning difficulties consequent upon structural or organic abnormalities of the central nervous system, and a larger group whose relatively mild learning difficulties may reflect the lower end of the normal distribution for the inheritance of intelligence and/or the effects of less than optimal environmental experiences.

The smaller group of children with learning difficulties consists of those who have detectable organic factors associated with their disabilities. This is a heterogeneous group which can be sub-divided into children with abnormal hereditary conditions, such as Down's Syndrome, and those with central nervous system damage arising from pre-natal influences, such as viral infections, anoxia, birth trauma, or accidents or illness in the early years of life. Detailed accounts of the classification of organic conditions can be found elsewhere (for example, Berg, 1974; Brison, 1967; Hogg *et al.*, 1990). In many of these cases the disability may be severe, but there may well be considerable variability in the profile of abilities. The extent of the learning disability is often difficult to determine where children also have physical or sensory disabilities. In the majority of cases these children may well be the only members of their families with learning difficulties, and their pattern of emotional development will be greatly influenced by the ability of their individual families to support and cherish them, sometimes under exceedingly difficult circumstances.

Within the last decade, the phenomenon of 'secondary mental handicap' has also begun to receive more attention (for example, Sinason, 1986). It is argued that perceptions of and reactions to primary disabilities, on the part of the person with the disability as well as on the part of carers and other acquaintances, can give rise to reactive patterns which may be maladaptive and self-perpetuating. There is also now considerable evidence that children with learning difficulties are vulnerable not only to deprivation of vital information about their own sexuality (Craft, 1987) but also to a greater risk of abuse of all kinds (McCormack, 1991). Effective therapeutic work in this area often requires a willingness to acknowledge one's own preconceptions and to recognize that children with learning difficulties experience emotions as least as painful and complicated as those of other children (Sinason, 1989, 1991).

The larger group of children with learning difficulties is defined as 'functional reaction alone manifest' in the AAMD classification (Heber, 1959, p. 39). Within this category, the largest sub-group consists of individuals whose retardation is described as 'cultural-familial'. These children often have siblings or one or both parents who have intelligence scores in the low average or borderline range (that is, around 75–100). Frequently, they come from home backgrounds which are disadvantaged relative to the rest of society. Decisions related to coping with unhappiness in children from such backgrounds involve professionals in making an assessment of environmental and social factors as well as being prepared to work with the whole family or wider support network. Poor housing and inconsistent or less than adequate parenting are potential causes of unhappiness in all children, but the effects are likely to be even more marked when the children themselves have special needs and lack effective skills to modify their environment. A smaller sub-group includes children whose functional mental retardation is associated with emotional disturbance. These children will frequently be characterized by their unhappiness, though the unhappiness may not always be at a conscious level. Emotional disturbance can arise from a wide range of sources, and some of these are discussed in the following sections.

INDIVIDUAL DIFFERENCES IN EARLY EXPERIENCE

One question which we need to address is whether unhappiness as experienced by children with learning difficulties is in any way qualitatively different from the range of experiences of unhappiness encountered in other children. The answers to this question would have to include 'maybe', 'sometimes' and a range of qualifications about different categories of learning difficulties and the ages of the children. There is good evidence that children show individual differences in temperament in the early days of life (Thomas *et al.*, 1968). These differences in temperament are likely to be constitutionally determined, reflecting both genetic and pre-natal influences. The early behaviour of the child's carers will be influenced in part by their reactions to the newborn's physical appearance and temperament and the extent to which the infant is able to meet their expectations. In the case of the parents of children with learning difficulties, much will depend upon their understanding of disability, and their expectations will in turn have been influenced by what they have been told by professionals and other family members.

The child's emotional development reflects a complex transaction with the parents and other carers (Sameroff and Chandler, 1975). Children with learning difficulties may have a range of early life experiences which may not always be typical of the experience of the wider population. Sometimes medical reasons necessitate a period of intensive care immediately after birth, with consequential reduced opportunities for contact and early stimulation. When the likelihood of disability has been known since before the birth, the parents will be anxious but will often have already started on the complex processes of adjustment and preparation for the child's needs. Psycho-analytic theorists refer to a need to mourn for the loss of the normal child they had been expecting but never had.

It is not possible to generalize about the range of parental emotions in such situations, and just occasionally one or both parents is or are not able to accept the care of a child with a severe disability. When awareness of the child's learning difficulties does not become clear until some time after the birth, there is frequently a period of disbelief and a challenging of diagnoses by the parents. Optimism for improvement may be held throughout the childhood period and in some cases there will be anger and criticism over the educational provision suggested by the local authority. These observations give an indication of the highly charged emotional environment in which some children with learning difficulties may spend their early years, even when they have loving and devoted parents. Further evidence of the stresses on the whole family when children with severe disability or chronic illnesses are being cared for is shown in the slightly higher incidence of emotional problems and academic underachievement in the siblings than in the general population. In social learning theory terms, children with severe learning difficulties are more likely than other children to have been exposed to models who were themselves experiencing unhappiness.

For all children the gradual emergence of personality characteristics is greatly influenced by early social interactions. The development of a secure attachment to the mother figure is a complex and protracted process, and Bowlby and others have suggested that this primary attachment may be the prototype for later affectional bonds (Bowlby, 1969). Attachment in infancy is a complex, two-way interaction, and for the child with learning difficulties there may be delays in the formation of cognitive representation of the primary attachment figure. There may also be delayed responsivity, particularly to verbal stimulation. It is not always easy for mothers to sustain a level of stimulation which is appropriate to the child's level of cognitive development over an extended period. Again, concern about the child's welfare and ability to cope may sometimes result in parents being protective to the extent of restricting the opportunities for exploration of the environment. Parents of some children with learning difficulties become concerned that their offspring appear to be too trusting and lack a sufficient degree of wariness for strangers.

DEPRESSION AND UNHAPPINESS

It is possible to distinguish between unhappiness and depression in adults by conducting a structured clinical interview. The distinction is less clear cut in children generally, and it is even more difficult to make in the case of children with learning difficulty. Depression is usually defined as a syndrome involving suppression of affect or mood, but also causing changes in motor behaviour, sleep pattern and appetite over a period of weeks or months. While the depressed child would usually be considered to be unhappy, transitory periods of unhappiness or agitation will not necessarily indicate depression.

In addition to sadness, the common symptoms of depression in children include low self-esteem, anxiety, poor concentration, and difficulties in relating appropriately to other children and to adults. Unhappy children with learning difficulties sometimes appear to have a lowered threshold of irritability in social situations and react aggressively towards others. One possible explanation is that they are seeking ways to reduce their intense feelings of sadness. Nevertheless, it would be a mistake to label all aggressive acts in children with learning difficulties as symptoms of depression.

One suggested interpretation of depression in children is that they perceive themselves as having little control over the powerful influences in their lives. The actual degree of control is less relevant than their perception of their ability to control what happens to them. Children with learning difficulties will often experience frustration and lack of understanding over the apparent power of others to control their environment. An important coping strategy in such situations is to teach simple skills which allow children to experience feelings of control.

Behavioural interpretations of childhood depression seek to identify not only causes but also which features of the child's environment are likely to be maintaining the depressed behaviour. It sometimes emerges that the child is receiving quite a lot of attention and sympathy from parents and others because he or she seems unduly miserable. It has already been suggested that the parents of children with learning difficulties may themselves show an above-average tendency to depression as a consequence of their reaction to the child's disability. In addition, they may be likely to have strong empathy for the child who is perceived as vulnerable, thus reinforcing the depressed behaviour.

The treatment method of choice in these cases should be family therapy in the first instance. There are several issues which need to be addressed in the early sessions. Firstly, it needs to be determined whether the family has come to terms with the child's disabilities. Are there residual feelings of guilt or anger? Are there realistic views about the future of the family and of the child? It will quickly become apparent whether or not the unhappy child is being overprotected. If so, the parents will have to be persuaded to initiate a gradual programme of dependency weaning, despite their anxieties over safety. The parental couple may need help to re-establish their own boundaries. An estimate of the child's optimism about the future needs to be made, but without creating further emotional trauma for the parents.

Matson (1989) reviews a number of inventories and checklists suitable for assessing depression in childhood. Unfortunately, few of the direct measures have normative data on children with learning difficulties. It is always necessary to evaluate the suicide risk in depressed children with learning difficulties. Acts of self-mutilation, risk-taking and attention-seeking behaviour can have disastrous consequences. Expressions of dissatisfaction with life from children must always be taken seriously. Cognitive behavioural methods designed to improve self-esteem depend upon the child's level of verbal comprehension. Severely withdrawn children with learning difficulties are more likely to respond to individual psychotherapy. Such children need gentle encouragement to explore the intensity of their feelings through play and action.

COMMUNICATION

The initial problem confronting the therapist meeting any withdrawn or unhappy child for the first time is to establish a process of interactive communication. The child's non-verbal behaviour will provide some indication of emotional state, but there will often be an unwillingness on the part of the child to answer even the simplest of questions. Facial expression, body posture and the willingness or refusal to make eye contact all signal the child's mood. It is most important that the first few minutes of the meeting should not be allowed to develop into a struggle for power. However, if the results of previous assessments are not available, it is important to obtain an estimate of the child's comprehension of spoken language. Children are all too easily alienated by adults who appear to be talking down to them, but they quickly become confused and withdraw even further into themselves when they cannot understand what is being said to them. For school-age children, a suitable measure of receptive vocabulary which covers the range from 2½ years to 15 years can generally be obtained by administering the British Picture Vocabulary Test (BPVT) (Dunn *et al.*, 1982). This is a multiple-choice test which relies on pointing responses from the child. At the lower levels the stimulus words are concrete nouns which are relatively easy to match to the correct line drawings, but further up the scale action verbs, adjectives and abstract nouns are used. A quick, although less accurate, estimate of receptive vocabulary can be obtained by using the Short Form of the BPVT, which samples the same age range with a set of 32 items and will involve most children in fewer than 20 responses.

A more detailed assessment of the unhappy child's linguistic abilities will often be justified. Children with severe learning difficulties not uncommonly have speech problems together with poor comprehension. The expression of worries and emotions is a struggle and the child can experience feelings of isolation in social situations. Unhappiness is very often a consequence of not being able to understand explanations. Teaching children with learning difficulties and poor linguistic skills a simple form of sign language such as Makaton can sometimes result in a dramatic change for the better in their sociability.

It has already been indicated that intelligence tests have often been used to categorize children with learning difficulty. However, the Piagetian model of stages of cognitive development is in some ways better able to provide insight into the child's understanding of social relationships than the psychometric model of the growth of intelligence. Piaget considered that all children pass through a hierarchical sequence of stages. He did not specifically discuss the problems of children with learning difficulties, but there is evidence that they pass through the stages at a slower rate and are less likely to reach the higher stages. Development is construed as an active process, with the child's own cognitive structures adapting as a result of interaction with the environment (Piaget, 1954). The first stage is the sensorimotor period, which in normal development involves most of the first two years after birth. The infant's representation of the world is thought to be at the level of simple actions and images. Only gradually is object permanence acquired; that is, the awareness that objects and other people continue to exist when they are out of perceptual range. There is considerable debate over whether Piaget underestimated the rate of attainment of object permanence, but it seems possible that, for children whose development is slower than the norm, delays in the ability to form mental representations of absent figures may lead to an extension of those phases during which infants characteristically show low tolerance for separation experiences as well as lowered thresholds for frustration or delay of gratification. It is possible to speculate that these delays might leave children with learning difficulties more vulnerable to unhappiness as they pass through this stage.

Piaget's stage theory becomes more relevant to a discussion of children with learning difficulties when we consider his second major stage, the pre-operational period, which in normal development covers the age range 2–7 years. At this stage in development the child is considered to have symbolic representations of the external world and to be capable of intuitive thought processes. However, Piaget drew attention to the limitations of this level of functioning. The child has difficulty in understanding that others have viewpoints which differ from his or her own. While Piaget is sometimes criticized for overemphasizing the importance of egocentricity, one has only to reflect on the difficulties of using a logical line of reasoning when in dispute with a pre-school child to perceive the qualitative difference between this stage and later stages. The pre-operational child is also considered to have difficulty in understanding that rules and agreements are social conventions which can be changed by negotiation. Morality at this stage is very much a case of accepting the rules of powerful others and sometimes taking risks on getting caught for transgressions. However, the pre-operational child is not very good at calculating the likelihood of success in risk-taking behaviour. In a similar vein, one might say that the child with learning difficulties is also unlikely to be very successful at calculating risks. Many children with learning difficulties may either only just reach or not proceed far beyond this pre-operational stage.

Finding rules difficult to understand, and feeling unfairly treated or that all decisions will be taken arbitrarily by powerful others, can make children despair of understanding how to do things and, perhaps more seriously, of trying to change situations in which they are experiencing discomfort or misery. In order to understand the thought processes which might be sustaining negative behaviour, thoughts and self-attributions, the first task of the cognitive behavioural therapist will be to attempt to establish the level of reasoning the child may be using. The popularity of self-advocacy and self-help programmes for children and older people with learning difficulty increasingly reflects a recognition of the need to understand the world from the point of view of the person with learning difficulties, particularly where challenging behaviours are at issue (Flynn and Ward, 1991).

A brief consideration of Piaget's two later stages of cognitive development will provide some insight into ways in which children with learning difficulties that are a consequence of developmental delay sometimes appear to lack the reasoning skills shown in the problem-solving behaviour of other children of the same age. It is important to recognize that delay gives rise to qualitative differences in reasoning. The concrete operational stage, which normally occurs during the age range 8–11 years, involves the development of cognitive structures that allow the child to comprehend and construct classification systems. Number systems also begin to make sense and the child has a much better understanding of causality. The child becomes able to consider more than one point of view and can make transitive inferences. Children with learning difficulties need careful help and support to attain this level of functioning, and it is important that they are not exposed to repeated experiences of failure. The final stage in the Piagetian system is the period of formal operations, which normally begins around the age of 11 years. This stage involves the attainment of combinatorial thinking. The child becomes able to consider the hypothetical as well as the here and now. Scientific reasoning becomes possible and concepts such as the future and infinity begin to make sense. It would be wrong to assume that the child with learning difficulties is not capable of thinking and worrying about these concepts. Incomplete understanding of moral or philosophical dilemmas, which require careful and sensitive discussion at an appropriate linguistic level, can be a source of considerable confusion and distress.

CONTAINING DIFFICULT BEHAVIOUR

Children with learning difficulties, possibly because some of them have minimal neurological problems, appear to be slightly more likely than other children to be restless and impulsive in their behaviour. Some of them show the typical features of attention deficit disorder with hyperactivity (American Psychiatric Association, 1987; Barkley, 1981). Other children become restless and uninterested in the classroom situation as a result of their early experiences of failure. It is often very difficult to contain such children in school and to prevent them from becoming disgruntled and disruptive, as is acknowledged by the extensive body of literature that offers advice on this subject.

The increasing trend towards making provision whenever possible within mainstream schools rather than in special schools has been referred to earlier. Many parents and professionals felt that segregation in special schools was potentially damaging to the child's self-esteem, even though such schools may have been exceptionally well equipped to meet educational needs. It was also felt that lack of regular contact with children of a wide range of abilities removed some of the necessary challenge from education. On the other hand, an argument in support of special schools was that children with learning difficulty were protected from unhealthy competition and also from taunts and insults.

UNHAPPINESS AND SPECIFIC LEARNING DIFFICULTIES

In the past, many educationalists used the term 'specific learning difficulties' to refer to children of average or above-average general intelligence who were underachieving in one or more areas of their academic performance. It was recognized that these children were different from slow learners and that their special educational needs would also be different. Such children have always presented a challenge to teachers and educational psychologists, both in terms of the need for careful assessment of their strengths and weaknesses and because of the emotional difficulties and unhappiness which so often follow experiences of failure. The situation is even more complicated because of the need to identify those children whose learning problems are consequent upon emotional problems which are affecting the motivation to learn and the capacity to pay attention in the classroom situation.

The largest single group of children with specific learning disorders is made up of those who are experiencing difficulties in the acquisition of reading and spelling abilities. Over the years there has been a protracted debate on whether there is a syndrome of specific developmental dyslexia. Many educationalists have preferred to focus on the distinction between backward readers, whose attainments in most areas is significantly below that expected for their chronological age, and retarded readers, whose reading alone is significantly below their intellectual level (Rutter and Yule, 1975). Others have felt that providing the parents and the child with an explanation of the problem is in itself supportive and properly focuses the need for continued remedial support.

It is hard to capture the misery and frustration which so often accompany failure at reading. Until the problem is properly identified, many children are criticized by parents and teachers for being lazy or for not trying hard enough. They will have started using carefully graded reading schemes and watched their classmates move on in apparent triumph. All too frequently, the resultant attention-seeking activities and difficult behaviour are seen as the main problem rather than as a reaction to the underlying difficulties which they are masking. Also, as they get older these children are sadly limited in their ability to obtain pleasure and comfort from reading books on their own.

PROMOTING SELF-ESTEEM

Happiness in all children depends upon achieving a state of content with the self and with others. Contentment with the self includes attaining feelings of security and freedom from threat, but it also involves acquiring self-esteem and a sense of purpose. These are rarely permanent attainments and there is usually an awareness of lack of control over the environment. Children with learning difficulties may experience low self-esteem and may also be less able to use effective metaprocesses for self-evaluation. They tend also to be less in control than other children over what happens to them, and less able to understand why things happen to them. In this sense, they may be both more vulnerable to feelings of unhappiness and less well equipped to shake off feelings of despair.

Achieving content with others is closely related to contentment with the self. For the young child, social relationships begin with interactions with the mother or primary carer, and the early years are mostly dominated by interaction with the immediate family. It has been suggested in this chapter that, for a variety of reasons, children with learning difficulties may be exposed to more negative emotions than other children even when they are cared for in loving homes. Assisting the family to maintain its functioning as a stable and healthy system while meeting the needs of the child is likely to be more effective than focusing solely on the child's problems. Similarly, it is crucial to continue to pay attention to the child's wider social network, where all too often negative attitudes towards learning disabled children still prevail.

Perhaps the greatest threat to the learning disabled child's happiness is the difficulty of attaining contentment in social relationships. Children are notoriously cruel towards people who are visibly different from the 'norm', and it has long been known that relations between children of low academic ability and their peers can be strained. There is also evidence that some children with severe learning difficulties may have problems in identifying other people's emotional states (Sternina, 1990). However, it is only relatively recently that the need for open acknowledgement of the potential loneliness of such children has been recognized (for example, Anderson and McNicholas, 1991). All children, at times, need help to achieve satisfactory relationships but, for reasons that we have touched on earlier, some children with learning difficulties may be less likely to obtain the help they need. Perhaps the best that we can hope for is that the future will bring further advances in our response as a society to the right of all individuals to be listened to with respect.

REFERENCES

American Psychiatric Association (1987) *Diagnostic and Statistical Manual of Mental Disorders*, 3rd edn, Washington, DC: American Psychiatric Association.

Anderson, R. and McNicholas, S. (1991) *Best Friends*. London: A. & C. Black/Jet Books.

Barkley, R.A. (1981) *Hyperactive Children: A Handbook for Diagnosis and Treatment*. Chichester: John Wiley.

Berg, J.M. (1974) Aetiological aspects of mental subnormality: pathological factors. In A.M. Clarke and A.D.B. Clarke (eds), *Readings from Mental Deficiency: The Changing Outlook*, pp. 82–177. London: Methuen.

Berger, M. and Yule, W. (1985) IQ tests and assessment. In A.M. Clarke, A.D.B. Clarke and J.M. Berg (eds), *Mental Deficiency: The Changing Outlook*, 4th edn, pp. 53–96. London: Methuen.

Bowlby, J. (1969) *Attachment*. Vol. II of *Attachment and Loss*. London: Hogarth Press. 2nd edn. (1982), Harmondsworth: Penguin.

Brison, D.W. (1967) Definition, diagnosis and classification. In A.A. Baumeister (ed.), *Mental Retardation: Appraisal, Education and Rehabilitation*, pp. 1–19. Chicago: Aldine Publishing Press.

Clarke, A.M. and Clarke, A.D.B. (1985) Criteria and classification. In A.M. Clarke, A.D.B. Clarke and J.M. Berg (eds), *Mental Deficiency: The Changing Outlook*, 4th edn, pp. 27–52. London: Methuen.

Craft, A. (1987) *Mental Handicap and Sexuality. Issues and Perspectives*. Tunbridge Wells: Costello.

DES (Department of Education and Science) (1978) *Special Education Needs*. (The Warnock Report). London: HMSO.

DES (1981) *Education Act*. London: HMSO.

DES (1987) *The National Curriculum 5–16*. London: HMSO.

Dunn, L.M., Dunn, L.M., Whetton, C. and Pontille, D. (1982) *British Picture Vocabulary Scale*. Windsor: NFER-Nelson.

Elliott, C., Murray, D.J. and Pearson, L.S. (1983) *British Ability Scales – Revised*. Windsor: NFER-Nelson.

Flynn, M. and Ward, L. (1991) 'We can change the future': self and citizen advocacy. In S.S. Segal and V. Varma (eds), *Prospects for People with Learning Difficulties*, pp. 129–48. London: David Fulton.

Grossman, H.J. (ed.) (1983) *Classification in Mental Retardation*. Washington, DC: American Association on Mental Deficiency.

Heber, R. (1959) A manual on terminology and classification in mental retardation. Monograph supplement to *American Journal of Mental Deficiency*, **64**.

Hogg, J., Sebba, J. and Lambe, L. (1990) *Profound Retardation and Multiple Impairment. Vol. 3: Medical and Physical Care and Management*. London: Chapman & Hall.

McCarthy, D.A. (1972) *Manual for the McCarthy Scales of Children's Abilities*. San Antonio: Psychological Corporation.

McCormack, B. (1991) Sexual abuse and learning disabilities: another iceberg. *British Medical Journal*, **303**, 143–4.

Matson, J.L. (1989) *Treating Depression in Children and Adolescents*. New York: Pergamon Press.

Montgomery, D. (1990) *Children with Learning Difficulties*. London: Cassell.

Piaget, J. (1954) *The Construction of Reality in the Child*. New York: Basic Books.

Quicke, J. (1984) The role of the educational psychologist in the post Warnock era. In L. Barton and S. Tomlinson (eds), *Special Education and Social Interests*, pp. 122–45. Beckenham: Croom Helm.

Richardson, K. (1991) *Understanding Intelligence*. Milton Keynes: Open University Press.

Ruble, D.N. (1983) The development of social-comparison processes and their role in achievement-related self-socialisation. In E.T. Higgins, D.N. Ruble and W.W. Hartup (eds), *Social Cognition and Social Development: A Sociocultural Perspective*, pp. 134–57. Cambridge: Cambridge University Press.

Rutter, M. and Yule, W. (1975) The concept of specific reading retardation. *Journal of Child Psychology and Psychiatry*, **16**, 181–97.

Sameroff, A.J. and Chandler, M.J. (1975) Reproductive risk and the continuum of caretaking casualty. In F.D. Horowitz, S. Scarr-Salapatek and G. Siegel (eds), *Review of Childhood Development Research*, Vol. 4, pp. 187–244. Chicago: University of Chicago Press.

Sarason, S.B. and Doris, J. (1969) *Psychological Problems in Mental Deficiency*, 4th edition. New York: Harper & Row.

Sinason, V. (1986) Secondary mental handicap and its relationship to trauma. *Psychoanalytic Psychotherapy*, **2**, 131–54.

Sinason, V. (1989) Uncovering and responding to sexual abuse in psychotherapeutic settings. In H. Brown and A. Craft (eds), *Thinking the Unthinkable: Papers on Sexual Abuse and People with Learning Difficulties*, pp. 39–49. London: Family Planning Association Education Unit.

Sinason, V. (1991) Interpretations that feel horrible to make and a theoretical unicorn. *Journal of Child Psychotherapy*, **17**, 11–24.

Sternina, T.Z. (1990) Mentally retarded children's comprehension of another person's emotional state. *Soviet Psychology*, **28**, 89–104.

Terman, L. and Merrill, M.A. (1973) *Stanford-Binet Intelligence Scale: Manual for the Third Revision Form L-M*. Boston: Houghton Mifflin Co.

Thomas, A., Chess, S. and Birch, H.G. (1968) *Temperament and Behavior Disorders in Children*. New York: New York University Press.

Wechsler, D. (1974) *Wechsler Intelligence Scale for Children – Revised*. New York: Psychological Corporation.

Wodrich, D.L. and Kush, S.A. (1990) *Children's Psychological Testing: A Guide for Nonpsychologists*, 2nd edn. Baltimore: Paul H. Brookes Publishing Co.

Chapter 8

Coping with Unhappy Clever Children

Robert Povey

It is difficult to find a phrase which describes 'clever' or 'gifted' children without seeming to taint them with elements of 'self-satisfaction', 'priggishness' or 'elitism'. Reference to children with 'marked aptitude' in particular spheres of activity (ILEA, 1988) comes, perhaps, closest to a non-controversial description of the type of child with whom we are concerned. In particular, it avoids the problems of *exclusivity* by which, for example, 'clever' or 'gifted' pupils have often tended to be confined to a limited group of 'high-IQ' pupils or those with outstanding all-round academic achievements (see discussion in Renzulli, 1978). The term recognizes that 'children of marked aptitude' can be drawn from high-flyers in areas outside the usual 'academic' curriculum (for example, in sport or dance) as well as in the traditional academic subjects. The drawback with the phrase, however, is that it is somewhat cumbersome and lacks the snappiness of terms such as 'clever' or 'gifted'. As a shorthand measure in the present chapter, therefore, I shall use the term 'clever' to denote children who show cleverness (that is, have a marked aptitude in) any sphere of worthwhile activity.

INCIDENCE OF UNHAPPINESS IN CLEVER CHILDREN

Within the ranks of clever children there will be a wide range of individuals exhibiting many different characteristics both intellectual and affective. The *heterogeneity* of such a group (even when confined, say, to a limited IQ range) is, in many respects, one of its most important characteristics (Maltby, 1984, p. 209), and yet we tend to ignore this when making sweeping generalizations about the characteristics of such children. (See Povey, 1980, p. 14 for a fuller discussion on this point.) It follows that we are likely to find among any group of clever children a proportion of children adjudged by themselves (and others) as predominantly happy as well as a number who are unhappy. There is little evidence to suggest that clever children are inherently more unhappy than their less clever peers. Indeed, the findings from longitudinal research projects such as the classic Terman studies (Terman, 1925; Terman and Oden, 1959) and from other more recent studies (such as Freeman, 1979) tend to suggest that the intellectually able child is rather better adjusted than the child of lower ability. In a recent American study carried out by Gallucci (1988), the levels of adjustment of 83 children (47 males and 36 females) with IQs of 135+ on the Stanford-Binet were assessed by counsellors, parents and teachers. No greater incidence of psychopathology was evident in this sample than in the normative group; and this remained true for children with IQs greater than 150 when compared with a group having IQs between 136 and 140. In another study, Tidwell (1980) examined the psycho-educational profiles and self-reported perceptions of 1,593 tenth-grade Californian students (804 males and 789 females) on a wide range of issues. Apart from their higher mean IQ (Stanford-Binet mean IQ = 136.9; SD 15.25), the students exhibited few atypical responses. They participated fully in school and extracurricular activities, gained average scores on the self-esteem inventory (although in verbalizing their views they showed a distinct reluctance to acknowledge their personal merits), and the majority (74 per cent) considered themselves as 'happy' or 'very happy'.

There is, however, some evidence that *underachieving* clever children tend to become unhappy adults, aware of and frustrated by the fact that their achievements are well below their potential (Terman, 1930). Crocker (1987) puts such findings down to the use of predominantly middle-class samples in research on clever children. He suggests, in effect, that the values and aspirations of middle-class parents are being visited upon their 'underachieving' children, who respond by showing a restless, unhappy and dissatisfied approach to life. In a small-scale study, Crocker examined 28 grammar-schoolboys, all with IQs above 125 on NFER 11 + examination tests. At the end of the first year in the secondary school, about half of these pupils were placed in A and B streams and half in C and D streams on the basis of school results. The pupils were then followed through to O-levels, when the A and B stream pupils predictably took and passed more subjects than the C and D pupils. In fact, the findings offer a classic example of the 'self-fulfilling prophecy' (see Povey, 1980, p. 19) by which pupils tend to take on the characteristics of the stream to which they have been allocated. The fact that the B and C stream pupils produced a significantly higher average grade than the upper-stream pupils can be explained to a large extent by the fact that any reduction in *quantity* of schoolwork and exam-load is likely to lead to a consequent *increase* in available revision time and performance level per subject. Crocker makes brief reference to this explanation but prefers, in general, to lay emphasis on the somewhat depressing view that these (for the most part 'working-class') pupils should be seen as under-achieving in relation to one criterion only (that is, their IQ). He argues (p. 176) that they are performing, in a contented way, just as much as they want to do and as much as 'their parents, their extended families and society at large' expect them to do; and he concludes that 'happy, stable (working class) youngsters' may be forced to join 'a fiercely competitive social situation that is not of their own choosing' (p. 177). While this situation may sometimes arise, Crocker's view seems to represent a rather defeatist acceptance of the 'status quo' and a sad rejection of the value of education as a means by which disadvantaged children can be helped to broaden their cultural and occupational horizons. It is surely at least as plausible to suggest that the exclusion of such youngsters from a sufficiently broad curriculum during the early stages of their secondary schooling is tantamount to an 'enforced' reduction in their chances of obtaining more varied, and arguably more fulfilling, career opportunities. Fortunately, however, the inequalities in opportunity arising from such school experiences are likely to be mitigated to a large extent by the implementation of the Education Reform Act 1988 (DES, 1988), under which all pupils are *required* to participate in certain 'core' and 'foundation' subjects in the National Curriculum.

The main conclusion from the studies reviewed so far, therefore, seems to be that clever children (apart, perhaps, from those who are underachieving) are, in general, as happy or unhappy as childen who are less clever; and the small-scale study reported below tends to confirm this view.

WHAT MAKES CHILDREN HAPPY OR UNHAPPY? A SMALL-SCALE STUDY

Sixty-one children in the 9–11-year age range were asked by their teachers to write about the things which made them feel happy and unhappy. At the top of one side of the paper they copied the phrase: 'I feel happy when . . .'. They were then given the open-ended task of writing, from their own experiences, as many responses to this initial phrase as they could produce. When they had completed this task the children were asked to turn over the page and copy the following phrase: 'I feel unhappy when . . .'. They completed this second task in the same way.

The subjects were divided into two groups: a 'clever' group ($N = 13$; 7 boys and 6 girls) with NFER Verbal Reasoning Quotients (VRQs) of 120+ (representing the top 10 per cent of the sample) and a 'less clever' group ($N = 48$; 29 boys and 19 girls) with VRQs of 119 and below. The full range of VRQs in the latter group was 83 to 119: 6 pupils with VRQs below 100, 29 between 100 and 119, and 13 between 115 and 119.

As with any open-ended task, the exercise produced a wide range of responses, in both quantity and quality. The number of responses ranged from two to forty with, in general, more responses per pupil for the 'happy' than for the 'unhappy' exercise. The mean number of 'happy' responses for the total group was 12, and two-thirds of the sample gave between 8 and 17; whereas the mean number of 'unhappy' responses was 8, with two-thirds offering between 5 and 12 responses. There were no significant differences in mean number of responses between the 'clever' and 'less clever' groups. Any response which was given by at least 10 per cent of the pupils (that is, by 6 or more pupils) was assigned a specific 'response category' label (see Table 8.1). The remaining responses are referred to as 'miscellaneous' in the ensuing discussion. These included responses relating to specific school subjects, teachers or events which gave pleasure or led to unhappiness.

The most marked feature of the response categories was the consistency with which they occurred within both 'clever' and 'less clever' groups. Very few differences emerged either between these groups or between the responses of boys and girls. For the purposes of tabulating the results, therefore, the findings for the *total* sample are presented (see Table 8.1). Where the few relatively clear differences in response patterns between ability or sex groupings did occur, these are referred to in the text. Quotations, however, have been restricted to those from 'clever' pupils on sources of *unhappiness* in order to provide specific illustrations of some of the points made in other parts of the chapter.

It can be seen from Table 8.1 that 'Relationships' were given by this sample of schoolchildren as the most frequent source of happiness *and* unhappiness. Parents, relatives, friends and animals all feature in the pupils' responses, irrespective of ability

Table 8.1.   *Percentage of pupils in total sample giving various categories of response as sources of 'happiness' or 'unhappiness'*

Happiness		Unhappiness	
Category	%	Category	%
Relationships	100	Relationships	100
Special occasions	75	Negative feelings	80
Material possessions	67	Physical ill-health	72
Participation	67	Material possessions	28
Achievement	56	Participation	28
Positive feelings	41	Lack of achievement	21
Leisure	39	Weather	16
Weather	12	Leisure	13

Notes:

1 *Explanation of response categories*: 'Relationships' include responses relating to both humans and animals; 'Special occasions' include such events as outings, birthdays and Christmas; 'Material possessions' include gifts which are both given and received, and (for unhappy feelings) damaging or losing possessions; 'Positive feelings' (happiness) include such reponses as 'being loved' and 'given attention', and 'Negative feelings' (unhappiness) such responses as 'being rejected'; 'Participation' involved taking part in activities (happiness) or 'being excluded' (unhappiness); 'Achievement' (happiness) or 'Lack of achievement' (unhappiness) relate to both academic and non-academic pursuits; 'Leisure' denotes engaging in leisure pursuits (for happiness), and for unhappiness this translates as having nothing to do/being bored in leisure time; 'Weather' includes any response relating to weather conditions; 'Physical ill-health' (for unhappiness only) relates to ill-health in both self and others. Table 8.1 gives the percentage of responses for the total sample in relation to each of the main response categories.

2 *Scoring*: For the most part the categories are mutually exclusive but a 'Relationship' response might occasionally be relevant to more than one category; for example, 'being told off by parents' could count as a 'Relationships' response *and* a 'Negative feelings' response. Similarly, 'playing with friends' could count as 'Relationships' and also 'Participation'. However, for the purposes of Table 8.1 the percentage score for each category represents the proportion of pupils giving *at least one* response scored *exclusively* under that category.

level or gender. 'Making friends' and 'being with the family' were common responses as sources of happiness in this category:

> Timothy (chronological age [CA] 9 years 9 months; VRQ 136): 'I feel happy when mum gives me a hug at night.'

> Andrew (CA 10 years 6 months; VRQ 127): 'I feel happy when . . . seeing my dad, sitting in front of the fire with my mum, sometimes when playing with friends, playing with my mum's boyfriend.'

Animals were frequently referred to as sources of happiness, especially by girls (48 per cent for girls as opposed to 28 per cent for boys):

> Veronica (CA 10 years 5 months; VRQ 126): 'I feel happy when my aunt's cat comes and sits on my lap and starts purring, I have a special happy feeling when I bury my hands in its fur.'

Similarly, problems with relationships were seen as an important source of unhappiness:

> Gillian (CA 10 years 4 months; VRQ 127): 'I feel unhappy when my brother starts arguing with me.'

> Robert (CA 10 years 10 months; VRQ 135): 'I feel unhappy when . . . friends say they don't like me anymore.'

These relationship problems could also be viewed as a source of unhappiness under the 'Negative feelings' category, as could 'teasing and rejection by friends'. Such negative feelings were mentioned by 80 per cent of the sample as sources of unhappiness:

> Robert (again): 'I feel unhappy when somebody teases me about my stuttering . . . friends saying they don't like me anymore; friends not letting me play with them; people criticizing me; my friends rejecting me for someone else.'

'Positive feelings' (such as feeling accepted, being praised or given attention) are clearly seen as important for feelings of happiness, but they tend to receive less *explicit* comment by the pupils when contrasted with the 'Negative feelings' relating to 'unhappiness' (41 per cent as opposed to 80 per cent). It is as if the positive feelings involved in 'playing with' or 'being with' relatives or friends do not require to be 'spelt out' in quite the same way as feelings of rejection. The 'clever' boys were also about twice as likely as the girls or less clever boys to include such responses as important sources of happiness. *Empathic* feelings are also evident in the pupils' responses in relation both to happiness and unhappiness:

> Natalie (CA 10 years 8 months; VRQ 122): 'I feel happy when I see other people happy and enjoying themselves' and 'I feel unhappy when I see other people crying.'

For 'happiness', the second most frequent response related to 'special occasions' such as outings, birthdays and Christmas. Girls (in both the 'clever' and 'less clever' groups) reported special occasions as important sources of happiness much more frequently than boys (92 per cent to 64 per cent):

> Rebecca (CA 10 years 9 months; VRQ 127): 'I feel happy . . . when it's my birthday or when it's my favourite cousin's birthday.'

The acquisition or giving of 'Material possessions' was a prominent source of happiness (roughly two-thirds of pupils in both groups giving such responses, 'getting' reponses outnumbering 'giving' responses by about 7 to 1 in this particular age group!):

> Trevor (CA 10 years 0 months; VRQ 121): 'I feel happy when it's my birthday because I get presents.'
>
> Timothy (again): 'I feel happy . . . when I see people's faces light up when I give them things.'

'Damage to possessions' also figured as a source of unhappiness in 28 per cent of the sample. Another, more prominent source of unhappiness, was 'Physical ill-health' (72 per cent mentioning this as experienced by the pupil himself or herself and/or when observed in other people and in animals). Although *personal* ill-health was the most frequently quoted response, ill-health or death in others was mentioned by a substantial number of pupils (28 per cent):

> Kevin (CA 10 years 2 months; VRQ 124): 'I feel unhappy when . . . I'm hurt and nobody takes any notice; one of our pets gets hurt; I fall over and get dirty.'
>
> Timothy (again): 'I feel unhappy . . . when one of my friends' brothers dies.'

'Participation' (or not being allowed to participate) in activities such as games or 'play' was seen as a source of both happiness (67 per cent) and unhappiness (28 per cent):

> Keith (CA 10 years 2 months; VRQ 124): 'I feel happy when . . . I'm in a football team; I'm in a hockey team; friends come over to play.'

Terry (CA 10 years 0 months; VRQ 121): 'I feel unhappy . . . when I get left out of games.'

'Achievement' was reported as a source of happiness by 56 per cent of the pupils and 'Lack of achievement' was related to unhappiness by about a fifth of the pupils. In this particular sample the clever pupils mentioned unhappiness resulting from poor achievement rather more frequently (31 per cent) than the less clever group (19 per cent):

Rosemary (CA 10 years 9 months; VRQ 127): 'I feel happy when I get good exam results . . . I feel unhappy when I do my violin wrong and make a bad note.'

James (CA 11 years 2 months; VRQ 108): 'I feel happy when I get high marks in an exam . . . I feel unhappy when I don't do well in a subject. When I fail an exam.'

'Leisure' activities were seen as sources of happiness by both clever and less clever pupils; but lack of leisure activities ('boredom' or 'nothing to do') was only mentioned as a source of unhappiness by the less clever pupils. The influence of the weather, on the other hand, was seen as relevant to both happy (12 per cent) and unhappy moods (13 per cent) by a small proportion in both groups.

In summary, it seems clear that clever children (at least in this small sample of 9–11-year-olds) tend to feel happy, or unhappy for the same sorts of reasons as the less clever children. Relationships appear to occupy a central role with respect to feelings of happiness/unhappiness for all the children in this study, irrespective of ability or sex. Where differences between the ability groups do appear, however, they tend to mirror differences which have emerged in previous studies. For example, the clever children tended to be more strongly affected by failure to reach their academic (or other) goals than less clever children; and the able pupils also tended to be less affected than their less clever peers by ennui in leisure time. As Freeman (1985, p. 10) observes, able children tend to have a great variety of interests to keep them occupied; but, as we shall see later, boredom in relation to assigned classroom tasks is sometimes a source of unhappy frustration in clever children.

SPECIFIC EXAMPLES OF UNHAPPINESS IN CLEVER CHILDREN AND HOW TO COPE WITH THEM

Since many of the sources of unhappiness in clever children are identical to those relating to other, less able children, the coping strategies adopted by parents and teachers for such children are likely to be very similar to those adopted for unhappiness more generally. So for ill-health, for example, parents would provide comfort and medical treatment as necessary, whatever talents the child possessed. For children with exceptional sporting talents parents, teachers and coaches may be more careful about what in other circumstances might be considered 'minor' injuries, but, in general, the principles of coping with the unhappiness arising from the injury would be much the same, that is, the provision of appropriate treatment and reassurance. There are a number of characteristics exhibited by clever children, however, which can lead to unhappiness and which require more particular handling by parents and teachers, the first being unhappiness which arises from the child's self-expectations.

Self-expectations

Being clever in several spheres of activity looks like a recipe for multidimensional contentedness; but in reality this can be very far from the truth. Young adults who were brilliant all-rounders as children often disappoint others because they have failed to develop one or other of their particular talents. Similarly, clever children often disappoint *themselves* by failing to live up to their own high aspirations: 'At some point, you will probably tell yourself that you have no talent. Your mind will vacillate between believing you are a genius and believing that you are a failure. Neither being true, you may become extremely depressed or confused and your opinion of yourself will begin to break down' (quoted in Deslisle, 1985 p. 369). This tendency among clever children to feel upset over achievement levels was also illustrated in the study of 9–11-year-old children reported earlier. It may be recalled that the group of clever pupils tended to report feeling unhappy as a consequence of what they saw as poor achievement more frequently than the less clever group. Thus, while low self-esteem is not a predominant characteristic of clever children (see Tidwell, 1980), it is nevertheless sufficiently prevalent to merit special comment.

The point is that some children, however competent they are adjudged to be on 'external assessments' of their work, see themselves on the basis of their own 'internal judgements' to be 'failures'; and this can be particularly difficult to recognize and understand in children who are widely acclaimed for the brilliance of their achievements. Observers will usually put such protestations of worthlessness down to 'false modesty', whereas it can be symptomatic of deep unhappiness. Norbert Wiener, for example, who was one of the great mathematicians of the twentieth century, suffered from 'a prolonged period of unhappiness, accompanied by a profound lack of self-esteem' (Howe, 1990, p. 84). His problems were in large measure probably a result of 'the contradictions and impossible demands of an intense, insecure, over-critical family' whose unacceptably high aspiration levels Wiener had assimilated from a very young age; and they illustrate the fact that low levels of self-esteem are not confined to poor achievers. Parents and teachers, therefore, need to recognize that even the most clever pupils need the reassurance which comes from receiving acceptance and praise from others. As Suzanne Packer (gifted actress and sister of the Olympic hurdler, Colin Jackson) put it in an interview about her own and her brother's experiences: 'High achievers don't get the attention they should . . . A lot of A-grade pupils are very unhappy because people think they don't need encouragement and support' (Martingale, 1992).

Similarly, it should be remembered that despite the child's high level of accomplishment in some activities there is no guarantee that this degree of maturity is paralleled by the same level of emotional development. The child may appear to be dependent on incongruously high levels of emotional support in comparison with the mature and independent way he or she copes with intellectual, sporting or artistic pursuits. It is salutary to remind ourselves from time to time that clever individuals still need the same measure of *explicity demonstrated* approval, encouragement and affection from parents and teachers which their less advanced peers enjoy. An oversized portion of praise and approval can sometimes lead, of course, to an off-putting sense of conceit and self-satisfaction in both parents and child. Fortunately, clever children often seem to disapprove of such overindulgence, and this acts as a corrective to embarrassing levels of parental pride. The omission of adequate levels of praise and approval from parents and teachers, on the other hand, can lead to reduced levels of self-esteem.

Parental handling

There is, in fact, a considerable amount of evidence pointing to the relevance of parental handling to the happiness or unhappiness of clever children and, as we have already seen, relationships are considered by clever children to be of prime importance in this context. In general, clever children seem to thrive and be most well adjusted in family environments which include such features as a positive intellectual climate with reasonably high parental expectations, a strong involvement of the parents with the child, and a relationship of mutual trust between them (Monks and van Boxtel, 1985, p. 289). Some researchers, notably Torrance (1983), have drawn attention to the importance of a 'mentor' (often the parent) in encouraging creative, independent achievement, and there are many examples of coaching mentors in the development of high sporting, musical and academic achievement (see Radford, 1990, Ch. 4). Boris Breskvar, for example, was associated with the tennis player Boris Becker (and also with Steffi Graf) from a very early age. He took Boris Becker as a pupil, at the age of 6 years, and worked with him nearly every day for the next nine years. In music there are numerous examples of mentors, perhaps the most famous being the devotion of Leopold Mozart to his son's musical education (see Shuter-Dyson, 1985, p. 163). A recent example of an intellectually gifted child with a parental mentor can be seen in the case of Ruth Lawrence (for a fuller discussion of her case and other child prodigies see Radford, 1990). With the aid of her father's coaching Ruth gained O-level mathematics at the age of 9 and A-level at 10, at which age she also won an open scholarship to St Hugh's College, Oxford. Her father was at her side during her brilliant university career, which resulted in the award of a first-class honours degree at the age of 13 and a postgraduate research career. The lives of other childhood prodigies also point to the importance of a mentor, and the view that such a life-style need not necessarily lead to unhappiness is expressed by the father of one such prodigy, John Adams (who gained an O-level at 8 and an A-level at 9). John's father wrote a book about his and his son's experiences entitled *Your Child Can be A Genius – And Happy*! (Adams, 1988).

The regimes implemented by such mentors can sometimes, however, become too narrowly focused and 'oppressive' for the pupil, and can result in profound unhappiness. Perhaps the clearest example is that of John Stuart Mill, the nineteenth-century philosopher and economist. He was an infant prodigy who was educated by his father under an incredibly demanding regime, in which his classical education began at the age of 3 with the learning of Greek. The impression one gains from his autobiography (Mill, 1971) is that he took this educational regime in his stride for the most part and enjoyed a good deal of the work. Nevertheless, it was an extremely rigorous and lopsided education, in which intellectual pursuits predominated over the development of social skills. Contact with other children was severely limited and 'no holidays were allowed, lest the habit of work should be broken, and a taste for idleness acquired' (pp. 22–3). Mill's father set impossibly high standards ('my father . . . demanded of me not only the utmost that I could do, but much that I could by no possibility have done', p. 6), to the extent that the young Mill considered himself 'rather backward' in his studies 'since I always found myself so, in comparison with what my father expected of me'. It is not entirely surprising, therefore, that in his 20s Mill appears to have suffered a severe depressive reaction to this narrowly oppressive life-style. He reports that 'the whole foundation on which my life was constructed fell down . . . I seemed to have nothing left to live for' (p. 81). It is possible, of course, that he would have had a depressive illness whether he had been subjected to such a rigorous intellectual regime or not, but parental pressures seem likely to have played a significant role in its genesis.

An interesting finding reported by Freeman (1979, 1980) indicates that children labelled by their parents as 'gifted' tend to present more problems and to show more signs of unhappiness than other gifted children. She studied a sample of high-IQ children between the ages of 5 and 16 whose parents had joined the National Association for Gifted Children (NAGC). Comparing these children with others of similar IQ levels, she concludes that they 'are undoubtedly different from their peers. They are difficult to bring up and show maladjusted behaviour at school. They also have more physical ill-health. Doubtless they are more unhappy' (Freeman, 1980, p. 90). It is difficult to determine to what extent such behaviour is a consequence of different parental attitudes to their clever children, and to what extent it is the child's behaviour which gives rise to the different parental approaches. Freeman argues that the unhappiness of her 'target' children is not necessarily related to cleverness *per se* and that the reasons for the parents joining the NAGC probably had as much to do with the children's behavioural difficulties as with their intellectual prowess. Nevertheless, the practice of giving 'global' labels such as 'gifted' or 'clever' to children on an individual basis is generally not to be recommended. It tends to embarrass the child and sets him or her apart from (or worse still against) less able peers; and it also has the effect of setting standards (often based on the parental as opposed to the children's ambitions) which the children may have difficulty living up to.

Freeman (1983, pp. 183-7) gives a very useful list of advice for parents of clever children, which includes several of the points already discussed in this chapter. One point not included in Freeman's excellent list of suggestions, however, is the importance of *consistency* in parental handling. This is a point which is relevant to all children, of course, but it has been shown that this factor is particularly important in relation to 'difficult' gifted children. Based on studies of gifted delinquents, Brooks (1985, p. 306) concludes that the 'gifted child adjusts more successfully when given a stable home background . . . Over-permissiveness or over-strict regimes within the home or school appeared to enhance the degree of risk (to delinquent behaviour), but the most significant risk-factor emerged as erratic and inconsistent handling.'

Self-perception

Unhappiness can often arise in the clever child as a result of problems in self-perception. Wallace (1983) places great emphasis on the clever child's feeling of being different, the feeling of being 'out of step with their family, their friends and their time' (p. 10). Clever children can sometimes be born into families in which the nature and demands, for example, of academic or musical study are entirely outside the experience of any family member. This does not mean that the family will not be able to encourage and support the child in his or her studies, but it can lead to misunderstandings, stresses and unhappiness brought about through the child feeling 'like a fish out of water'. Such problems can often be surmounted with the aid of understanding teachers who are willing to spend time in close home–school liaison at times of potential conflict, and in fostering the child's talents at school. Despite such efforts, however, some clever children will choose to deal with the problem of 'feeling different' by withdrawing into a world of their own, a strategy which is nicely illustrated by the comment of William (CA 8 yrs 3 months; VRQ 140): 'I feel happy when I go swimming under water because you can get away from everything else and be alone.' Another way of coping with these problems is to allow the clever child the opportunity of meeting other children who are similarly gifted. Some local authorities organize such opportunities (see Roberts and Wallace, 1980; Wallace, 1983, Part 2). Wallace reports the experiences of Linda (aged 13), who had attended the Essex curriculum-extension courses. Linda's comments illustrate the damaging effects which classmates' negative, rejecting reactions can have on the self-perception of clever children (cf. Robert's comments quoted on page 97):

> Linda wrote: 'I have discovered a lot about myself during the last few days . . . at last, I don't feel that I am some kind of exceptional freak. Other people have the same problems as I do: being ostracized by classmates seems to be a common problem amongst us, and attempting to be "one of the crowd" by speaking the same way and acting the same way as others seems a common remedy.'
>
> (Wallace, 1983, p. 11)

Their difficulties in self-perception and in relating to the interests and activities of their chronological peer group can present considerable problems for clever children. In a sense they are 'too old for their years' and often possess a heightened sensitivity to adult problems. Wallace (1983, p. 12) describes a child of 7 with a precocious understanding of adult issues who could discuss the problems of world poverty, the rising crime rate and racial prejudice; but he would be kept awake at night worrying about the future – and to compound his problems, when he did get to sleep he would suffer from nocturnal enuresis! His problems were faced by understanding parents and a sympathetic school which tried to introduce him to less serious, more relaxing and humorous 'play' activities, in line with the sort of activities enjoyed by his chronological peers. At the same time he was offered the opportunity of satisfying his intellectual appetite by taking part in curriculum extension courses with pupils of similar ability.

School environment

Factors in the school environment can play an important part in a clever child's happiness or unhappiness. One problem resides in the tendency of some teachers to regard their clever pupils as commodities which belong to them for the purposes of showing them and the school in a good examination light. In such circumstances the pupil can feel abused and unhappy. The feeling is summed up most starkly in a poem written by a clever 15-year-old girl in her O-level year (see Wallace, 1983, p. 147):

> It is not
> how do I feel?
> Is this
> important to me?

No question asked.
It is only:
She is
property.

It is not
do I think?
Have I feelings
at all?

Only there is a
brain in there
somewhere.
Plain academic.

It is not
help me,
help me
to be happy.

It is only:
her exam results will
reflect well on us.

On the other hand, having talents which go unrecognized in the classroom can also lead to pupil boredom and unhappiness. In a sample of Oxfordshire secondary schools, Denton and Postlethwaite (1985) found that teachers were quite good at identifying potential high achievers in specific subjects such as maths and English. They also found, however, that teachers tended, rather too frequently for comfort, to classify pupils on the basis of 'broad generalizations concerning their abilities, and of views of the pupils' motivation and attitude' (p. 134). Where this occurs and teachers lack a sufficiently in-depth knowledge of a subject-specific profile for their pupils, it is likely that they will set tasks at an inappropriate level (usually far too low in the case of clever children). As a consequence, boredom and disaffection will frequently ensue among clever pupils. Some will simply do 'the stint' (see Bridges, 1969, 1980), doing just as much (or little) as the teacher's task requires and the pupil can get away with, and no more; others will while away their time 'acting the clown' or thinking up and carrying out unpleasant activities to annoy the teacher. Such children's real abilities often go unrecognized, hidden as they are by a smoke-screen of 'disruptive' and 'unco-operative' behaviour.

To a substantial number of clever pupils, the lack of challenge in classroom tasks will lead to a prevailing mood of frustration and unhappiness with the school environment; but with more careful matching by teachers of learning task to pupils' interest and ability levels, many of these problems can be overcome. It is not necessary for the teacher of clever pupils to be the 'fount of all knowledge'. Indeed, the majority of teachers are likely to be less clever than the cleverest of their pupils. What the teacher needs to do is to recognize this fact and to concentrate on acting as a *facilitator* of the pupil's learning experiences by allowing the pupil scope to develop his or her own learning programmes, extending the curriculum in depth rather than in quantity (for example, 'examine possible reasons for this phenomenon' rather than 'give me five more examples' or 'do ten more of the same'). In other words, teachers should concentrate on offering opportunities for *curriculum enrichment* (see Povey, 1980, especially chs 9 and 12) and on effective *enquiry techniques*, getting the pupil to ask probing questions ('How?' and 'Why?') rather than producing an extensive list of facts. Out-of-school clubs, including those organized by the National Association for Gifted Children (NAGC), can also provide a valuable source of extension activities.

Clever pupils can also be difficult to identify, sometimes as a consequence of disguised ability (as in the 'disruptive clown') and sometimes as a consequence of handicapping conditions, especially when these relate to the impairment of communication skills. Poor articulation and impaired language skills in children are often taken to denote a parallel impairment of intellectual skills, as are difficulties in reading and writing (see Whitmore, 1985, pp. 105–8). Thus children with cerebral palsy, dyslexia or autism, for example, are in danger of having their abilities underestimated and their latent potential stifled by inappropriate (and sometimes demeaning) curriculum experiences, which can lead to increasing frustration and unhappiness. To prevent such frustration we need to concentrate on the development of more effective identification procedures, so that such children are recognized at an early stage and provided with curriculum experiences appropriate to their individual needs. (For a discussion of the possibilities of developing such an approach with dyslexic children, see Povey and Tod, 1993.)

CONCLUSIONS

In summary, the sources of unhappiness in clever children are most likely to be very similar to those which affect their less clever peers. It has been possible, however, to identify a number of aspects in which the possession of 'marked aptitude' in particular areas seems to have a specific bearing on a child's happiness or unhappiness. The tendency for clever children to inflict excessive levels of self-expectation on themselves, to feel different from and to find difficulty in integrating with their peers are a few of the features which tend to cause unhappiness; and it is important for parents and teachers to be sensitive to ways in which they can help to alleviate these problems. Curriculum extension and enrichment projects are suggested as ways in which clever children can be given the sort of challenges which will enable them to develop their skills on an individual basis or in the company of similarly gifted peers. It is suggested that close liaison between home and school is a key to effective coping in many instances, together with sensitive, consistent handling by parents and flexible, individual teaching approaches by teachers. Finally, the essential role of early recognition is stressed as a prerequisite for the development of successful and happy education for clever children.

REFERENCES

Adams, K. (1988) *Your Child Can Be a Genius – and Happy!* Wellingborough: Thorsons.
Bridges, S. (1980) Experiments at Campion School. In R. Povey (ed.), *Educating the Gifted Child*. London: Harper & Row.
Bridges, S. A. (1969) *Gifted Children and the Brentwood Experiment*. London: Pitman.
Brooks, R. (1985) Delinquency among gifted children. In J. Freeman (ed.), *The Psychology of Gifted Children*, pp. 297–308. Chichester: John Wiley.
Crocker, A. C. (1987) Underachieving, gifted working class boys: are they wrongly labelled underachieving? *Educational Studies*, **13**, 169–78.

Denton, C. and Postlethwaite, K. (1985) *Able Children: Identifying Them in the Classroom.* Windsor: NFER-Nelson.

DES (Department of Education and Science) (1988) *Education Reform Act 1988.* London: HMSO.

Deslisle, J.R. (1985) Vocational problems. In J. Freeman (ed.), *The Psychology of Gifted Children*, pp. 367–78. Chichester: John Wiley.

Freeman, J. (1979) *Gifted Children: Their Identification and Development in a Social Context.* Lancaster: MTP Press.

Freeman, J. (1980) Giftedness in a social context. In R.M. Povey (ed.), *Educating the Gifted Child*, pp. 80–91. London: Harper & Row.

Freeman, J. (1983) *Clever Children: A Parent's Guide.* Feltham, Middlesex: Hamlyn.

Freeman, J. (ed.) (1985) *The Psychology of Gifted Children.* Chichester: John Wiley.

Gallucci, N.T. (1988) Emotional adjustment of gifted children. *Gifted Child Quarterly*, **32**, 273–6.

Howe, M.J.A. (1990) *Sense and Nonsense about Hothouse Children.* Leicester: The British Psychological Society.

ILEA (Inner London Education Authority) (1988) *Report of Inspection of Provision for Pupils of Marked Aptitude.* London: ILEA.

Maltby, F. (1984) *Gifted Children and Teachers in the Primary School 5–12.* Lewes: The Falmer Press.

Martingale, M. (1992) Relative values: high performance. *The Sunday Times* (magazine supplement), 1 March, p. 9.

Mill, J.S. (1971) *Autobiography*, ed. J. Stillinger. Oxford: Oxford University Press.

Monks, F.J. and van Boxtel, H.W. (1985) Gifted adolescents: a developmental perspective. In J. Freeman (ed.), *The Psychology of Gifted Children*, pp. 275–96.

Povey, R.M. (1980) *Educating the Gifted Child.* London: Harper & Row.

Povey, R.M. and Tod, J. (1993) The dyslexic child. In V. Varma (ed.), *How and Why Children Fail.* London: Jessica Kingsley Publishers.

Radford, S. (1990) *Child Prodigies and Exceptional Early Achievers.* London: Harvester Wheatsheaf.

Renzulli, J.S. (1978) What makes giftedness? *Phi Delta Kappan*, **60**, 180–4.

Roberts, S. and Wallace, B. (1980) The development of teaching materials: principles and practice. In R.M. Povey (ed.) *Educating the Gifted Child*, pp. 120–42.

Shuter-Dyson, R. (1985) Musical giftedness. In J. Freeman (ed.), *The Psychology of Gifted Children*, pp. 159–84. Chichester: John Wiley.

Terman, L.M. (1925) *Genetic Studies of Genius. Vol. 1: Mental and Physical Traits of a Thousand Gifted Children.* Stanford, CA: Stanford University Press.

Terman, L.M. (1930) *The Promise of Youth.* London: Harrap.

Terman, L.M. and Oden, M. (1959) *Genetic Studies of Genius. Vol. 5: The Gifted Group at Mid-Life.* California: Stanford University Press.

Tidwell, R. (1980) A psycho-educational profile of 1,593 gifted high school students. *Gifted Child Quarterly*, **24**, 63–8.

Torrance, E.P. (1983) Role of mentors in creative achievement. *The Creative Child and Adult Quarterly*, **8**, 8–16.

Wallace, B. (1983) *Teaching the Very Able Child.* London: Ward Lock Educational.

Whitmore, J. (1985) New challenges to common identification practices. In J. Freeman (ed.), *The Psychology of Gifted Children*, pp. 93–114. Chichester: John Wiley.

Chapter 9

Coping with Unhappy Children Who Exhibit Emotional and Behaviour Problems in the Classroom

James Gray

The behaviour of pupils in class varies considerably, from quiet to noisy, active to inactive, hard-working to non-working, and so on, and teachers recognize this as being perfectly normal. However there are also the pupils whose behaviour is outside this 'normal' range, and who stick out as being unusual or abnormal. They may just show extreme forms of 'normal' behaviour such as total silence, incessant movement, or an apparently total failure to learn; or they may exhibit more bizarre forms of behaviour. Some of these pupils attract attention, and the most extreme cases have tended to have some kind of special educational provision made for them.

Epidemiological work such as that of Rutter *et al.* (1970) suggests that school pupils suffer from a wide range of emotional and behavioural problems. Despite this, current provision concentrates very largely on the pupils who appear to be failing to learn, and on those whose behaviour causes disruption or leads to violence. The best explanation for this mismatch between problems and provision seems to be the fact that provision is made largely in response to demand, and demand is strongest when teachers suffer most. Indeed, authors such as Galloway and Goodwin (1988) assert that the principal function of the special educational system is to relieve mainstream teachers of pupils who worry them. This assertion is supported by the shortage of provision for pupils whose behaviour is withdrawn or self-effacing and so causes little problem. This is despite the suggestion of authors such as Pye (1989) that these pupils may well have personal needs as great as, or greater than, those of the disruptive pupils.

The shortage of special educational provision for withdrawn pupils could be taken to imply that teachers are not concerned about these pupils, but this is not the case. Dawson (1982) asked a sample of teachers to identify and describe pupils who caused them an unusual degree of concern. Although pupils with 'conduct problems' appeared most frequently, social isolates and children with physical problems, home problems and learning problems were all reported. Evidently, teachers are concerned about these less troublesome pupils whose behaviour they see as unusual, but their attention is drawn to the ones who disrupt lessons.

In this context, it is interesting to speculate on which of the identified pupils would be seen as being 'unhappy'. Ask a group of observers in a classroom to identify the unhappy pupils, and there would probably be considerable unanimity: withdrawn pupils, social isolates and the victims of bullying would be likely to top the list. With deeper knowledge of the pupils, others might be added, particularly those with unsettled home backgrounds.

By contrast, the numerous pupils in the 'conduct problem' group of Dawson's sample were described in phrases such as 'aggressive, disruptive and foul mouthed'. It is not surprising that they caused their teachers concern: what is more questionable is whether they would be seen as 'unhappy'. Characterization as 'unhappy' is based largely on sympathy, and certain types of behaviour are more likely to arouse sympathy than others. Pupils are not likely to elicit much sympathy when they exhibit behaviour that is described in terms characteristic of 'conduct problems'.

This, then, suggests a paradox. The pupils who disrupt lessons receive the attention of teachers and special educational provision, but they probably receive very little sympathy: withdrawn pupils may have the sympathy of teachers, and they are probably seen to be unhappy, but they receive relatively little provision or help. This suggests that both these groups of pupils merit further consideration. The plight of withdrawn pupils has recently been discussed by Pye (1989), and some of their problems are discussed in other chapters of this book, so this chapter will consider the contrasting group – the pupils who disrupt lessons. Their numbers are large, and their impact great (Elton, 1989), but despite this, it will be argued that disruptive behaviour is poorly understood.

Specifically, it will be argued in this chapter that unhappiness may indeed be closely associated with classroom misbehaviour, and that the underlying problems of these pupils are easily overlooked. In itself, this makes a humanitarian case for greater understanding of these children, but it will also be argued that appreciation of their plight may be of considerable help to the teachers involved in the very difficult task of coping with them. In order to do this, it is necessary to consider the processes involved in misbehaviour and the perceptions of those involved.

DISRUPTION AND DISRUPTIVE PUPILS

Terms such as 'behavioural problems' or even 'disruption' share an important characteristic with 'happiness' or 'unhappiness': they are all very hard to define objectively. Happiness is a subjective experience, so it cannot be defined objectively. As Argyle (1987) comments, 'if people say they are happy then they *are* happy' (p. 2). By the same token, disruption of a lesson is an individual's perception of what went on, and this makes it very hard to identify particular behaviours that are disruptive. By analogy with happiness, if a teacher says that his or her lesson was disrupted then it was disrupted.

However, one does not have to be quite so accepting if a teacher says that a particular pupil is disruptive. If many teachers describe one pupil as disruptive then it suggests that the pupil's behaviour does result in disruption of lessons. If only one teacher characterizes a particular pupil as disruptive, it may suggest that the teacher or the context in which that teacher meets the pupil contributes to the disruption that results. The fact that labelling the pupil as disruptive may contribute to the process of disruption will be discussed below.

Despite these caveats, it is important to note that there are pupils who frequently disrupt lessons, in many contexts, and with many teachers (Galloway *et al.*, 1982). For these reasons, the term 'disruptive pupil' will be used in this discussion to refer to those pupils who regularly become involved in incidents that disrupt their lessons. It is also clear (Elton, 1989) that the prime concern for teachers is just these disruptive pupils rather than the much rarer ones who become involved in acts of physical violence to teachers. Understanding disruptive pupils is of great importance to schools and to anybody who is concerned with young people.

There are four perspectives on the phenomenon of disruption that are of particular importance to anybody wishing to understand it. They are the pupils' self-perception, the pupils' social performance with their peers, the pupils' perceptions of their teachers and of disruption, and the teachers' perceptions of their pupils and of disruption. These will be discussed in the following sections.

PUPILS' SELF-PERCEPTION

Research described in detail elsewhere (Gray, 1987) investigated the self-image of 354 13–14-year-old pupils by means of a self-report questionnaire. This instrument was derived from those of Lindsey and Lindsey (1982) and Barker-Lunn (1970). Disruptive pupils were identified as is indicated above, by means of asking staff to nominate those pupils who had disrupted their lessons in the preceding weeks. Pupils nominated by more than one member of staff were taken as being regularly disruptive.

Factor analysis of the questionnaire results produced two factors that were significantly associated with a pupil's nomination as disruptive. These were characterized as 'self-control and social skills at relating to adults' and 'academic self-image'. Disruptive pupils tended to have low scores on both of these variables. The pupils who regularly disrupted lessons had poor social skills at relating to adults, or low academic self-image, or both. The pupils who were most heavily nominated by the staff as disruptive had low scores on *both* of these factors.

Self-reported poor social skills at relating to adults implies (Trower *et al.*, 1978) that these disruptive pupils did not feel able to deal with adults successfully, and that they did not get what they wanted out of their unavoidable contacts with adults. This would tend to make the child feel passive, put-upon and unable to influence the outcome of any dealings with adults, and in the school context, that means teachers. 'Low academic self-image' is another way of saying that the disruptive pupils in the survey probably believed that they could not do the work they were given.

Teachers may not recognize these descriptions as applying to their disruptive pupils, but it is important to accept that these were the feelings expressed by the pupils themselves. In this context, the perceptions of the teacher cannot take precedence over the self-perceptions of the pupils. Somehow the two sets of perceptions have to be reconciled, and this will be considered below.

One way of making intuitive sense of these descriptions of disruptive pupils is to consider how they may generate the disruptive behaviour. Figure 9.1 suggests some of the links that may be involved. It will be noted that the disruptive pupil is seen as being in the coils of two vicious circles. Although there are several ways into the circles, including factors such as the family background, there are no ways shown for the pupil

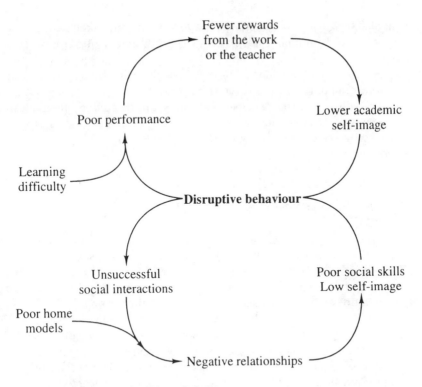

Figure 9.1 *Disruptive pupils – the vicious circle (1)*

to get out of them. This is because it requires a major change to at least one of the elements to break the circle. By contrast, generation of any one of the elements could be seen to initiate a pupil into a career of disruption.

The top circle represents the pupil's academic functioning, with 'disruptive behaviour' producing 'poor performance', which in turn produces 'fewer rewards' and a 'lower academic self-image', and these links seem fairly self-explanatory. In the final link, a low academic self-image is very likely to generate disruptive behaviour, because any attempt to get the pupil to work raises the enormous threat of failure (Burns, 1979). The pupil can avoid failure by ensuring that the challenge does not occur; in other words by making sure that the teacher cannot pursue the work of the lesson. Disruption avoids this perceived threat, and protects the pupil from failure.

The social dimension of disruption is represented by the bottom half of Figure 9.1. Here, disruptive behaviour produces the 'negative contact with the teacher' that is so familiar, and often ends up with the pupil being punished in some way. Over time, this leads to the pupil forming a poor relationship with the teacher(s), and from this the pupil cannot develop either the social confidence or the social skills that are needed for relating to adults in authority. Lack of confidence in a relationship, and ignorance of the necessary social skills, are likely to produce socially unacceptable behaviour, and that is a common characterization of disruption. The teacher who is involved may have other descriptions for this type of behaviour, but those will be discussed below.

A pupil who feels threatened by the work may just be able to negotiate his or her way round the conflict with the teacher. But if he or she also lacks the social skills for relating to adults such as the teacher, these attempts are not likely to be very successful. This two-edged problem may explain the predicament of the most seriously disruptive pupils.

These self-perceptions of the pupils who are involved in disruption provide one perspective on the phenomenon. However, disruption involves more than one person, so the ways in which the actors perceive each other are of comparable importance, as are the perceptions of the onlookers, the other pupils in the class. These will all be considered before returning to some of the further implications of the pupils' self-assessment.

PUPILS' SOCIAL PERFORMANCE WITH THEIR PEERS

If, as has been suggested above, teachers do not see disruptive pupils as unhappy, it may be partly explained by their failure to perceive accurately the social functioning of those pupils. Howarth (1985) found that teachers were generally inaccurate in assessing the popularity of pupils, particularly disruptive boys. Teachers tended to estimate that these boys were more popular than sociometry showed them to be.

In another study (Gray, 1987), disruptive pupils were found to receive as many positive nominations from their peers as did other pupils. This involved identifying 'somebody I like to be with', but when the opposite was called for, 'somebody I do not like to be with', disruptive pupils were nominated far more heavily than others. The disruptive pupils had some friends, but outside that group they were widely disliked. These findings are consistent with those of Galloway *et al.* (1982), that over one-third of the sample of suspended pupils had few, if any, friends.

All these findings suggest that disruptive pupils are not accurately perceived by adults, particularly by their teachers. Teachers' perceptions of their pupils are heavily coloured by their own involvement with the pupils, and their own anxieties about their position. In addition, it seems that disruptive pupils are not the social success they might be. This in turn suggests not merely that these pupils' social functioning is poor in relation to adults, but that they have problems generally in their dealings with other people.

PUPILS' PERCEPTIONS OF THEIR TEACHERS AND OF DISRUPTION

Several pieces of work have investigated the ways in which pupils view their teachers, and others have investigated the ways in which pupils explain their own disruptive behaviour. As we will see, there are significant similarities and differences between these sets of work, and both of them offer an important perspective on the pupils' predicament.

There is considerable agreement in the work investigating the ways in which pupils view and assess their teachers. Gannaway (1976) found that pupils used a series of criteria by which to judge their teachers. The series was as follows:

Can the teacher keep order?
Can the teacher have a laugh?
Does the teacher understand pupils?

Docking (1980) found very similar characteristics used to describe the 'good' teacher, and he summarized them as follows:

Strict but fair
Approachable
Interested in pupils

These and other, similar pieces of work show the importance to pupils of the teacher keeping order, but also of the ability of the teacher to relate to pupils in a positive way. The lack of any mention of the work that teachers try to teach may come as something of a surprise to some teachers, and is in significant contrast to the emphasis of so much of teacher training.

This type of study has been extended by other workers to consider pupils' explanations of disruption. Ball (1980) found that disruption was the result of pupils' attempts to resolve classroom situations that were unclear to them. Frequently this involved trying to find out the extent of the teacher's power or rights to control the classroom. This corresponds well to the common staffroom descriptions of pupils 'testing out' new teachers or students, and also reflects the importance attached to that aspect of the teacher's role, as indicated by the work referred to above.

Tattum (1982) found that pupils explained disruptive behaviour in somewhat different terms. He found five areas of explanation offered by pupils. These were summarized as follows:

'It was the teacher's fault.'
Not being treated with respect.
Inconsistency of rule application.
Everybody messes about, it's only having a laugh.
It is the fault of the school system.

This idea of pupils explaining their disruptive behaviour in terms of it being the teacher's fault is taken slightly further in the work of Marsh *et al.* (1978). These authors found that disruptive pupils explained misbehaviour generally in terms of it being the teacher's fault. They found that the pupils identified specific teacher acts that were viewed by the pupils as 'wrong'. Disruptive behaviour was the pupils' retribution to the teacher for these wrongs. The most important were:

Nagging
Weakness
Insulting pupils
Unfairness

Two important conclusions would seem to come from all this work on pupils' views of the classroom, their teachers and disruption. This first is that classroom control is seen by pupils as very important, indeed as central to the role of the teacher. Teachers, teacher trainers and others involved in school cannot afford to ignore this. The second conclusion follows from the first. In one way or another, it seems clear that pupils put the 'blame' for disruption in the classroom on the shoulders of the teacher. They see it as a result of the teachers' failure to carry out their expected role. The implications of this will be considered later, but it is first necessary to consider the opposite view of the classroom – the teacher's.

TEACHERS' PERCEPTIONS OF THEIR PUPILS AND OF DISRUPTION

Teachers' perception of disruption is essentially that the pupils are breaking the rules. Hargreaves *et al.* (1975) identify three levels of rule (institutional, situational and personal), different categories or themes of rule that apply in the classroom (such as the 'talk theme' and the 'movement theme'), and different stages in the progress of a lesson at which particular rules are likely to apply (such as 'entry' and 'clearing up'). As far as the teachers were concerned, disruption was what happened when pupils did not observe the rules that were in force at any given moment. The comparison between this perception and the pupils' perception, described above, is interesting, and will be discussed further in the next section.

Teachers have also been asked by researchers to explain the disruptive behaviour of individual pupils, and a good example of that work comes from Lawrence *et al.* (1984). These authors categorized teachers' responses under five headings:

Personality reasons
Reasons relating to the work of the school
Developmental reasons
Random reasons
The pupil's friends

These findings are consistent with work by the present author (Gray, 1987) which investigated the personal constructs used by teachers to distinguish between disruptive and non-disruptive pupils. Five common constructs were elicited:

Easily distracted	Not easily distracted
Malicious	Not malicious
Rude	Polite
Lazy	Hard-working
Short attention span	Long attention span

When these constructs were given to staff against a list of pupils' names, there was a very strong association between a pupil's scores on all of them and his or her nomination as disruptive. In other words, disruptive pupils tended to be described by their teachers in terms towards the left-hand side of the scales above.

Two conclusions come from this very brief review of teachers' perceptions of classroom disruption. The first is that teachers clearly feel that they are in the position of authority; that they make the rules, and pupils should obey those rules. The second conclusion comes from this, and it is that teachers tend to put the 'blame' for disruption on to the pupils. This view will be compared with the pupils' view in the following section.

COMPARISON OF TEACHER AND PUPIL PERCEPTIONS OF DISRUPTION

In comparing the two preceding sections, several points become clear. There seems to be only one point of similarity, and that is the fact that both teachers and pupils consider that classroom control is important, and that the teacher has a central role in achieving that control. From that point on, there is very little agreement between the two groups.

The teachers seem to consider that the basis for their authority and control is the rules, and that they have a right to impose those rules. By comparison, the pupils consider the obligations of the teacher, particularly the obligation to be fair and understanding. Teachers consider disruption to constitute failure of pupils to obey the rules in force: pupils consider disruption to be caused directly by the teacher or as retribution for the teacher's failure to meet his or her obligations to the pupils. It seems to be a conflict between rights and obligations.

Clearly these two sets of understandings of the phenomenon of disruption are the direct opposites of each other. The implications of this can best be understood by considering the attributional frameworks being employed by the two groups. Both teachers and pupils appear to be attributing the cause of the problem externally, and putting the 'blame' for the disruption on to the other party. It is rare for members of either group to mention a cause of disruption that could be described as internal. So teachers and pupils tend not to recognize that they are in any way to blame for what happened: disruption tends to be described as being the fault of the other party.

Work on attribution (for instance, Kelly and Michela, 1980) identifies the danger of the situation described above. It has been found very generally that individuals who use external attribution to explain the cause of problems tend to be unable to resolve the problem, and continue to fail. Suddenly, the fact that teachers and pupils blame each other for disruption becomes serious, because it suggests that neither can do anything about it, and that will make disruption continue.

In this way attribution theory shows how teachers' and pupils' blaming each other for disruption is likely to make the problem persist. Labelling theory shows how it is likely to make things worse. In their analysis of disruption, Hargreaves *et al.* (1975) take the teachers' perceptions of disruptive pupils as a starting point, and consider some of the effects. They identify a process whereby teachers' initial speculation becomes stabilized in the form of fixed labels that are used to describe a pupil. These authors identify two results of this process of labelling. First, the teacher's expectations come to be circumscribed not by the pupil's behaviour but by the label attached to the pupil. In this way teachers come to predict the pupil's behaviour, predict that it will be unacceptable, and disregard evidence to the contrary. Secondly, the teacher's behaviour towards the pupil generates what is described as 'secondary deviance'. In other words, the way that the teacher treats a pupil labelled as disruptive removes from the pupil any opportunity to behave in a non-disruptive way, and forces him or her into new forms of disruption. This would perhaps be the case if a teacher started a lesson with a cautionary comment such as, 'Let's not have any trouble from you today.' This teacher's behaviour towards that pupil could well be seen as 'nagging, insulting or unfair' – after all, the pupil has not done anything yet – and these descriptions were all among the list of teacher offences that evoked disruptive retribution from pupils (Marsh *et al.*, 1978). In this way, teacher labelling forces a pupil into continued disruption.

This analysis suggests that the model representing the condition of pupils who disrupt (Figure 9.1) could become superceded once a pupil becomes labelled as 'disruptive'. For such a pupil, the two vicious circles represented in Figure 9.1 would be likely to persist, but an additional circle involving the teacher's labelling and expectations would be added to it (see Figure 9.2). A pupil who gets embroiled in the sequence of events represented by Figure 9.2 would seem to have an intractable problem. By the time he (and more boys than girls seem to become firmly labelled

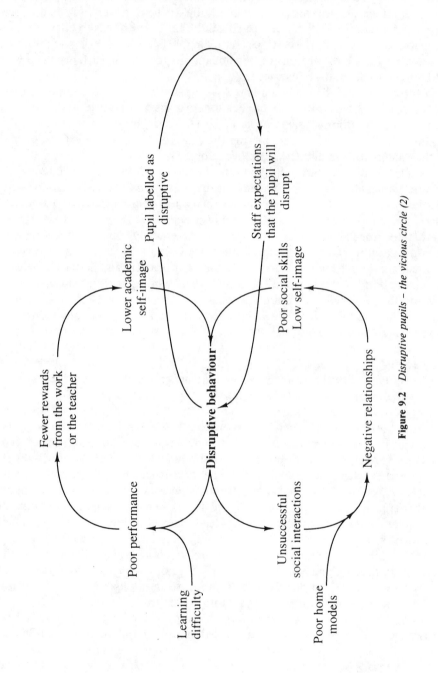

Figure 9.2 *Disruptive pupils – the vicious circle (2)*

as disruptive) leaves school, his social skills with adults and his academic self-image would seem to be severely damaged. This is in direct contrast to anybody's aims of education, and this is one reason why the condition of these pupils needs to be taken very seriously indeed.

Disruptive pupils should also be taken seriously for three other reasons. The first is that they have an enormous adverse effect on events in the classroom, and this is to the detriment of all the other pupils. The second is that disruption is a major source of stress for teachers (Elton, 1989). The third is that the pupils who disrupt need help, and this will be discussed in the following sections.

THE UNHAPPINESS OF DISRUPTIVE PUPILS

This chapter started with a recognition of the fact that some pupils in a classroom might evoke sympathy while others would not, and among this latter group one would expect to find the disrupters. The intervening sections have been devoted to explaining the phenomenon of disruption that these pupils are involved in. It is now time to return to a consideration of the plight of these pupils.

In his review of the phenomenon of happiness, Argyle (1987) identifies a number of factors that are of particular importance in relation to an individual's happiness. Many of these are unrelated to the present consideration; for instance, leisure, money, class and culture. However, two of the most important are of direct and immediate relevance to a consideration of disruptive pupils. These are 'social relationships' and 'work'.

Social relationships

The discussion in the preceding sections suggests that disruptive pupils do not have a rich set of social relationships. They have a few friends, but a large number of their peers do not like them. They are unpopular with the powerful people in the school, namely the teachers. Disruptive pupils are generally unpopular in the school. Perhaps it is even more important to note that the pupils expressed themselves as feeling that they did not have control of their social functioning. This would both make their social interactions unsatisfactory and make social contact anxiety-provoking, rather than positive and supportive.

In concluding his discussion of 'social relationships' and their effect on happiness, Argyle notes the following:

> Social relationships are a major source of happiness, relief from distress and health.
> (Positive) relationships increase happiness by generating joy, providing help, and through shared enjoyable activities. They buffer the effects of stress by increasing self-esteem, suppressing negative emotions and providing help to solve problems.
>
> (p. 31)

This suggests that disruptive pupils do not have the social relationships that can be a source of happiness to other pupils.

Work

The description of disruptive pupils in the preceding sections noted their low achievement and their poor academic self-image. Argyle's conclusions on the relationship between work and happiness include the following comments:

> Job satisfaction can be divided into several components, of which the most important is intrinsic satisfaction with the work itself. This is stronger when the work has skill variety and autonomy, . . . and when there is evidence of successful performance.
> Job satisfaction affects overall life satisfaction, as well as health and mental health.
>
> (p. 50)

The descriptions given are very different from the situation of the disruptive pupil. It is likely that under the heading of 'Job satisfaction' disruptive pupils will also be deprived of aspects of their life that could make them happy.

It would seem from the above paragraphs that disruptive pupils lack two of the major elements of life that could make for positive happiness. Argyle points out that 'happiness' is not just the opposite of 'miserableness', so this is not quite the same as saying that they are likely to be miserable. Despite this caveat, it seems that disruptive pupils really should be included in the group of pupils who are likely to be unhappy. In the same way that generating poor social skills and a low academic self-image is the antithesis of the aims of education, generating unhappiness is not part of the aims of a school. This suggests that schools are failing by their own standards with disruptive pupils.

Such criticism may initially appear to be negative, but the positive side of it needs to be emphasized, and that will be discussed in the following section.

COPING WITH DISRUPTIVE PUPILS

In the preceding two sections, the need to help disruptive pupils was spelt out. It is based on the humanitarian recognition of the fact that they are unhappy, that they are liable to leave school with impaired self-images and social skills, and finally that disruption damages the education of other pupils and causes considerable stress to teachers. These are the reasons for helping these pupils, but that leaves a two-fold problem: how to recognize the needs of individual pupils, and what to do to help.

The recognition of the need to help disruptive pupils arises from the analysis of disruption above, but so does another point. The elements that appear to require intervention most are the teachers' labelling of pupils, and the pupils' academic self-image and social skills, and these things are linked.

In one element of the work outlined above, teachers were asked to rate pupils on constructs that had previously been elicited from other teachers (Gray, 1987). It has already been noted that they rated disruptive pupils as being easily distracted, malicious, rude, lazy and having a short attention span. When these results were analysed further, it was found that teachers' ratings corresponded very closely to the disruptive pupils' own ratings on self-assessment. The teachers' rating of a pupil on the scales of 'rude' and 'malicious' were closely related to the pupil's own self-assessment of social skills. Teachers' ratings of a pupil on 'attention span', 'laziness' and 'distractability' were closely related to the pupils' self-assessed scores for academic self-image.

This finding raises the first optimistic point. The teachers were clearly capable of recognizing the specific problems that the disruptive pupils had. The teachers recognized pupils' poor social skills, and described this (very appropriately) as rudeness; they recognized pupils with a low academic self-image, but described the pupil as lazy or distractible. This suggests that teachers recognize manifestations of the pupils' problems, but they tend to view them in self-referred terms. In other words, they recognize the effect the pupil has on them, the teachers. In itself this is unsurprising, because actors in a situation tend to be chiefly aware of their own position, and ascribe motives to the other actor based on their own experience. The positive aspect of this finding, though, is that it opens up the possibility of the teachers doing something to help the pupils. If a teacher can be persuaded to translate his or her perception that a pupil is 'lazy' into the recognition that the pupil may feel unable to do the work, it opens up avenues of positive action that the teacher may take. Similarly, if the teacher can translate the perception that a pupil is 'rude' into recognition of the fact that the pupil probably lacks social skills, it becomes possible for the teacher to do something to help the pupil.

These changes from 'lazy' to 'lacking confidence' and from 'rude' to 'lacking social skills' may sound trivial and pompous. However, they are important because they open up the possibility of action. This represents a specific example of the move away from categorization of 'handicapped' pupils to recognition of their special educational needs as advocated in the Warnock Report (DES, 1978). The linguistic move that is being advocated also brings these pupils' special educational needs right into the domain of the teacher. The way to help people with poor social skills is by training (Trower *et al.*, 1978). Pupils need to be taught these skills, and there is every reason for teachers to recognize themselves as expert in that activity of teaching. Perhaps relatively few teachers are specialists in 'social skills training' but teachers are skilled at teaching, and such interpersonal skills can be taught to people very successfully. Teachers have the necessary skill and opportunity to meet these special needs of their disruptive pupils, and some of the pastoral work carried out in schools today does attempt to address this need.

Similarly, a pupil's academic self-image is so much a part of a teacher's considerations that recognizing 'lazy' pupils as having a poor academic self-image immediately brings the remedy into the teachers' domain. A teacher can address that need in a pupil in the normal class in the normal course of lessons. In fact, teachers spend much of their training learning how to make it easy for pupils to learn the curriculum. Recognizing the fact that disruptive pupils may be starting from a position of belief in their own inability to learn means that the teacher has to start from a slightly different point. Success and reinforcement have to be built into every stage of a piece of work, particularly the basic stages, rather than assuming that the pupils have already mastered those basics.

The first two problems that disruptive pupils seem to have – academic self-image and social skills – clearly lie in the province of teachers. Although the third, labelling, also closely involves the teachers, it is somewhat less simple for them to address. This is because it is virtually impossible to avoid some of the elements of the labelling process. Confronted with the hundreds of pupils that a secondary teacher teaches each week, it is impossible to develop a deep understanding of and relationship with each one.

Inevitably people in that situation develop a set of descriptions. They use categories to describe the pupils' appearance and the way in which the pupil behaves, and this helps recognition when next they meet. However, using categories to describe pupils is very different from labelling them. Labelling carries with it the prediction that the pupil will behave in a particular way, and these expectations can very easily become self-fulfilling.

I have argued elsewhere (Gray and Richer, 1988) that a major cause of teachers' moving from describing pupils to labelling them is because of the effects of stress on the teacher. Stress makes it increasingly necessary to try and understand a situation, and predictions make a situation less threatening than the unknown or unpredictable. Stress also makes people increasingly egocentric. In the classroom context this makes a teacher tend to see only his or her point of view, fail to notice events that might contradict the predictions that have been made, and put the blame for any problems that arise on to the pupils.

From this, it would seem that teacher stress is not just an occupational hazard, it is also a major source of classroom disruption. Needless to say, this in its turn is likely to be a source of future stress, so teachers, like pupils, can become locked in a vicious circle of disruption. This suggests that one way to help deal with the problem of disruption may be to help teachers manage the stress of their jobs. A specific aspect of this would be to improve the training of teachers in understanding both the processes of disruption and the individuals involved. In addition, this would be considerably improved if teacher training focused more on classroom management skills (Elton, 1989) and on understanding both the processes involved in classroom management and the disruption that results from failure of those skills. In this way it may become possible for teachers to prevent petty disruption escalating, and to prevent themselves and their pupils becoming enmeshed in the vicious circles of disruption. My future work must be aimed at that goal.

REFERENCES

Argyle, M. (1987) *The Psychology of Happiness*. London: Methuen,

Ball, S. (1980) Initial encounters in the classroom. In P. Woods (ed.), *Pupil Strategies*. London: Croom Helm.

Barker-Lunn, J.C. (1970) *Streaming in the Primary School*. Slough: NFER.

Burns, R.B. (1979) *The Self-Concept: In Theory, Measurement, Development and Behaviour*. London: Longman.

Dawson, R. (1982) What concerns teachers about their pupils. *Journal of the Association of Educational Psychologists*, **9**, 37–40.

DES (1978) *Special Educational Needs* (The Warnock Report). London: HMSO.

Docking, J.W. (1980) *Control and Discipline in Schools: Perspectives and Approaches*. London: Harper & Row.

Elton, R. (1989) *Report of the Committee of Enquiry into Discipline in Schools*. London: HMSO.

Galloway, D.M. and Goodwin, C. (1988) *The Education of Disturbing Children*. London: Longman.

Galloway, D.M., Ball, T., Blomfield, D. and Seyd, R. (1982) *Schools and Disruptive Behaviour*. London: Longman.

Gannaway, H. (1976) Making sense of school. In M. Stubbs and S. Delamont (eds), *Explorations in Classroom Observation*. London: John Wiley.

Gray, J.R. (1987) Social skills and classroom disruption. D.Phil. thesis, University of Oxford.

Gray, J.R. and Richer, J. (1988) *Classroom Responses to Disruptive Behaviour*. Basingstoke: Macmillan.

Hargreaves, D., Hestor, S. and Mellor, F. (1975) *Deviance in Classrooms*. London: Routledge and Kegan Paul.

Howarth, R. (1985) A comparison of three methods of investigating social structures in the classroom. Dissertation for the Special Diploma in Education, University of Oxford.

Kelly, H.H. and Michela, J.L. (1980) Attribution theory and research. *Annual Review of Psychology*.

Lawrence, J., Steed, D. and Young, P. (1984) *Disruptive Children – Disruptive Schools?*. London: Croom Helm.

Lindsey, W. and Lindsey, K. (1982) A self-report questionnaire about social difficulties for adolescents. *Journal of Adolescence*, **5**, 63–9.

Marsh, P., Rosser, E. and Harré, R. (1978) *The Rules of Disorder*. London: Routledge and Kegan Paul.

Pye, J. (1989) *Invisible Children*. Oxford: Oxford University Press.

Rutter, M., Tizard, J. and Whitmore, K. (1970) *Health, Education and Behaviour*. London: Longman.

Tattum, D. (1982) *Disruptive Pupils in Schools and Units*. Chichester: John Wiley.

Trower, P., Bryand, P. and Argyle, M. (1978) *Social Skills and Mental Health*. London: Methuen.

Chapter 10

Coping with Unhappy Children Who Have Educational Disadvantages

Theo Cox

This chapter is concerned with educationally disadvantaged children and will attempt to answer the following questions:

- Who are the educationally disadvantaged?
- What are the causes and effects of educational disadvantage?
- In what sense are educationally disadvantaged children unhappy?
- What educational measures can be taken to ameliorate educational disadvantage?

WHO ARE THE EDUCATIONALLY DISADVANTAGED?

Over the past 25 years a number of terms have been coined, particularly in the USA, to describe children who are disadvantaged on account of their social, cultural or economic backgrounds. These include 'poor', 'needy', 'deprived', 'underprivileged', 'underachieving' and 'socially or culturally disadvantaged'. Some of these terms gradually dropped out of use as they came to be perceived as derogatory or demeaning, and current usage favours the term 'disadvantaged' (whether socially, culturally or educationally). To avoid the confusion likely to arise from the use of such global terms it is necessary to elaborate and define them. Since social, cultural or economic disadvantage is likely to impair children's educational achievement and progress, and thereby their ultimate career prospects, it is appropriate to highlight this aspect in a working definition of this term. Thus Passow (1967, p. 16) defined the disadvantaged child as one who 'because of social or cultural characteristics, for example social class, race, ethnic origin, poverty, sex, geographical location etc, comes into the school system with knowledge, skills and attitudes which impede learning.' Presumably the author would accept the converse form of this definition, which would refer to children entering school *without* the knowledge, skills and attitudes which assist learning. Wedge and Essen (1982, p. 11) defined disadvantaged children as 'that group of children who fail to thrive, who fail to mature as much or as quickly physically, or who fail to achieve as well in school as other British children.'

Membership of the 'lower working class' (that is, having semi- or unskilled jobs or being long-term unemployed) is often included in operational definitions of disadvantage, as it is associated with low income, poor housing and other adverse features; but we must bear in mind that membership of a particular social class, on its own, is not a reliable predictor of a child's likely educational achievement, for there is wide variation in this respect among children *within* a particular social class. Also we need to understand the mechanisms through which class membership appears to influence educational achievement.

In addition to socio-economic factors, membership of an ethnic minority group within the prevailing culture is also sometimes included as a possible indicator of disadvantage, partly because of its links with poverty and social disadvantage (as in the case of many lower-working-class black families in the USA) but also because of negative discriminatory attitudes and practices which members of the 'mainstream culture' may adopt towards minority group children and their families (see chapter 10). In this chapter, however, this factor will not be discussed further, since the focus is upon 'indigenous' children in Britain. Its importance as a contributory factor to educational disadvantage is acknowledged, however.

CAUSES AND EFFECTS OF EDUCATIONAL DISADVANTAGE

While studies carried out over the past 40 years have convincingly demonstrated a strong association between children's social-class membership and their educational achievement (for example, Davie *et al.*, 1972; Osborn and Milbank, 1987), relatively few studies have examined the progress and achievement of children specifically defined as disadvantaged. Using an operational definition of disadvantage in terms of family size, income and housing, Wedge and Essen (1982) found that the educational attainment and school behaviour of their disadvantaged group of children were significantly poorer than those of the remaining children in their large National Child Development Study sample, three-quarters of the disadvantaged children having low average reading and mathematics test scores at age 16.

I carried out a longitudinal study of disadvantaged children, which originated in the Schools Council's Compensatory Education Project based at University College Swansea, and focused upon a sample of approximately 100 children attending infant schools serving 'deprived' catchment areas in England and Wales. Half of these children, the disadvantaged group (DG), came from homes judged to be culturally and materially disadvantaged on the basis of a structured parental interview in the home; the other half, the comparison group (CG), came from more advantaged homes within the same deprived areas. In relation to those of the comparison group the homes of the disadvantaged group were characterized by lower income level, poorer quality of housing and accommodation space, lower social class (by father's occupation), more limited provision of play materials and books for the children, and a lower level of parental interest in the child's educational development. The two groups were matched for age, sex, non-verbal reasoning ability and school. The educational progress and achievement of the children throughout their infant school careers were assessed by means of teachers' ratings and individually or group-administered tests.

The children were followed up at age 11 in a further project funded by the Schools

Council, and also at age 15 in a project funded by the Social Science Research Council. In both follow-up studies the children's homes were revisited and reassessed in terms of their quality of cultural and material provision, and, with few exceptions, the homes of the DG children were found to have remained disadvantaged in relation to those of the CG children. Further measures of the children's educational progress and achievement were taken by means of tests and teachers' ratings, and the study as a whole provided a detailed picture of the children's school progress at key stages in their educational careers; at ages 5–7 years, 11 and 15 years. The findings of this study have been published in a number of books and articles (see, for example, Chazan and Williams, 1978; Cox and Jones, 1983; Cox, 1982), and will only be briefly summarized here.

In all three stages of the study the DG children, as a group, performed significantly more poorly than their CG peers on the main measures of educational attainment used, namely reading, spelling, writing (11 and 15 years only), oral expression and mathematics. In the case of reading and oral expression the 'achievement gap' between the two groups widened significantly between the ages of 7 and 15. The children were also rated as less well adjusted to school socially and emotionally. Roughly one-third of the DG children had received some form of special educational provision for their learning difficulties, especially in reading, during their junior and secondary schooling, compared with only 6–10 per cent of CG children. At the late-secondary-school stage, the DG children had a poorer mean attendance record than their CG peers, and nearly three times as many of them left school at the earliest possible date (78 per cent versus 28 per cent). Only three DG pupils (6 per cent), compared with 20 CG pupils (43 per cent), gained five CSE examination passes at Grades 2 to 4 or better (or the equivalent GCE O-level passes).

The main conclusion of this study was that culturally and materially disadvantaged home environments appeared to have an adverse and long-term influence upon the children's educational progress and attainment throughout their school careers, especially in the key areas of literacy skills and mathematics but also, to some extent, in aspects of oral language skills. The second conclusion was that many of the DG children showed a lack of motivation and commitment to their secondary-school education, so that roughly three-quarters of them left school as soon as they legally could, with very little or nothing by way of publicly recognized educational qualifications.

A case study drawn from this longitudinal research project, that of 'Ian', illustrates important aspects of educational disadvantage, including its cumulative adverse effects. Ian was the eighth of nine children living with their parents in a rented council terraced house with all basic amenities, including a safe outdoor play area. The house was in a reasonable state of repair except for some problems caused by damp, and was in a fair decorative state although the furniture was rather shabby. Living conditions were grossly overcrowded, however, and Ian shared a bed with at least one other sibling. The father, judged to be in fair health, had a semi-skilled job, but his wage provided a family income little above subsistence level. The mother seemed to be in normal health but rather overburdened by her circumstances. Ian had very few books or toys and neither parent read to him, but an older child in the family was said to read to him occasionally. His father often played with him and, although he did not attend any form of pre-school, he experienced a good deal of social contact with other children during his early years.

During his three full years at his infant school Ian made virtually no measurable progress in basic literacy and numeracy and did not even enter into the school's graded reading scheme. His scores on standardized reading and spelling tests at age 7 fell below the lowest norms for his age group. This pattern of a lack of measurable progress in the basic skills continued throughout the junior school, despite his placement in remedial classes during his second and fourth years. In his final junior year he was described by his special-class teacher as lacking in concentration, unresponsive to teaching and resentful when corrected. He was also characterized as inconsistent in his behaviour, contra-suggestible and moody. He was still a non-reader and, by now, showed an active dislike of reading activities. He was found to have a defect of vision that needed correction, and was judged by his teacher to have poor speech and hand control and to be in poor general health.

On transfer to secondary school Ian was placed in a full-time remedial/special class and appeared to settle in quite well, although his teacher commented in frustration that he would not wear his glasses. He was followed up again when in his fifth and final year at school, at age 15-plus years. On standardized attainment tests given to the group at that stage he obtained reading and spelling ages of around 7 years, and he fell below the lowest age norms for the mathematics test (10 years 6 months). He was therefore still virtually a non-reader, and his written essay on the subject of 'my school', set as part of the study, showed many misspellings, reflecting a lack of awareness of letter–sound correspondence, very basic sentence structure and limited vocabulary. His school attendance in his final year was very poor and he frequently truanted with the knowledge of his parents. He left school at the very earliest date possible – before his sixteenth birthday.

A further visit to his home during his fifth year revealed that his father had been unemployed for a number of years and appeared to be in poor health. An older sibling still at home was also unemployed and the parents reported having debt problems. The father expressed concern about Ian's failure to learn to read and took the view that the school was mainly responsible for this, adding that he himself could not read very well (although he was very articulate), and that older children in the family had also failed to learn to read at school. He admitted that Ian was often absent from school and attributed this to his unhappiness about being unable to read.

During a personal interview before leaving school Ian expressed an aspiration to be a panel-beater or to join the army, but his expectation was that he would be a petrol-pump attendant on leaving school. (He already had a part-time job in a service station.) Information subsequently provided by the school indicated that he had first gained employment as a general assistant in a local firm, and later as a building labourer, after a period of unemployment.

Ian's home circumstances were clearly very disadvantaged in terms of poverty, overcrowding and extremely limited educational stimulation and support from his parents. In addition, the fact that older children from the same family had failed to learn to read at school (according to the father) may have lowered Ian's teachers' expectations of his academic potential, and the apparent tradition of family unemployment may have further weakened his academic motivation. Also, his defective vision seems to have gone uncorrected due to his refusal to wear glasses. This combination of adverse home background and physical factors with negative attitudes on the part of Ian and his parents proved totally resistant to the remedial efforts of his teachers, in both ordinary and special classes. His resistance to learning seemed to be linked with a history of poor relations with his teachers, dating from his early school years, and it is also possible that their negative perceptions of Ian as a pupil and their low expectations of his educational potential, given his family background, may have vitiated their efforts to teach him. Thus Ian's severe educational disadvantage appeared to stem from a combination of home, school and personal factors.

However, not all of the disadvantaged children underachieved or showed special educational needs, for the study yielded some remarkable examples of children who overcame their environmental handicaps to reach average or even above-average levels of attainment (see Cox and Jones, 1983). Moreover, although the disadvantaged children *as a group* obtained significantly lower attainment test scores than the control group, there were some DG pupils who outperformed some of their CG peers. Other studies of disadvantaged children have confirmed that certain individuals overcome their disadvantages by their achievements in scholastic or career terms, and these studies have tried to identify those family, personal or other factors which appear to distinguish such 'resilient' disadvantaged children from the rest (Pilling, 1990; Osborn, 1990).

It is clear from this and other similar studies that a range of home background factors can have a powerful influence upon children's educational development, although this must not be regarded as totally deterministic. Another potentially major source of influence is the school; the amount of research on this topic is small compared with that on the contribution of home background factors, although it is growing. Mortimore *et al.* (1988) carried out an in-depth, longitudinal study of the educational attainment and progress of 2,000 pupils in 50 randomly selected London primary/junior schools between the ages of 7 and 11. They found that while parents' social class, based on the father's occupation, was powerfully related to the children's *initial* attainments in reading, writing and mathematics on entry to their junior schools or departments, the nature of the primary/junior school attended was a more powerful influence than social class upon the *progress* in these areas made by the children during their junior years. This did not mean that the schools reversed the pattern of social-class differences in attainment found initially, for that pattern was maintained during each of the junior years. Rather, they found that the effective schools in their sample tended to boost the educational performance of *all* of their pupils, regardless of their social background, in contrast to the less effective schools.

Mortimore *et al.* also found some evidence that the teachers in the sample schools showed some differences in their attitudes and classroom behaviour towards children from different social backgrounds. In particular, they observed that some teachers appeared to have different expectations of pupils from manual backgrounds, regardless of the children's objective performance on educational tests. They tended to supervise the work of these children more closely than that of the children from non-manual backgrounds. Mortimore *et al.* regard such differential teacher expectations and behaviour as a potential impediment to the future attainments of the children from manual backgrounds, and as something which should therefore be challenged. Their findings lent support to those of Rutter *et al.*'s earlier (1979) study of the differential effectiveness of a sample of London secondary schools with regard to the pupils' attainments and behaviour, but went beyond these in quantifying the size of the school effects in relation to those of the home.

IN WHAT SENSE ARE EDUCATIONALLY DISADVANTAGED CHILDREN UNHAPPY?

While we must be careful not to overgeneralize about the likely effects of educational disadvantage upon children, because of the demonstrated resilience of some of them, we can say that experience of such disadvantage puts children at risk of 'unhappiness', in the sense that depressed educational performance may impair their long-term career and life prospects. This does not necessarily mean that disadvantaged children who underachieve are emotionally unhappy, since they may defend against their lack of scholastic success by lowering their educational or career aspirations or even by rejecting the aims and values of the school altogether. However, research has shown a link between educational failure and lowered self-esteem, particularly that aspect of self-esteem which relates to the role of the pupil (Burns, 1982). Moreover, comparisons between disadvantaged children and those from more favoured circumstances generally show that the former appear to be less well adjusted, socially and emotionally, and to show a higher incidence of behaviour problems, particularly of the 'conduct disorder' variety (Davie *et al.*, 1972; Cox and Jones, 1983). Although one must be careful not to conclude from this that these children are less mentally healthy, and therefore unhappy, it should be recognized that the conditions which they experience (such as poverty, overcrowding and atypical family structures) are potential stress-inducing factors, certainly for their parents and at least indirectly for them. More research is needed on this question, for the research on the effects of educational disadvantage tends to have focused upon its academic consequences rather than its personal and emotional effects.

During the past decade the number of children experiencing adverse family conditions has significantly increased, in line with changes in economic conditions, demographic structures and social policies in the UK. Thus, according to Bradshaw (1990), more children are now living in low-income families and the number living in poverty has doubled. At the same time, the gap between the living standards of poor families and those of the rest of the population has grown wider, he argues, compounding the disadvantages experienced by their children. Employment prospects for relatively unqualified school leavers have also significantly declined.

WHAT EDUCATIONAL MEASURES CAN BE TAKEN TO AMELIORATE EDUCATIONAL DISADVANTAGE?

If educational intervention is to make its maximal impact on the life chances of disadvantaged children, it should be coupled with wider social and economic measures to improve the circumstances of their families and their employment prospects (Halsey, 1975; Bradshaw, 1990). However, even without this wider back-up, well-planned and well-delivered educational programmes aimed at simultaneously improving the quality of disadvantaged children's pre-school, school and post-school education and increasing the level of educational support offered by their parents should bring lasting benefits to the children and are, therefore, justified in their own right.

The Plowden Report on primary education (Central Advisory Council for Education, 1967) highlighted the problem of low standards in schools serving 'deprived areas', where the homes of many children appeared to provide little support and stimulus for learning, and argued strongly for a policy of positive discrimination in favour of such schools so as to enable them to provide a 'compensatory environment' for their pupils. Through this policy, extra resources were to be chanelled to these schools, including more experienced and better-qualified teachers and teachers' aides, and funds for the improvement of dilapidated school buildings. In addition, the Report advocated the expansion of nursery education to allow the part-time attendance of all 4- and 5-year-old children living in those deprived areas, as well as other measures. A range of criteria were suggested for the identification of the most deprived school areas, including a high proportion of unskilled or semi-skilled workers, of large or incomplete families, of overcrowding and of relative poverty as indicated by the receipt of free school meals.

In response to this major report, the government of the day funded a number of initiatives. One of these was the Urban Programme, under which money paid to selected local authorities was to be allocated to education, housing, health and welfare programmes. Another was the Educational Priority Areas research initiative (EPA), which took the form of a series of action research programmes centred on selected inner cities and areas in England and Scotland (but not Wales) and directed by Professor A.H. Halsey of Oxford University. The common aims of these programmes were to raise educational standards; to raise teacher morale; to improve links between home and school by increasing parental involvement in their children's education; and, finally, to assist in giving the local communities a sense of responsibility. The results from these various programmes were reported in a series of volumes (see Halsey, 1972).

Some criticisms of the Plowden Report's recommendations and of the government's subsequent policies and programmes have been summarized by Mortimore and Blackstone (1982). One of these concerned the notion of identifying a 'deprived area' as the focus for intervention in disadvantage. Some argued that designating specific school catchment areas as deprived was ineffective, in view of evidence that there were more disadvantaged families living outside such areas than were living within them (Barnes and Lucas, 1975). Another question raised was whether the target for intervention should be on individually identified 'at-risk' families living within designated deprived areas, or upon all children and families within them. Identifying individual children and families obviously carries the risk of socially stigmatizing them, even though the aim is positive discrimination, and it is also administratively expensive to do effectively. Channelling provision and resources to all children within a designated deprived-area school avoids this difficulty, but may result in tensions between different schools competing for the additional funds. Nevertheless, some form of school-based policy for intervention seems to offer the best way forward.

Given that state funds for intervening in disadvantage are inevitably limited, we need to ask whether such an investment is better focused upon a particular age group of children or spread across the whole age range from birth to 19. In practice the bulk of the investment, both in the UK and in the USA has so far been targeted at pre-school and early-primary-school children and their families. This is not surprising, since a very strong psychological case can be made for the importance of such early intervention. The pre-school years are widely regarded as the period of most rapid development, and it has been estimated by one psychologist that half of the variation in measured adult intelligence is predictable at age 5 (Bloom, 1964). On this premise, early environmental experiences could be expected to have lasting effects, and the idea of preventing educational failure by early intervention makes much sense.

Early educational intervention

The Plowden Report argued that (part-time) attendance at a nursery school is desirable for most children but especially so for children from socially deprived backgrounds, on account of their need for 'the verbal stimulus, the opportunities for constructive play, a more richly differentiated environment and the access to medical care that good nursery schools can provide' (paragraph 165). The Report recommended that the building of new nursery schools and extensions to existing schools should start in the designated educational priority areas and spread outward, and their suggested *minimum* goal was that all 4–5-year-olds living in such areas should have the opportunity of part-time attendance, with perhaps 50 per cent having full-time places.

The Plowden Committee's advocacy of nursery education for disadvantaged young children appeared to be based upon oral evidence and research regarding the extent to which it could compensate for social deprivation and, in particular, for the 'poverty of language' which was judged to be a major cause of their later educational failure. This notion of compensatory education underpinned the federally funded pre-school intervention programmes in the USA which started in the early 1960s and were aimed particularly at poor, lower-working-class black children. These came to be known as the Head Start programmes, and they continue to this day with ongoing federal or state funding. In contrast, although successive British governments have expressed concern over the failure of the educational system to create equality of opportunity for children from different social backgrounds, the substantial investment in nursery education urged by the Plowden Committee has never materialized. In a major study of the long-term effects of pre-school education in Britain, Osborn and Milbank (1987) found that 46 per cent of the most disadvantaged children in their national sample of nearly 9,000 children had received no form of pre-school education, compared with only 10 per cent of the most advantaged children. They point out that the expansion of pre-school educational provision during the period 1975–85 was accounted for mainly by the growth of the independent pre-school playgroup movement, which tends to serve middle-class families, and also the expansion of nursery classes attached to LEA primary schools, coupled with an increase in the number of under-5s being admitted to infant reception classes in those schools. Their research, however, showed that the quality of both the provision and the curriculum offered in the primary schools for 4–5-year-olds was less appropriate and favourable than that available in nursery schools, day nurseries and private playgroups.

Although the theory underlying the compensatory nursery education movement is clear, we have to ask whether the predicted educational benefits do actually materialize, especially in the longer term. A rigorous analysis of the long-term effects of 12 American Head Start programmes, selected for the quality of their planning and evaluation, revealed very encouraging results, including a significant reduction of the proportion of children placed in special classes or 'retained in grade', improved achievement motivation and a higher take up of post-secondary education or employment (Consortium for Longitudinal Studies, 1983). This is indeed positive evidence that early educational intervention can achieve lasting benefits for disadvantaged children, although Woodhead (1985) cautions against extrapolating these results to the British situation directly because of the special character of the samples of children selected for the Head Start programmes.

In Britain, a number of studies have demonstrated short- or medium-term educational gains for specially devised and structured early intervention programmes targeted on disadvantaged children, including some pre-school projects forming part of the EPA programme (see, for example, Smith, 1975; Kellaghan, 1977; and Chazan and Cox, 1976, for a review of the earlier programmes). Many of these programmes were designed specifically to produce linguistic and cognitive gains in the children receiving them, on the premise that the diffuse curriculum of the ordinary nursery unit did not meet these children's particular educational needs. The benefits associated with such programmes do not necessarily outstrip those achieved through good-quality general nursery education (Woodhead, 1976; Smith and Connolly, 1986). However, according to Hawkridge *et al.* (1968), there is strong support from the research literature that the most successful compensatory early education programmes are characterized by the following features:

1. careful planning and a clear statement of academic objectives;
2. the use of small groups and a high degree of individualization of instruction;
3. instruction and materials that are clearly relevant and closely linked to the programme objectives;
4. high-intensity treatment;
5. teacher training in the methods of the programme.

In addition, the active involvement of parents in the programme may be crucial for the longer-term success of early intervention (Bronfenbrenner, 1974).

Despite the emphasis in the research literature on the value of structured educational pre-school and early school programmes, Osborn and Milbank's (1987) study showed that ordinary pre-school education of the kind typically offered in our nursery schools and playgroups significantly benefited the children receiving it. The educational attainments and behaviour of a large sample of children receiving various kinds of pre-school education were compared with those of children not receiving such education at ages 5 and 10 years respectively. All forms of pre-school education were found to be beneficial, but the highest gains were achieved by the children attending nursery schools or playgroups and the lowest by children attending nursery classes attached to primary schools. These gains remained even after the children's test scores were statistically adjusted to take account of a number of important home and family background variables. Moreover, it was found that pre-school education boosted the educational achievement of the socially disadvantaged children at least as much as those of children from more favoured home backgrounds.

What of the role of the parents in their children's early education? As stated earlier, Bronfenbrenner (1974) argued that the active participation of parents in these programmes was essential for their longer-term success, on the grounds that parents can sustain the effects of the programmes even when they are discontinued, possibly through increased expectations of the children's educational performance. The children's increased achievement motivation may also serve to sustain their earlier educational gains (Sylva, 1989). Nursery schools and units provide an ideal basis for the encouragement and guidance of active parental involvement in their children's education, whether this is focused upon language and pre-literacy skills or spread more widely over the full range of children's development. Features of successful, school-based, parental involvement programmes have been described in the literature (see, for example, Donachy, 1987; Hirst and Hannon, 1990). A useful source book for nursery and infant teachers wishing to involve their children's parents in their education has been provided by Tizard *et al.* (1981).

Another possibility is to combine nursery education with health and social provision for pre-school children and their families in a children's centre, as originally suggested in the Plowden Report. A good example of such combined provision is the Pen Green Centre for under-5 children and their families in Corby, which provides both nursery education on a sessional basis throughout the day and a range of activities and services for the parents, including a toy library, a health workshop and a welfare rights course for single parents (Widlake, 1986). Parental involvement can also be achieved through educational home-visiting programmes, which may use health visitors (Child Development Project, 1984), Portage workers (Cameron, 1982), or teachers (Raven, 1980).

Primary and secondary education

No matter how effective the education offered to disadvantaged children at the pre-school stage, we cannot realistically expect it to inoculate them against the subsequent stresses and disadvantages they may face, or to guarantee their long-term educational success, despite the encouraging research results reported earlier. It is essential that the quality of the children's formal education is maintained throughout the primary- and secondary-school years, and that the parents should continue to receive support and encouragement to collaborate with teachers in their children's education. This means that the schools will need to be well staffed and resourced, as envisaged by the Plowden Committee, and that both teachers and parents maintain appropriately high standards and expectations of the children's educational performance and progress. This need is highlighted by a recent HMI report which commented on patchy standards of instruction and unstable staffing patterns in inner-city schools (DES, 1992). Mortimore (1990) voiced the danger that urban schools facing considerable social problems will deteriorate and their pupils will only have access to second-rate provision.

In their study of the effectiveness of primary schools Mortimore *et al.* (1988) identified several key factors associated with school effectiveness for all pupils, including those from disadvantaged backgrounds. Among these were intellectually challenging and clearly focused teaching, parental involvement and the creation of a positive learning climate. At the secondary-school level, reports by Rutter *et al.* (1979) and ILEA (1984) have made similar recommendations.

Given the fundamental importance of competence in language and literacy skills and knowledge to later academic achievement, I would argue that primary and secondary schools should take all possible steps to secure the development of basic competence in these skills in children from disadvantaged backgrounds. Teachers of such pupils will have to decide whether this can be achieved through the normal curriculum and normal teaching methods, or whether more focused and more structured teaching will be required, at least for a time. As discussed in relation to pre-school education, a case can certainly be made for the provision of structured language and cognitive programmes, provided that these complement rather than replace the normal curriculum. (See Curtis and Blatchford, 1981, for an example of such a complementary programme.) One of their advantages is that they guarantee a minimum amount of adult–child linguistic interaction of the facilitating kind that disadvantaged children do not have enough experience of in their own homes. This is particularly important, since infant-school reception classes often have much less favourable adult–child ratios than nursery schools or playgroups (Osborn and Milbank, 1987). If teachers do not make use of such programmes, they must rely entirely upon creating and exploiting the opportunities for adult–child dialogue within the context of the normal curriculum (Clark, 1988). Nursery and infant class observational studies by Tizard *et al.* (1984) and Wells (1985) have highlighted some important limitations in the quality of individual teacher–pupil talk in naturally occurring classroom situations, particularly in the case of working-class pupils, and have have offered helpful advice to teachers on how to improve such dialogue.

Given the particularly heavy demands made on teachers in schools serving disadvantaged areas, it is essential that, as well as having the most favourable teacher–pupil ratios and resources possible, such schools should seek to maximize the amount of contact such children will have with adults in instructional contexts, particularly in relation to language and literacy. Mention has already been made of pre-school parental involvement programmes; it is vital for these to continue during the primary-school years and, where necessary, into the secondary-school stage. There is now a solid body of literature testifying to the benefits of active parental involvement in the teaching of children to read, following the pioneering Haringey Reading Project, which was centred on a number of infant schools serving lower-working-class areas (Hewison and Tizard, 1984). (A useful review of this research has been provided by Topping and Wolfendale, 1985.) In addition, the involvement of secondary-school pupils in language and literacy work in primary schools represents another resource.

In order to cater for children who fail to make sufficient progress in the early stages of learning to read, such as 'Ian' in the longitudinal study described earlier, it will be essential for schools to have a well-planned back-up system for the early detection and remediation of reading difficulties, such as the Reading Recovery scheme (Clay, 1979), recently endorsed by the present government.

At the secondary-school stage there is a strong case for a radical overhaul of the present curriculum and examination system, if the pattern of low academic motivation, poor attendance and non-participation in public examinations revealed in my longitudinal study of disadvantaged children is to be changed for the better. One way of achieving this is by providing a special curriculum for such pupils which partly or even wholly replaces the normal curriculum. The Lower Attaining Pupils Programme (LAPP) introduced by the government in 1982 represents such a development. This was targeted on undermotivated and underachieving pupils, particularly in the fourth and fifth secondary-school years, for whom the existing public examination system did not cater and who were not benefiting fully from school. A wide range of curricular innovations was developed by the participating schools, although not all of these offered alternative curricula to the pupils targeted. The project as a whole was evaluated by the National Foundation for Educational Research (1988) and was appraised by HMI in a special report (DES, 1989). The latter commended many promising features of the various initiatives and judged that they had raised the general status of the pupils in their schools and had fostered their oracy and thinking skills in particular, but were less successful in raising their levels of literacy and numeracy. The report expressed major disappointment at the relatively poor school-attendance figures for these pupils, the teachers' insufficiently high expectations of their pupils' capacities, and the lack of sufficient curricular differentiation to meet their identified learning needs. They concluded that the LAPP experiences provided a valuable bases from which to make provision for lower-attaining pupils within the framework of the National Curriculum.

The HMI report on the LAPP project, however, did not discuss the central educational issue of whether to provide a special, alternative curriculum for the lower-attaining pupils. While the aims of such curricula are commendable, there is a serious danger that such initiatives will marginalize the pupils they seek to help, by cutting them off from the mainstream curriculum and thereby reducing their ultimate career and life prospects (Mortimore and Blackstone, 1982). The best way forward is to institute a more general reform of the secondary-school curriculum and examination system, within the framework of the National Curriculum, with the aim of achieving flexibility of subject content and teaching method in order to cater for widely differing interests, learning needs, abilities and aspirations among secondary pupils in general. The introduction of the GCSE examination system in 1986 was a wholesale reform of just this kind and its benefits to many pupils are widely recognized, although it falls short of what is required to boost the motivation and achievements of disadvantaged children, as Mortimore (1990) points out. He cites the relatively modest GCSE grades of significant numbers of pupils taking the examination, and their poor participation rates in further and higher education. Other major 'mainstream' innovations have been the introduction of the Technical and Vocational Education Initiative (TVEI) and the development of pupil records of achievement.

SUMMARY

To sum up, the following measures should be taken to combat the adverse effects of educational disadvantage:

1 the provision of high-quality nursery education at ages 4 and 5, coupled with active parental participation;
2 the provision of well-resourced and clearly focused teaching during the primary-school years, with particular emphasis upon developing competence in language and literacy, supported by a continuation of parental involvement;
3 the establishment in schools of a careful monitoring system which will identify cases of early reading or language difficulties so that well-planned intervention can take place;
4 the encouragement of teachers in schools with a high proportion of disadvantaged pupils to raise their levels of expectation of their pupils' capabilities;
5 the continuation of the general reform of the curriculum and examination system for secondary-age pupils, with the aim of providing for a wide range of pupils' abilities, needs and interests and of encouraging them to participate in further or higher education and training, a system which, itself, is now undergoing much needed reform.

Such measures will, of course, take place within the broad framework of the National Curriculum, which quite rightly is a curriculum of entitlement for all. The education of disadvantaged children should not be separate or different from that of children in general, but should be integral to it. Improvements to the wider educational system, such as those recommended by the government-appointed team of 'three wise men' concerning curriculum organization and practice in primary schools (Alexander *et al.*, 1992), are likely to carry particular benefits for disadvantaged children.

REFERENCES

Alexander, R., Rose, J. and Woodhead, C. (1992) *Curriculum Organisation and Classroom Practice in Primary Schools* London: HMSO.

Barnes, J.H. and Lucas, H. (1975) Positive discrimination in education: individuals, groups and institutions. In J. Barnes (ed.), *Educational Priority. Vol. 3: Curriculum Innovation in London EPAs.* London: HMSO.

Bloom, B.S. (1964) *Stability and Change in Human Characteristics.* New York: John Wiley.

Bradshaw, J. (1990) *Child Poverty and Deprivation in the UK.* London: National Children's Bureau.

Bronfenbrenner, U. (1974) *A Report on Longitudinal Programs. Vol. 2: Is Early Intervention Effective?* Washington, DC: Department of Health, Education and Welfare.

Burns, R. (1982) *Self Concept Development and Education.* London: Holt, Rinehart and Winston.

Cameron, R.J. (1982) *Portage: Pre-schoolers, Parents and Professionals.* Windsor: NFER-Nelson.

Central Advisory Council for Education (England) (1967) *Children and Their Primary Schools. Vol. 1: Report.* London: HMSO.

Chazan, M. and Cox, T. (1976) Language programmes for disadvantaged children. In V.P. Varma and P. Williams (eds), *Piaget, Psychology and Education.* London: Hodder and Stoughton.

Chazan, M. and Williams, P. (1978) *Deprivation and the Infant School.* Oxford: Basil Blackwell.

Child Development Project (1984) *Child Development Programme.* Bristol: University of Bristol Early Child Development Unit.

Clark, M.M. (1988) *Children under Five.* London: Gordon and Breach.

Clay, M. (1979) *The Early Detection of Reading Difficulties.* Auckland: Heinemann Educational Books.

Consortium for Longitudinal Studies (1983) *As the Twig Is Bent: Lasting Effects of Pre-School Programs.* Lawrence Erlbaum.

Cox, T. (1982) Disadvantaged fifteen-year-olds. *Educational Studies*, **8**, 1–13.

Cox, T. and Jones, G. (1983) *Disadvantaged 11-Year-Olds.* Oxford: Pergamon Press.

Curtis, A. and Blatchford, P. (1981) Meeting the needs of socially handicapped children. *Educational Research*, **24**, 31–42.

Davie, R., Butler, N.R. and Goldstein, H. (1972) *From Birth to Seven.* London: Longman.

DES (Department of Education and Science) (1989) *Education Observed 12: The Lower Attaining Pupils Programme 1982–88.* Middlesex: DES Publications.

DES (1992) *Standards in Education: The Annual Report of HM Senior Chief Inspector of Schools.* London: HMSO.

Donachy, W. (1987) Parental participation in a language programme. In M.M. Clark (ed.), *Roles, Responsibilities and Relationships in the Education of the Young Child.* Educational Review Occasional Publication no. 13. Birmingham: University of Birmingham Faculty of Education.

Halsey, A.H. (ed.) (1972) *Educational Priority. Vol. 1: E.P.A. Problems and Priorities.* London: HMSO.

Halsey, A.H. (1975) Sociology and the equality debate. *Oxford Educational Review*, **1**, 9–23.

Hawkridge, D.G., Chapulsky, A.B. and Roberts, A.O. (1968) *A Study of Selected Exploratory Programs for the Education of the Disadvantaged*. US Office of Education and Welfare Report, Project 089013.

Hewison, J. and Tizard, B. (1984) Parental involvement and reading attainment. *British Journal of Education Psychology*, **50**, 209–15.

Hirst, K. and Hannon, P. (1990) An evaluation of a pre-school home teaching project. *Educational Research*, **32**, 33–9.

ILEA (Inner London Education Authority) (1984) *Improving Secondary Schools* (The Hargreaves Report). London: ILEA.

Kellaghan, T. (1977) *The Evaluation of an Intervention Programme for Disadvantaged Children*. Windsor: NFER-Nelson

Mortimore, P. (1990) City limits. *First Annual Lecture on Inner City Achievement*. London: Times Educational Supplement Promotions.

Mortimore, P. and Blackstone, T. (1982) *Disadvantage and Education*. London: Heinemann.

Mortimore, P., Sammons, P., Stoll, L., Lewis, D. and Ecob, R. (1988) *School Matters*. London: Open Books.

National Foundation for Educational Research (1988) *The Search for Success: An Overview with 8 Short Reports and Broadsheets*. Windsor: NFER.

Osborn, A.F. (1990) Resilient children: a longitudinal study of high achieving socially disadvantaged children. *Early Child Development and Care*, **62**, 23–47.

Osborn, A.F. and Milbank, J.E. (1987) *The Effects of Early Education*. Oxford: Clarendon Press.

Passow, A.H. (1967) *Education of the Disadvantaged*. New York: Holt, Rinehart and Winston.

Pilling, D. (1990) *Escape from Disadvantage*. London: Falmer Press.

Raven, J. (1980) *Parents and Teachers: A Study of a Home Visiting Scheme*. London: Hodder and Stoughton.

Rutter, M., Maughan, B., Mortimore, P. and Ouston, J. (1979) *Fifteen Thousand Hours*. London: Open Books.

Smith, G. (1975) *Educational Priority. Vol. 4: The West Riding E.P.A.* London: HMSO.

Smith, P.K. and Connolly, K.J. (1986) Experimental studies of the preschool environment: the Sheffield project. *Advances in Early Education and Day Care*, **4**, 27–66.

Sylva, K. (1989) Does early intervention 'work'? *Archives of Disease in Childhood*, **64**, 1103–4.

Tizard, B. and Hughes, M. (1984) *Young Children Learning: Talking and Thinking at Home and at School*. London: Fontana.

Tizard, B., Mortimore, J. and Burchell, B. (1987) *Involving Parents in Nursery and Infant Schools*. London: Grant McIntyre.

Topping, K. and Wolfendale, S. (eds) (1985) *Parental Involvement in Children's Reading*. London: Croom Helm.

Wedge, P. and Essen, J. (1982) *Children in Adversity*. London: Pan Books.

Wells, G. (1985) *Language Learning and Education*. Windsor: NFER-Nelson.

Widlake, P. (1986) *Reducing Educational Disadvantage*. Milton Keynes: Open University Press.

Wood, D. (1980) *Working with Under Fives*. London: Grant McIntyre.

Woodhead, M. (1976) *Intervening in Disadvantage*. Windsor: NFER.

Woodhead, M. (1985) Pre-school education has long term effects but can they be generalised? *Oxford Review of Education*, **11**, 133–55.

Chapter 11

Coping with Unhappy Children Who Are from Ethnic Minorities

Kedar Nath Dwivedi

In addition to the distress and unhappiness described in other chapters in this book, ethnic minority children are also vulnerable to the distress and unhappiness caused by direct or indirect racial prejudice, disadvantage, discrimination and abuse, and by the undermining of their culture, identity and self-esteem. This chapter aims to touch briefly upon some of these issues.

RACE, ETHNICITY AND CULTURE IN THE UK

Race, ethnicity and culture are all rather vague terms. The word 'race' refers sometimes to social groups from different parts of the world, but at other times to certain morphological features. In fact, colour of skin and hair plays a major role in such perceptions. People with certain cultural characteristics, such as language, religion and racial identity, are often referred to as an ethnic group. However, the word 'ethnic' is usually abused and the terms 'ethnic population' or 'ethnic families' are used to refer to coloured populations or coloured families, as if white populations or families did not have any ethnicity!

'Racism' or 'racialism' refers to beliefs based on racial prejudice and practices of racial discrimination, whether deliberate or unintentional. People who are prejudiced tend to 'prejudge' individuals or groups without adequate knowledge and are unwilling to change their views in spite of sufficient factual evidence to the contrary. Thus, a larger proportion of coloured people than whites in the UK suffer from economic and social disadvantages such as unemployment or poor jobs, lesser opportunities for education and training, poor housing, etc. There is also a tendency to suppress or dismiss their culture in the name of integration, and most social policies tend to ignore minority cultures.

The word 'disadvantage' may sometimes be wrongly used to imply that the people who are disadvantaged are in some way 'inferior' or inadequate and have therefore brought this misfortune on themselves. Thus, they are themselves to be blamed for their own situation. There are similar attitudes towards developing countries. In fact, socio-economic disadvantages in developing countries are mainly due to unequal treatment and opportunities at a global level. Similar inequalities appear to be built into and perpetuated by the structure and organization of society in the UK (Mares *et al.*, 1985).

The 'melting-pot' concept of a single culture resulting from the blending of different ethnic groups has to give way to a pluralistic view of recognition and acceptance of differences among various ethnic groups. The 'multicultural' approach aims to promote greater understanding between the different cultures of a multicultural society and to alleviate inequalities based upon cultural differences. The 'multiracial' approach focuses more upon white perceptions of coloured communities and on race relations and racial inequalities. Most children, whether from majority or minority ethnic groups, have to learn to live with ethnic diversity.

The novelist Ruth Prawer Jhabvala (1987) observes:

> To live in India and be at peace, one must to a very considerable extent become Indian and adopt Indian attitudes, habits, beliefs, assume, if possible, an Indian personality. But how is this possible? And even if it were possible – without cheating oneself – would it be desirable? Should one try to become something other than what one is?
>
> (p. 21)

Historical background

The settlement and growth of ethnic minority communities in the UK took place in the 1950s and 1960s, when British employers actively encouraged people from the New Commonwealth to come and work for them because of labour shortages and a booming economy. About 60 per cent of the migrants then came from Jamaica, the remainder from Trinidad, Barbados and the smaller islands. The main areas of settlement were London, Manchester, Leeds, Nottingham, Bristol, Northampton and Reading (Edwards, 1979). The term 'Afro-Caribbean' is now commonly used to indicate people from the West Indies who are of African origin. In fact, the population of the West Indies includes many different ethnic groups, and people of Indian origin are the most numerous. However, the migrants from the West Indies to this country were mainly of African origin (Black, 1989).

For a Caribbean migrant, Britain was the 'historico-cultural navel of the West Indian Society' (Hiro, 1971). It was rather like 'coming home' to a society of which the migrant regarded himself or herself as an integral part. In the West Indies, schools were dominated by textbooks written in England, careers by the examination boards of Oxford and Cambridge, and surroundings by the monuments of English admirals and places named after English towns. But the expected welcome and the acceptance 'at home' turned out to be something very different: *The Times* (2 November 1976) declared 'our nation has never faced a greater danger'.

In the 1970s and early 1980s there were also some refugee migrations of Ugandan Asians and Chileans, among others. Most of the refugees from Uganda were of Indian origin. Apart from migrants from the Indian subcontinent (mostly for economic reasons, and either directly or via East Africa), there are also some South East Asian (for example, Chinese and Vietnamese) migrants in the UK.

Even though the non-white migrants to Britain in the 1970s were only one-third of the total number of migrants, the use of the word 'immigrant' in the newspaper headlines invariably meant black, and such a black presence in the country was often described as an 'invasion'. Invasion is a very emotive metaphor, as in the invasion of a country by enemy soldiers or of the body by cancer cells (Sontag, 1979). Moreover, in recent court judgments the definition of 'illegal entrant' has been enlarged. Thus an individual's status can be redefined as 'illegal' at any time if the individual on entry failed to disclose material facts, even though he or she was not specifically asked to do so at the time and did not realize they were relevant (Mares *et al.*, 1985).

About 10 per cent of the British population are from ethnic minorities. The majority of ethnic minority populations live in inner-city areas, and in certain areas there may be a large proportion of the population that is of ethnic minority origin. Nearly half of the coloured population in the UK were actually born in the country.

Attitudes to ethnic minorities

Black (1989) writes,

> an ethnic minority is a group of individuals who consider themselves separate from the general population and are seen by the population at large to be distinct because of one or more of the following: common geographical or racial origin, skin colour, language, religious beliefs and practices, or dietary customs.

(p. 1)

Many of the Asian, Cypriot and Turkish immigrants who were essentially sojourners, and whose return has been continually delayed, maintain close ties with their country of origin and often make generous contributions to community projects, schools, etc., in their 'home' country. Such demonstrations of generosity, loyalty and identity have also been resented by some people, as evidenced by the 'cricket' test of Norman Tebbit (which saw support of a particular country in a cricket match as proof of exclusive loyalty to that country). Coloured immigrants have often experienced the same negative attitudes whether they considered Britain or other countries as their 'home'.

Thus, a large number of migrant families experience dislocation, culture shock, loss of informal support systems, an alien, threatening and hostile culture, restrictive and humiliating immigration procedures, considerable social and psychological pressures and various forms of socio-economic discrimination. In Britain 'migrants' are often subjected to a stereotype of themselves and have projected on to them a variety of undesirable characteristics. Even their minor crimes, such as motoring offences, are recorded on a Special Branch Register (Du Sautoy, 1980) and until recently the migration procedures included vaginal examination to determine marital status and bone X-rays to confirm age.

Direct racial discrimination leads to less favourable treatment on racial grounds, while in indirect discrimination the intention may not be discriminatory – although the effect is. Storti (1989), through a superb collection of excerpts (mainly from English people in other countries), highlights the way we expect others to be like us but find they are not. Thus a cultural incident can lead us to react with anger or fear and prompt us to withdraw. What begins innocently as a reflex self-protection quickly hardens into a pattern of systematic evasion and withdrawal. This leads to a vicious cycle of retracting from the culture, feeling uncomfortable among people and withdrawing.

The whole process happens without our knowing it, and in fact mainly because of our lack of awareness.

EFFECTS ON CHILDREN FROM ETHNIC MINORITIES

Direct or indirect racial discrimination, disadvantages and inequality are manifest in most aspects of the life of ethnic minority groups: educational and training opportunities, employment, income, working conditions, housing, access to health care and welfare, local amenities and environmental quality. In times of recession and a high level of unemployment, a larger proportion of non-white families have the poorest prospects of employment and housing.

Economic circumstances, housing and environment also have a major influence on the way children are brought up, their health and nutrition, and the lives and values of the whole family. Long working hours, night shifts, poor wages, bad housing and overcrowding can lead to an increased risk of a number of health problems. For many ethnic minority families, the constraints of poor housing and an unfamiliar, industrial, inner-city environment are extremely restrictive. These constraints hamper their ability to bring up children as they would wish. The parents themselves may have enjoyed the open air and spacious rural surroundings with natural play-things during their own childhood in their countries of origin. For example, the quality of life for many Bangladeshi children in rural Bangladesh is far better than that in inner-city Britain.

Thomas Cottle (1986), through a series of interviews with a young adolescent girl, revealed the profound effect of economic hardship and housing conditions on her psychological development:

> Every trip to a shoe store, clothing store, grocery, pharmacy turns into someone giving someone a lecture on how money is lost, spent, thrown away . . .
> I can't even find a place to dress in when I want to. It's like I'm living in a tube station. Everybody's always coming or going. I don't even know who I am, half the time.
>
> (pp. 115–16, 118)

For most people from the ethnic majority, unless they themselves have been victims of discrimination (for example, on grounds of gender, class or colour) or have been emotionally close to someone who has been a victim, it is difficult to understand what it feels like to experience discrimination just because of the colour of one's skin. Thus, there is a tendency on the part of many white people to disbelieve or ignore it. This leaves vulnerable people, especially children, feeling hopeless when they experience racial discrimination, bullying and abuse in schools, playgrounds and other situations.

Case study

Kareem was referred to me at the age of 9 years by his consultant paediatrician. He lived with his mother (41 years old) and at times her boyfriend (who was in his early 20s) visited regularly or lived with them for brief periods. Kareen had been exhibiting outbursts of excessive, violent behaviour and it was becoming very difficult to cope with him both at home and at school. He had been seen by the paediatrician because of a recent attack of asthma. He also had a past history of myoclonic epilepsy at the age of 1 year, when a number of anti-convulsants were tried; ultimately he was put on an effective drug, but his mother stopped it around the age of 4 because she felt he was cured by 'faith healing' and prayer. As a toddler, too, Kareem was rather overactive and defiant.

Kareem's mother had a rather unhappy childhood. Her own mother was often cruel to her and also exhibited suicidal behaviour. Her father, in fact, committed suicide and her stepfather sexually abused her when she was 9 years old. She married a man who turned out to be homosexual and later left her and became a Christian priest. There were two children from this marriage: a daughter (22 years) and a son (18 years). The daughter had also suffered from grand mal epilepsy and the son from asthma. This son too had a history of violent outbursts and had taken an overdose at the age of 15 years. Both these children had left her already. In fact, this son took away all her life savings.

Kareem's father originated from Pakistan. The relationship between him and Kareem's mother lasted for a year and became rather violent. The mother feared that Kareem's father might take him to Pakistan, so she moved away from the father when Kareem was only a baby so that he could not find them. Kareem, therefore, had no memory of his father. His mother often suffered from phobic anxiety and depressive disorders. She too had attempted suicide, had received in-patient psychiatric treatment and had been on medication for a long time. Her agoraphobic symptoms were rather handicapping, so she had to depend heavily upon her immature boyfriend. He had a problem with drinking, violence and bizarre behaviour (for example, being seen without his clothes on). However, he could take her out for various appointments and felt 'needed' to control Kareem's violent outbursts.

Kareem found himself in a very strange predicament. On the one hand, he was required to be a 'parent' to his emotionally deprived, anxious, inadequate and infantile mother, and on the other his own demands were treated as infantile and crushed by a violent, immature man for whom Kareem had very little respect. Kareem's violent outbursts, which Kareem called 'Kareem-specials', were also 'gifts' to his mother, who used them as a basis to plead with her boyfriend to stay in their ambivalent relationship.

As the therapy sessions with Kareem and his mother continued in our clinic, Kareem began to articulate some of his feelings and wishes. His mother too began to acknowledge the way her own childhood emotional deprivations and abuse and her intense feelings of envy and jealousy were compounding her efforts to care for her son. We tried to explore the possibility of her receiving individual psychotherapy, but the opinion of the consultant psychotherapist was: 'there are indications of a very damaged personality structure, presumably influenced by childhood experiences, and one could not envisage psychotherapy [being] sustainable in this setting'.

Kareem had been expelled from his school but another school kindly accepted him, and here a teacher, with our assistance, began to take a special interest in him. She could see Kareem's temper brewing in time and intervene in an affectionate but effective manner. His attendance at the clinic and in a weekly psychotherapy group had already begun to help him hold in some of his negative feelings. The teacher's outreach work with the mother was admirable. This allowed the mother to express some of her feelings of jealousy (for example, 'he would do it for you but not for me') and made sense of these. Kareem's behaviour appeared to be transformed.

Then he had to move to a larger school. The teachers in this school, in spite of our efforts, remained rather unsympathetic to Kareem's feelings and his efforts to contain them. He was bullied and constantly provoked by other children and felt that the teachers were also blaming him. He had no knowledge of Pakistan, the culture or religion, and could not identify with images created by racist bullying from other children. This confusion of identity, combined with the intensity of the bullying and the attitude of rejection from the teachers, broke his capacity to contain his feelings and use them constructively. As he lashed out, the vicious cycle of violence, hurt, dread and abandonment was rapidly unleashed.

With a degree of hindsight it is obvious that Kareem's identity issues should have been explored and helped much earlier in therapy, though there were many other pressing problems needing attention.

Mental health

A recent study sponsored by the Confederation of Indian Organizations (Beliappa, 1991) conducted semi-structured mental health interviews of 200 Indians randomly selected from each of the language groups of Asians derived from Haringey's Electoral Register. The findings contradicted the myth of Asians somatizing their emotional distress. They did not appear to compartmentalize their experiences but, in fact, used a holistic model and linked such experiences within a normative structure of roles and expectations. The researchers, therefore, conceptualized the notion of 'distress' to denote the whole person being affected, a condition that signalled an urgent need to restore lost meaning with reference to expected roles.

Nearly 29 per cent of those interviewed reported such 'distress'. Their life experiences included excessive work load, lack of housing, isolation, language difficulties and racism: 'We expected respect, instead we were marginalised on the basis of the colour of our skin' (Beliappa, 1991, p. 12). The study revealed that there were very few avenues to express these feelings. There were a number of barriers to using available services, which tended to use stereotypical views and overgeneralizations rather than the user's frame of reference, or than taking account of their family dynamics, belief systems and cultural constraints (discussed later in this chapter).

As real help could only be sought from those organizations and individuals who understood their cultural viewpoint, and such resources and skills are in scarce supply, a large proportion of the people (35 per cent) turned inwards towards their own resources, such as prayer, boosting confidence, channelling energy into work, etc. Thirty-two per cent of respondents had major concerns relating to children's upbringing and education and the values being imbibed by them. Some examples of their concerns were as follows:

'There's no future for our children without good education. At the same time they cannot lose their identity and fit into English ways totally.'

'Our kids must be in a position to do better than us. But we worry whether they will because the State Education is inadequate. Children seem to be underachieving.'

'Our children are being exposed to external factors often alien to our culture, they have to be moderated.'

'The loss of our children is the price we have paid for coming here. We spent all our early years tending over them. But now they have grown apart and are often disrespectful. They question us on everything and for some of these questions we have no answers.'

(p. 18)

There are several studies of child mental health problems available in the literature. Some examples of the findings from abroad are mentioned below, followed by the findings of some of the studies in the UK.

Nurcombe and Cawte (1967), in a study of aborigines on an island off the coast of Australia, reported a rate of 9.7 per cent of children aged 2–15 years who showed some form of psychogenic disorder – most commonly consisting either of a 'tension discharge' or an 'anxiety-inhibition' syndrome. Similarly, a survey of 747 children between the ages of 4 and 12 years in Vellore (a city in south India) identified psychiatric disorders at a rate of 6.7 to 8.2 per cent (Verghese and Beig, 1974). The disorders identified included sleepwalking, enuresis, behaviour problems and also mental retardation. It is difficult to calculate the rate of psychiatric disorders exclusive of mental retardation from the data presented, but Graham (1980) estimated it to be in the region of 5 per cent.

Minde (1975) studied 577 children in three schools in Uganda, using the Rutter's questionnaire for teachers. Although 18 per cent of children scored more than 9 points on the scale, 8.3 per cent were difficult children and were further studied. Factors such as urbanization, lack of nourishment in the morning, family breakdowns and problems of discipline were also identified in the problem children. Lal and Sethi (1977) studied 272 children up to the age of 12 from families living in an urban community in north India and found that 11 per cent of children suffered from such psychological disorders. A study of 270 children from 1 to 15 years of age living in a Sudanese village indicated that 10 per cent of the children showed 'pronounced psychiatric symptoms' (Baasher and Ibrahim, 1976).

Cochrane (1979) found that Asian children in the UK showed lower rates of behavioural deviance on Rutter's teachers' questionnaire than the white children. The mean scores were 3.6 for children of Indian parents, 4.2 per cent for children of Pakistani parents, 5.7 for children of white parents and 6.8 per cent for children of West Indian parents. Asian children also had lower rates of admission to mental institutions than did white children, while the children of West Indian immigrants had higher rates. (The pattern for adults, incidentally, was similar to that for children.)

Rutter *et al.* (1974) studied 10-year-old school-children in an Inner London borough using the Rutter's questionnaires for teachers and parents, and also teacher and parent interviews on randomly selected children. They found that the proportions of disturbed children of West Indian and indigenous parentage were very similar, but there were differences in sex ratios and diagnostic types. There was a higher proportion of girls from West Indian families with conduct disorder. They estimated the prevalence of psychiatric disorder, on parental interview, as 25 per cent in children from non-immigrant families and 17.5 per cent in children from West Indian families. However, on the basis of teacher's interviews, the estimate was 27.6 per cent in children from non-immigrant families and 38.2 per cent in children from immigrant families.

Kallarackal (director of a school of social work in Kerala, India) and Herbert (from a school of social work in Leicester) surveyed all the children of Indian origin who were in the final and next-to-final classes in Leicester junior schools with predominantly Indian pupils. They included 261 boys and 260 girls and used Rutter's questionnaires for parents and for teachers. A randomly selected sample from these were matched with English controls and interviewed and further studied. They found that the English children were nearly three times more maladjusted than the Indian children (31 per cent and 11 per cent respectively). Of the Indian children, 54 per cent were Gujaratis and 41 per cent Punjabis. There were no broken homes in the Indian group, but 22 per cent of the English families were one-parent families. In fact 40 per cent of the English maladjusted children came from families with impaired relations, such as serious marital problems, prolonged absence of one parent, separation and divorce (Kallarackal and Herbert, 1976).

Earls and Richman (1980), in an epidemiological study of 3-year-old children, compared the prevalence of behaviour problems in 58 children of West Indian parents with 705 children of British-born parents. There were few significant differences in the patterns of behavioural disturbance between the two groups (15.5 per cent in West Indian and 14.3 per cent in the indigenous group) and none between West Indian boys and girls. The children of West Indian families were living in poorer housing and had experienced more separations but did not show higher rates of behaviour problems.

A retrospective study of case-note analysis of referral to the Department of Child Psychiatry at the London Hospital (Stern *et al.*, 1990) revealed that the Asian children referred to that department were grossly underrepresented when compared to the local population. Only 12 per cent of referrals were from Bangladeshi families, when the Inner London Education Authority (1985) suggested that some 33 per cent of school-age children in the area would have been of Bangladeshi origin. The nature of presenting problems in children of Bangladeshi families was similar to that in children of English origin. However, no pre-school children of Bangladeshi families were referred as a result of child sexual abuse, nor were there any pre-school referrals for sleeping problems, enuresis or encopresis from Bangladeshi families.

THE FAMILY

Children in Asian households are usually better protected against sexual abuse not only because of greater adherence to religious and moral values but also because of the extended family situation and the presence of several family members walking into and out of each other's rooms. The two preconditions of abuse, namely privacy and opportunity, rarely arise. If any member of the family tried to abuse a child he or she would be subject to the collective wrath of the entire family. There is also no tendency to have a succession of one-night stands, stepfathers or boyfriends (Laungani, 1989). So although the occurrence of sexual abuse in Asian families cannot be ruled out, there are many protective factors that make it less likely.

A general practitioner (Dutt, 1991) working with Bangladeshi families noted that in his practice the commonest conditions in children were bedwetting, head banging, vomiting and daytime wetting and soiling. He went on to add that Bangladeshi parents viewed these problems as misbehaviour. In our experience this is not unique to Bangladeshi parents. Shame and embarrassment aroused by some of these conditions often lead to a blaming attitude in a large proportion of parents irrespective of their ethnic status. The GP felt that Bangladeshi parents did not accept these problems as mental conditions and seldom co-operated fully with the attempts at help from child mental health services. But problems like enuresis and encopresis are seldom caused by psychiatric disturbance; in fact, psychiatric disturbance if present is often caused by these conditions. The child mental health services usually ask the whole family to attend their clinics and tend to focus on family relationships and family communications as a means of alleviating childhood disorders. Poor family co-operation with such family therapy approaches is not uncommon, even in ethnic majority families. Moreover, many ethnic minority families have added difficulties in making use of health and other services.

Obstacles to using services: language

Language can be a major obstacle. Though a mere 200,000 adults in Britain speak English only slightly or not at all, many health and other professionals take the view that everybody should learn to speak English. It is easily assumed that it is possible for every individual to do so: in fact, there are many reasons that make it impractical and even impossible for many people to learn English. Some people have never attended school; others who have small children and a home to run with limited resources have very little energy, time or resources left to study another language. The feeling of strangeness, inhibition, lack of information and transport, etc. can further hinder this. Existing English teaching methods and facilities are often inappropriate and unsuitable to the particular needs of many such people; and all this is in addition to the intrinsic difficulties of learning another language. If an adult health worker tried to learn another language he or she might realize how difficult it is (Mares *et al.*, 1985) – as Mel Brooks said (in Kenneth Tynan's *Show People*, quoted in Storti, 1989):

> When we got to our hundred and eighteenth French village, I screamed at the top of my lungs, 'The joke is over! English, please!' I couldn't believe a whole country couldn't speak English. One third of a nation, all right, but not a whole country.
>
> (p. 85)

Most health and other authorities do not have a proper interpreter service. They tend to use the children from the family, very inappropriately, for such purposes, or use other professionals who happen to know a bit of another language but have very little time to help in this matter. The establishment of a proper interpreter service, with due respect and sensitivity to the various issues involved, would make a lot of difference to ethnic minority families and their children in meeting some of their needs.

Obstacles to using services: negative attitudes

Ethnic minority families can also find that members of the caring professions convey a rather negative attitude towards their culture, language, religion, colour, etc. and carry with them a number of myths (Damle, 1989). This undermines the families' confidence in these services and leads to their avoiding such agencies or delaying seeking their help or acting upon their advice or instructions. Mares *et al.* (1985) illustrate how such negative attitudes can be conveyed even unintentionally or unthinkingly; for example, by talking to people in pidgin English, by making derogatory comments about their life-style ('you see, even your baby prefers our food to yours!'), by making fun of their mother tongue, by referring to all non-white people as 'immigrants', etc. Many feel an urgent need to change the 'inadequate' culture of ethnic minority families for their own good and even force people to do things against their own will. If this meets with resistance, it is labelled as excessive sensitivity or an unusual or peculiar attitude (such as extreme modesty).

Scott (1979) observed: 'English people are not mass-produced, they do not come off a factory line all looking, speaking, thinking, acting the same. Neither do we' (p. 13). Balarajan *et al.* (1991) reported that outpatient attendance by Indian, Pakistani and West Indian children is well below the level in white children. The district health authorities need to consult ethnic minorities and provide relevant services (Bahl, 1991).

Mental health professionals can be equally ethnocentric, as if minority communities never had anything like mental health 'treatment' until Western science came along and invented it. By making it unethical or illegal to practise counselling or therapy without proper credentials, the professionals may destroy the natural help-giving networks that may already exist. Mental health professionals set up services that are inappropriate for ethnic minorities and wait for them to come. Then, when they do not come, the professionals wonder why (Sue and Sue, 1990).

ETHNOCENTRIC EXPECTATIONS OF FAMILY NORMALITY

As the focus of family therapy is on family communications and relationships, Western European ethnocentric expectations of normality about family interactions often get inappropriately applied to ethnic minority families. Such values include individuation from the emotional field of the family, the nuclear family as the standard, free emotional expression, egalitarian role relationships and equal division of labour.

In the Western individualistic orientation, the family (the nuclear family) is viewed as a biological necessity and the extended family as a fringe benefit or a nuisance. Independence is a cherished ideal in Western culture, where high dependence is seen as a despicable state. Parents are often at pains to make their children independent as quickly as possible. Even in psychotherapy situations, whether individual, group or family therapy, dependence versus independence is seen as the fundamental issue in the development of the human personality. Thus, Western cultures are becoming a breeding ground for narcissistic disorders (Lasch, 1980); Eastern child-rearing practices have a great deal to contribute to help overcome this rising tide.

In contrast, Eastern cultures place more emphasis on dependability than on independence (Roland, 1980). Parents are usually at pains to ensure that their children grow up in an atmosphere where parents are a model of dependability. There is an atmosphere of indulgence, prolonged babyhood, physical closeness, common sleeping arrangements and immediate gratification of physical and emotional needs. It is a culture of spoilt children creating a strong bond, a sense of security and inner strength. As care-givers are supposed to be always present, toys and other transitional objects do not play an important role. There is also an emphasis on contentment rather than achievement. The young ones are loved just for 'being' rather than 'doing' the right things.

However, as the child grows, expectations change tremendously. Parents use their own example, shaming and authority to try to teach children to mature emotionally. This includes developing tolerance for one's feelings, heightening sensitivity to others' feelings and controlling the expression of hurtful feelings. It also involves mastering one's narcissistic individuality and developing one's involvement in family role expectations, myths, rituals, honour, etc. (Roland, 1980).

Krystal (1988) points out that maturation of affectivity includes amongst other things the development of a capacity to tolerate feelings without having to act them out or evacuate them quickly, and the ideal time for the development of this capacity is the latency period in a child's life. This training in emotional continence requires active support from the care-givers, just as training in walking, talking and developing urinary and faecal continence does.

Thus, Eastern children are expected to grow up to value the sacrifice of narcissistic individuality and to respect the authority of elders. Instead of direct confrontation leading to loss of face, there is a tendency to make indirect references through folk parables or sayings (Toupin, 1980). According to Eastern wisdom (Atwood and Maltin, 1991), feelings are like the weather, an important part of human life. As it is not possible to have a state of weatherlessness, similarly we always have one or the other feeling: pleasant, unpleasant, subtle, gross, etc. The feelings are always changing as well, and are not controllable by will (Dwivedi, 1990). The best way to handle them is to recognize them, to accept them, and to go about one's business. However, one is responsible for one's actions whether through body or speech. One has to learn to master the control of actions that can be harmful to oneself or to others, as actions indirectly affect future feelings, according to the Karmic law (Guenther, 1957).

Maslow (1968) highlighted the hierarchical organization of motives, ranging from hunger and thirst to self-actualization. Wilber (1980) suggested that self-transcendence lies beyond self-actualization, and according to Asian psychologies, selfless service is regarded as a human motive of a still higher order (Walsh and Shapiro, 1983; Walsh, 1988). Boss was the first Western psychiatrist to examine Asian practices, and realized that, compared with the extent of yogic self-exploration, 'even the best Western training analysis is not much more than an introductory course!' (Boss, 1963, p. 188).

From the point of view of Eastern (Hindu–Buddhist) psychology, mental health would be defined as:

> the ability to live in harmony with oneself and nature, to understand one's relationship to the universe, to show tolerance and compassion to one's fellow human beings, to endure hardship and suffering without mental disintegration, to prize non-violence, to care for the welfare of all sentient beings, and to see a meaning and purpose in one's life that allows one to enter old age or to face death with serenity and without fear.
>
> (Atwood and Maltin, 1991, p. 374)

There now appears to be an increased interest amongst many physicists (Panda, 1991), philosophers and psychotherapists in understanding and appreciating the wisdom behind the principles underlying Eastern (Hindu–Buddhist) cultures. The new physics sees the universe as a dynamic web of interrelated events, all following from the properties of the other parts, which is very much in the spirit of Eastern thought (Atwood and Maltin, 1991).

Having been brought up in a Western culture, even well-meaning professionals such as teachers, social workers, counsellors, psychotherapists, psychologists, family therapists, doctors, nurses, etc. may see Eastern family life as 'oppressive', often projecting on to it the features of extended Victorian family life of the past. Many become passionately involved in rescuing Asian children and youngsters from their 'primitive' and 'oppressive' family values. As one school counsellor remarked: 'If he does not feel separate from his parents in school, there is no way he could discover for himself what kind of lifestyle he would want to adopt when he leaves his parents.' A deputy headmistress felt disappointed, as: 'We teach the girls to be independent and critical thinkers, but at home, they are taught the virtues of collective responsibility and unquestioning respect to the elders in the family' (quoted in Ghuman, 1991, p. 121).

Asian families are criticized as being too self-contained, constricting and not being prepared to adjust to the British way of life (Littlewood and Lipsedge, 1989). Ahmed (1986) points out that the very fabric of British society is permeated with racist cultural imperialism, manifesting itself in education, school, history books, children's story books, the media and social work literature, and leading to subconscious assumptions about the superiority of Western child-rearing practices and denigration of others. Ethnic minority cultures are often described in a way which make them seem bizarre or backward or imply that their problems are somehow caused by the nature of their culture (Mares *et al.*, 1985).

Even researchers studying acculturation have missed the essence of Eastern culture or have tended to measure trivia (such as the items on the Acculturation Scale; Ghuman, 1991) in the name of measuring cultural values. There is an interesting Sufi story of a man searching for his keys under a street-lamp. Someone trying to help him asked him where exactly he had lost his keys. The man explained that he had lost his keys somewhere in the bush, but it was very dark there, so he was searching for them under the street-lamp where there was enough light.

STRESS IN CHILDREN FROM ETHNIC MINORITIES

There are many people in any culture who, due to a variety of influences or personality disorders, tend to deviate from their cultural norms. Social dislocation, loss of supporting network, alcohol and drug abuse, etc. further increase their vulnerability. Certain psycho-social circumstances can make people behave in culturally incongruent ways that they themselves may find regretful.

Some ethnic minority children are distressed by their life circumstances, life events, disadvantages and other sources of stress. In times of emotional distress, there is no other effective solution than an emotional contact with the extended family. Many dislocated ethnic minority families in this country do not have such supportive emotional networks easily accessible.

For example, Kuldeep, an 8-year-old boy with parents of Punjabi Indian origin, was referred to our service as he appeared reluctant to attend school, insisted on sleeping in his mother's bed and was frightened of dying. He had become very clingy, demanding and tearful. This was precipitated by his father's suicide. Kuldeep had been very close to his mother but rather distant to his father and did not even call him as 'Dad'. The relationships between the parents were very stormy and they had been going to divorce, when the father died. Kuldeep felt that his father killed himself because Kuldeep did not call him 'Dad'. It was difficult for him to share with his mother the complexity of his feelings towards his father. At school he had already been on the receiving end of teasing and bullying with racist overtones, and he therefore felt further threatened by the school rather than being able to seek comfort from it. His isolation was compounded by his mother's isolation in the light of the intensity of hostility from her in-laws.

There can be a variety of protective factors in the family life of people from Eastern cultures. The intensity of the relationships between extended families is often helpful in maintaining a respect for ideals of refraining from violence, abuse, alcoholism, family breakdown, etc. These are instilled through a sense of honour, pride and shame, reinforced by the intensity of interactions between extended families and close-knit communities. However, the migrant family networks have to compete with other, wider influences which can at times be extremely powerful. Kuldeep's father had started heavily abusing alcohol, and this progressed to violence, family breakdown and suicide. This was compounded by the effect of shame unleashed in the community of significant others. In a non-resonant cultural context, the protective devices became rather destructive.

Emotional support by caring professionals can help alleviate a great deal of stress. Dayal (1990) points out that the emotional availability of such professionals to ethnic minorities is often limited. Some fail to respond on the grounds that they cannot understand the cultural ways of ethnic minority families (Fernando, 1988), while others look for and quickly find 'cultural conflict'-type explanations. Devereux (1953) coined the term 'culturalistic pseudo insight' to describe the confusion of attributing to culture what is actually an explanation of the individual personality. Such a labelling and focus tend to fuel and escalate cultural conflict: as William Hazlitt wrote, 'The first thing an Englishman does on going abroad is to find fault with what is French, because it is not English' (*Notes of A Journey through France and Italy*, quoted in Storti, 1989, p. 47). Such experiences have also led to young Asians, at times of distress, presenting to white professionals with problems in a way that is more likely to elicit a sympathetic response; for example, a complaint of ill-treatment, fear of arranged marriage, etc. (Ahmed, 1986). The contrasting perceptions of the concept of 'arranged marriage' symbolize the phenomenon whereby, on looking at the well-known picture, one sees either a vase or two faces.

Racism tends to denigrate and dehumanize ethnic minorities, leading to depression, low self-esteem and a sense of worthlessness among them (Fernando, 1988; MacCarthy 1988). Goldberg and Hodes (1992) highlight the role of racism in distorting the processes by which adolescents, especially girls of Asian origin, negotiate increased autonomy. Adolescents begin to resist parental protectiveness, and this escalates because of their experience of cultural racism. Self-poisoning by a number of Asian adolescent girls symbolizes the acting out of the view of the dominant group that the minority is 'harmful' or 'poisonous' – a form of projective identification. Attempted suicide by overdosing is more common amongst Asians, especially young women, than amongst the non-Asian British (Glover *et al.*, 1989; Merrill and Owens, 1986, 1988).

Case study 1

I met a 15-year-old girl, Rashida, the eldest of seven children in a single-parent family of Pakistani origin. Her father migrated to the UK from Pakistan at the age of 19. He went back to Pakistan to get married and Rashida was born there. Rashida and her mother joined him in the UK when Rashida was nearly 18 months old. He was 48 years old when I met him, had been suffering from a long schizophrenic illness and had had in-patient psychiatric treatments. He was now living with his brother and was maintained on an anti-psychotic medication.

Rashida had been a healthy, enjoyable and lovable baby and toddler. Being the first grandchild, she was even spoilt by her grandparents and other relatives, who were full of admiration and warmth. However, the emergence of mental illness in her father was manifested in violent, unpredictable and bizarre behaviours and very often a fierce and frightening demeanour. This led to Rashida and her mother taking refuge in a women's refuge. They found the attitude of many white women in the refuge to be racially derogatory. Rashida began to have strong negative feelings towards her ethnic associations, reinforced by the attitudes and atmosphere in her school. Parental separation led to a sense of shame in her community and loss of valuable social support. In such an atmosphere, even when they moved out of the refuge and her mother tried to keep Rashida in touch with her cultural values, through dress, language and making use of religious educational opportunities, Rashida began to resist identification with Pakistani culture. She began to defy and turn against her mother's attempts.

As the conflict between Rashida and her mother escalated, Rashida complained of ill-treatment by her mother and also the fear of an arranged marriage. She was taken into care, lived in a children's home and expressed a strong desire not to have to do anything with her parents or come into contact with them at all. Her mother made several attempts to get in touch, but Rashida remained adamant. Rashida stopped speaking of her parents as parents and referred to them as 'that man' and 'that lady'. She felt that they could not have been her real parents, that she must have been adopted by them and that at least one of her natural parents must have been white. She was full of hatred for them and described them, particularly her father, as 'monsters' or 'demons'.

Such an intensity of 'blind hatred' is a common feature of a narcissistic disorder. In narcissistic disorders, there is an element of grandiosity as a defence against a damaged self-concept. This is achieved by stripping off and externalizing all the bad aspects of oneself. The person develops 'blind hatred' towards many others, who are assigned sub-human status and have no right to exist. A narcissistic individual is unable to appreciate that such 'monstrous' people may be or ever have been good or kind to that individual. As there is an externalization of all traits, there is also a tendency to idealization transference (Horowitz, 1989; Horowitz *et al.*, 1984; Kohut, 1972). Certain other people, therefore, are idealized and identified with.

Case study 2

Another major source of unhappiness amongst ethnic minority children may be their poor self-esteem, created by the process of socialization that can flood them with negative images of ethnic minority status. Many black children cared for by white care-givers (for example, through adoption, fostering or residential institutions) harbour negative attitudes towards black people. There are many examples of black people who have difficulty in acknowledging the fact that they are black and have problems of identity confusion. Many have no sense of their cultural or racial pride, no knowledge or appreciation of positive role models from their ethnic group.

Joan, a 9-year-old child, was referred to us by her GP for her difficult behaviour. She had already been referred to our clinic before on three occasions, first by the health visitor and then twice by the school teacher. On one occasion, the family did not attend at all, and on the other two occasions they turned up for the initial assessments but not for treatment sessions.

Joan lived with her mother, stepfather and two younger stepchildren. Joan's mother, Maureen, had felt emotionally deprived as a child, kept getting into trouble at school and had reacted by repeatedly running away. She (Maureen) became pregnant at the age of 14 and was expelled from school. Her father was so disappointed in her that he never talked to her again. Her baby girl was therefore adopted. Maureen still grieves over this loss. Maureen married a young West Indian man, Ted. Maureen's parents did not approve of her marrying a black man at all and she lost contact with both of them. Ted was a tall (6′4″), slim young man and heavily involved in drug abuse and violence. Maureen had Joan from this marriage, but when Joan was only 3 months old Ted tipped boiling water over her, leading to the baby's hospitalization and reception into care. When Joan was 1½ years old, the family split up and Joan and Maureen lived together. A few months later, Ted committed suicide through a drug overdose. Maureen, having lost her parents, her husband and her first baby, found Joan to be the only object available for expressing emotional comfort, indulgence, anger, hatred, rejection or neglect.

Maureen then found a young white man, John, who also had a history of emotional deprivation in his childhood and a string of delinquent behaviours leading to his admission to an approved school. John did not have any children from his previous marriage. Maureen and John got married and had two young children. Maureen felt that Joan got on better with John than with her. However, John too felt at the end of his tether and threatened to leave Maureen if Joan continued with her ways.

The parents were most annoyed by her stealing. These were usually items of food (biscuits, bread, etc.) or small items of play. Her parents felt that she had a voracious appetite and even ate iron tablets and drank shampoo. She urinated behind radiators, on the landing and in other inappropriate places. She had no friends, was often withdrawn and clammed up when questioned.

Over a few individual play therapy sessions, Joan described how she got teased at school. She also discussed how angry she felt both at home and at school and how helpless and hopeless she became when she was angry, teased and nagged. In fact, at school, the children called her 'Paki', which completely baffled her. Her parents were also very critical and derogatory towards her (late natural) father. Their attitudes and language were overtly racist and Joan saw no possibility of her parents protecting her from racial bullying at school. Her mother often described Joan as taking after her late father in appearance, build, behaviour and mental disturbance. It was difficult to elicit any affectionate response from her parents towards her.

We offered weekly group therapy, individual and family therapy sessions, but none was taken up properly. In one of the sessions Maureen did acknowledge the intensity of her projections on to Joan, but her fragile relationship with her husband got in the way of turning this into a healing effort. The school teacher, on the other hand, was more empathic and did take some steps both to comfort and protect Joan, though it was very difficult in that school context.

IDENTITY MODELS

Sue and Sue (1990) have refined the five-stage Minority Identity Development Model (MID) and have applied it to ethnic minority as well as white identity development. The five stages start with conformity (whites as well as minorities having positive attitudes towards whites and negative attitudes towards non-whites, but denying that there is racism) and move through dissonance, through resistance and immersion, through introspection, and finally to integrative awareness (characterized by positive identity and appropriate appreciation of positives in each other). Storti (1989, p. 92) quotes Rudyard Kipling's 'We and They':

All nice people, like us, are we
   And everyone else is they:
But if you cross over the sea,
   Instead of over the way,
You may end by (think of it) looking on
   We as a sort of they!

A process model of identity clarifies the way differing ethnic attitudes and behaviours reflect different stages of development rather than permanent characteristics of a group or acculturation (Phinney, 1990). Maximé (1986) has described some useful ways of working with identity problems in ethnic minority children, and Coward and Dattani (1993) have promoted group work with ethnic minority children to help with identity issues.

NOTE

I am very grateful to Pratima Dattani, Ethnic Minorities Development Officer, Coventry, for a number of suggestions, and to my son, Rajaneesh Dwivedi, for repeated wordprocessing of the manuscript.

REFERENCES

Ahmed, S. (1986) Cultural racism in work with Asian women and girls. In S. Ahmed, J. Cheetham and J. Small (eds), *Social Work with Black Children and Their Families*, pp. 140–54. London: Batsford.

Atwood, J. D. and Maltin, L. (1991) Putting Eastern philosophies into Western psychotherapies. *American Journal of Psychotherapy*, 45(13), 368–82.

Baasher, T. A. and Ibrahim, H. H. A. (1976) Childhood psychiatric disorders in the Sudan. *African Journal of Psychiatry*, 1, 67–78.

Bahl, V. (1991) Ethnic minority health care. *Health Trends*, 30, 88.

Balarajan, R., Raleigh, V. S. and Yuen, P. (1991) Hospital care among ethnic minorities in Britain. *Health Trends*, 23, 90–3.

Beliappa, J. (1991) *Illness or Distress? Alternative Models of Mental Health*. London: Confederation of Indian Organizations (UK).

Black, J. (1989) *Child Health in a Multicultural Society*. London: British Medical Journal.

Boss, M. (1963) *A Psychiatrist Discovers India*. New York: Basic Books.

Cochrane, R. (1979) Psychological and behavioural disturbance in West Indians, Indians and Pakistanis in Britain: a comparison of rates among children and adults. *British Journal of Psychiatry*, 134, 201–10.

Cottle, T.J. (1986) A bedroom for Sheila Cooperton. In J. Cheetham, W. James, M. Loney, B. Mayor and W. Prescott (eds), *Social and Community Work in a Multiracial Society*, pp. 115-20. London: Harper & Row.

Coward, B. and Dattani, P. (1993) Race, identity, and culture. In K.N. Dwivedi (ed.), *Groupwork with Children and Adolescents*. London: Jessica Kingsley (in press).

Damle, A.D. (1989) Transcultural issues in community psychiatry. *Community Psychiatry: Its Practice and Management*, **2**, 22-5.

Dayal, N. (1990) Psychotherapy services for minority ethnic communities in the NHS – a psychotherapist's view. *Midland Journal of Psychotherapy*, **11**, 28-37.

Devereux, G. (1953) Cultural factors in psychoanalytic therapy. *Journal of American Psychoanalytic Association*, **1**, 629-55.

Du Sautoy, S. (1980) Register lists all offences by aliens. *Guardian*, 16 August. (Quoted in Littlewood and Lipsedge, 1989, p. 139.)

Dutt, G.C. (1991) How cultural beliefs hamper psychiatric treatment. *ODA News Review*, **2**, 14.

Dwivedi, K.N. (1990) Purification of mind by Vipassana meditation. In J. Crook and D. Fontana (eds), *Space in Mind*, pp. 86-91. Shaftesbury: Element Books.

Earls, F. and Richman, N. (1980) The prevalence of behavioural problems in three-year old children of West Indian-born parents. *Journal of Child Psychology and Psychiatry*, **21**, 99-106.

Edwards, V.K. (1979) *The West Indian Language Issue in British Schools: Challenges and Responses*. London: Routledge & Kegan Paul.

Fernando, S. (1988) *Race and Culture in Psychiatry*. London: Croom Helm.

Ghuman, P.A.S. (1991) Best or worst of two worlds? A study of Asian adolescents. *Educational Research*, **33**, 121-32.

Glover, G., Markes, F. and Nowers, M. (1989) Parasuicide in young Asian women. *British Journal of Psychiatry*, **154**, 271-2.

Goldberg, D. and Hodes, M. (1992) The poison of racism and the self poisoning of adolescents. *Journal of Family Therapy*, **14**, 51-67.

Graham, P.J. (1980) Epidemiological approaches to child mental health in developing countries. In E.F. Purcell (ed.), *Psychopathology of Children and Youth: A Cross-cultural Perspective*, pp. 28-45. New York: Josiah Macy, Jr, Foundation.

Guenther, H.V. (1957) *Philosophy and Psychology in the Abhidhamma*. Delhi: Motilal Banarasidas.

Hiro, D. (1971) *Black British, White British*. London: Eyre & Spottiswoode.

Horowitz, M.J. (1989) Clinical phenomenology of narcissistic pathology. *Psychiatric Clinics of North America*, **12**, 531-9.

Horowitz, M.J., Marmar, C., Krupnick, J. *et al.* (1984) *Personality Styles and Brief Psychotherapy*. New York: Basic Books.

Inner London Education Authority (1985) *Research and Statistics 1026/86. Language Census*. London: ILEA.

Jhabvala, R.P. (1987) *Out of India*. New York: Simon & Schuster.

Kallarackal, A.M. and Herbert, M. (1976) The happiness of Indian immigrant children. *New Society*, 26 February, 422-4.

Kohut, H. (1972) Thoughts on narcissism and narcissistic rage. *Psychoanalytic Study and Child*, **27**, 360-400.

Krystal, H. (1988) *Integration and Self Healing: Affect, Trauma, Alexithymia*. Hillside, NJ: Analytic Press.

Lal, N. and Sethi, B.B. (1977) Estimate of mental ill health in children of an urban community. *Indian Journal of Paediatrics*, **44**, 55-64.

Lasch, C. (1980) *The Culture of Narcissism: American Life in an Age of Diminishing Expectations*. London: Abacus.

Laungani, P. (1989), quoted in *Hospital Doctor*, 9 March.

Littlewood, R. and Lipsedge, M. (1989) *Aliens and Alienists: Ethnic Minorities and Psychiatry*. London: Unwin Hyman.

MacCarthy, B. (1988) Clinical work with ethnic minorities. In F.N. Watts (ed.), *New Developments in Clinical Psychology, 2*. Chichester: British Psychological Society, John Wiley.

Mares, P., Henley, A. and Baxter, C. (1985) *Health Care in Multicultural Britain*. Cambridge: Health Education Council and National Extension College.

Maslow, A. (1968) *Toward a Psychology of Being*. Princeton, NJ: Van Nostrand.

Maximé, J.E. (1986) Some psychological models of black self-concept. In S. Ahmed, J. Cheetham and J. Small (eds), *Social Work with Black Children and Their Families*, pp. 100-16. London: Batsford.

Merrill, J. and Owens, J. (1986) Ethnic differences in self poisoning: a comparative study of Asian and white groups. *British Journal of Psychiatry*, **148**, 708-12.

Merrill, J. and Owens, J. (1988) Self poisoning among immigrant groups. *Acta Psychiatrica Scandinavica*, **77**, 77-80.

Minde, K.K. (1975) Psychological problems in Ugandan school children: a controlled evaluation. *Journal of Child Psychology and Psychiatry*, **16**, 49-59.

Nurcombe, B. and Cawte, J.E. (1967) Patterns of behavioural disorder amongst the children of an Aboriginal population. *Australian-New Zealand Journal of Psychiatry*, **16**, 119-33.

Panda, N.C. (1991) *Maya in Physics*. Delhi: Motilal Banarasidas.

Phinney, J.S. (1990) Ethnic identity in adolescents and adults: review of research. *Psychological Bulletin*, **108**, 499-514.

Roland, A. (1980) Psychoanalytic perspectives on personality development in India. *International Review of Psychoanalysis*, **1**, 73-87.

Rutter, M., Yule, W., Berger, M., Yule, B., Morton, J. and Bagley, C. (1974) Children of West Indian immigrants - I. rates of behavioural deviance and of psychiatric disorder. *Journal of Child Psychology and Psychiatry*, **15**, 241-62.

Scott, P. (1979) *The Day of the Scorpion*. New York: Avon.

Sontag, S. (1979) *Illness as Metaphor*. London: Allen Lane.

Stern, G., Cottrell, D. and Holmes, J. (1990) Patterns of attendance of child psychiatry outpatients with special reference to Asian families. *British Journal of Psychiatry*, **156**, 384-7.

Storti, C. (1989) *The Act of Crossing Cultures*. Intercultural Press.

Sue, D.W. and Sue, D. (1990) *Counselling the Culturally Different*. New York: John Wiley.

Toupin, E.S.W.A. (1980) Counselling Asians: psychotherapy in the context of racism and Asian-American history. *American Journal of Orthopsychiatry*, **50**, 76-86.

Verghese, A. and Beig, A. (1974) Psychiatric disturbance in children - an epidemiological study. *Indian Journal of Medical Research*, **62**, 1538-42.

Walsh, R. (1988) Two Asian psychologies and their implications for Western psychotherapies. *American Journal of Psychotherapy*, **42**, 543-60.

Walsh, R. and Shapiro, D.H. (1983) Beyond health and normality. In R. Walsh and D.H. Shapiro (eds), *Explorations of Psychological Well-being*. New York: Van Nostrand.

Wilber, K. (1980) *The Atman Project*. Wheaton, IL: Quest.

Name Index

Subject Index

*(Where numerals are in **heavy** type, this represents a subject covered by a chapter).*